BEWITCHED
BY BURMA

BEWITCHED BY BURMA

A UNIQUE INSIGHT INTO BURMA'S COMPLEX PAST

ANNE CARTER

Matador
9 Priory Business Park
Kibworth Beauchamp
Leicestershire LE8 0RX, UK
Tel: (+44) 116 279 2299
Fax: (+44) 116 279 2277
Email: books@troubador.co.uk
Web: www.troubador.co.uk/matador

ISBN 978 1780882 710

Contents

List of Illustrations

Acknowledgements and Thanks

My grateful thanks to the United Society for the Propagation of the Gospel for allowing me to reproduce much of the Rev. George Tidey's narrative of the trek from Burma to India after the Japanese invasion. This is much appreciated.

I also want to say thank you to all members of my family for their encouragement and help, particularly to my brother and sister, Douglas Garrad and Liz Anderson; to my sons Thomas, Peter and Michael Carter, and to all my grandchildren, especially Juliette for drawing the map of Burma, and Mark and Matthew for their interest throughout. I am most grateful to my friend Joan Wheatley for her wise advice after reading the original manuscript, to the Rev. David Haokip for providing me with a copy of the Lord's Prayer in Burmese, to my mentor Keith Woods for assisting me through many a computer problem and to Marguerite Smith for compiling the index. Thank you, too, to my good friends in Burma for their heart-warming assistance on my recent visit to their beautiful country.

Finally, it goes without saying that this book could not have been written without the work of the letter writers and diarists on which it is based, so a huge thank you to them all. Any faults in the narrative are entirely of my own making, and where these occur I beg the reader's forgiveness.

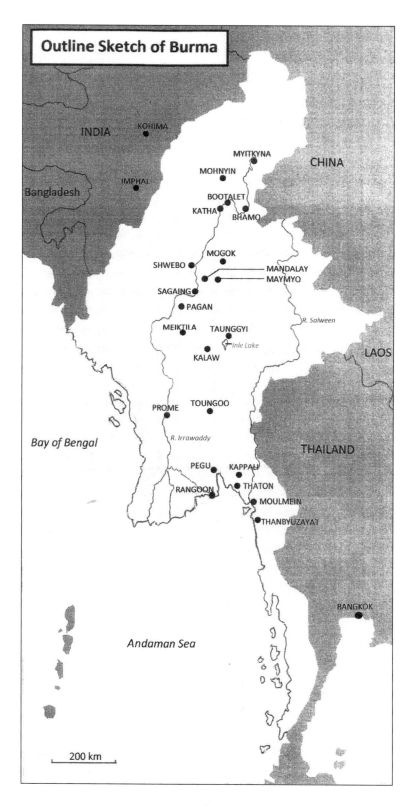

Outline Sketch of Burma

INDIA

KOHIMA

Bangladesh

IMPHAL

MYITKYNA

CHINA

MOHNYIN

BOOTALET

KATHA

BHAMO

MOGOK

SHWEBO

MANDALAY

SAGAING

MAYMYO

PAGAN

R. Salween

MEIKTILA

TAUNGGYI

Inle Lake

KALAW

LAOS

TOUNGGOO

PROME

R. Irrawaddy

Bay of Bengal

THAILAND

PEGU

KAPPALI

RANGOON

THATON

MOULMEIN

THANBYUZAYAT

BANGKOK

Andaman Sea

200 km

Prologue

Every life is made up of a torrent of moments: calm when waters run smoothly, agitated when currents try to swirl us off course, and stormy when the depths are whipped into a whirlpool of frenzy, and it's a huge struggle simply to keep afloat.

So it was with the life of the early church in Burma, and of the small part we were destined to play in it. Between us, eight members of our English family were to spend forty-five unforgettable years there, following in the remarkable footsteps of our intrepid forebears. We were there from 1906 to 1951 – from mid Colonial times to the dying days of the Raj, from the devastation of World War II to the rebirth of the country as an independent nation – and what years these were! This tale is an attempt to tell a small slice of the story of our life in the Anglican Community in Burma, in which we shared, from its beginnings until the time of our departure.

For me, Burma was the centre of the universe. I was born there in 1924, the eldest of three. My childhood was idyllic, surrounded as I was by my loving family, and by many gentle, brown and smiling faces, for the Burmese idolise children.

Yet, as my eighth birthday approached, I grew anxious. This was the dreaded cut-off point, the age at which European children were often sent 'home' to avoid falling foul of tropical illness and to be educated, their final humiliation being to live with strangers in a cold climate, completely isolated from their parents for years to come.

I remember almost wearing out my knees morning, noon and night for many weeks, praying that this wouldn't happen to me. And it didn't. My father suddenly got very ill and we all had to come home in a great hurry. I felt guilty, convinced that my endless requests to the Almighty had caused this calamity, and that the whole thing was my fault. It was a long time later, only after Father's full recovery, that I was able to let these feelings go, and even then not fully. We had to leave my beloved uncle and godfather behind in Burma and this left a permanent legacy of sadness, for we were a close-knit family.

Once settled in England, however, our home was full of Burmese treasures – statues of Buddha and elephants on the mantelpiece, woven cane baskets and betel-nut boxes in the hall, and lacquer ware everywhere. But above all, the house was alive with Burmese stories, for my parents and my aunt who lived with us (a grandmother figure) were great raconteurs.

These stories became a very part of me, as I listened and learned and tried to remember. It was then that I started to hoard Burmese bits and pieces: stamps, newspaper cuttings, postcards and photographs, telling myself that one day I would use my collection to write about Burma.

Years passed as I lived through war service and university, marriage, probation work and teaching, motherhood and grandmotherhood, while Burmese thoughts were put on hold, but never forgotten. All this time, and little by little, my collection of letters and diaries was growing, stored haphazardly in a couple of trunks (tin-lined to avoid the ravages of damp and white ants) and awaiting the day when I could begin to pull their contents together. Now, nearly eighty years later, I'm compelled to put pen to paper following two unexpected happenings. The first was a remarkably successful pilgrimage to our old haunts in Burma in late 2007, arranged by my three sons – who accompanied me throughout – and the second the astonishing discovery of a hoard of 250 of my father's letters from the 1920s and '30s, hidden away for over three generations in a cobwebbed attic.

This then, is a last ditch attempt by an octogenarian to tell her story of the Burma she loved as a child, using extracts from diaries and letters as a substantial part of the text. Much written material has not survived so there are large gaps in the narrative from time to time, with longer accounts in other years where letters have been kept. The result is something of a tangled tale, but so is the history of family life.

CHAPTER ONE

Burmese Myths and Legends

"Ow, my head hurts!" sobbed a small voice from the depths of a large, bamboo wastepaper basket, lying askew on the cabin floor. They were choppy seas aboard the *S.S. Kemmendine* on that hot June afternoon of 1932 and it must have been a particularly big swell in the Bay of Bengal that made the ship shudder so violently that it was able to dislodge a small child from the top bunk and hurl her to the floor, amid a heap of discarded rubbish, which helped to break her fall.

I was that slightly bruised and battered eight year old, and the incident has remained vividly fixed in my mind ever since, continually playing and re-playing itself like a favourite film on a television screen. I was sharing a cabin with my aunt – an inveterate story teller – and after my tumble, in order to comfort me, she began on a wonderful series of nightly tales about Burma, the country of my birth.

The author Anne Garrad as a child.

'Aunt Fan', the most unselfish person I have ever known, certainly lived up to her name. She was my father's sister, the practical person who kept things cool, who soothed away hurts and difficulties by bringing a breath of fresh air into every heated situation, and it is partly to celebrate and preserve her memory that I'm writing this story. People whose lives are often unnoticed and unmarked are sometimes the most important players in life.

Some of the tales she told were little more than legends, woven together by mystery and magic, sadness and farce, but I have never forgotten the force of them (but not of course their detail) and ever since our return to England, I've been trying to explore their authenticity.

Our forty-five years in Burma were lived, of course, in a totally different world from that of the Myanmar of recent years, currently suffering desperate poverty under a seemingly relentless military regime. The 1920s and '30s were still the era of the British Raj, when an omnipotent Governor General reigned supreme, and when Burma was the rice bowl of the Far East. The railways (built by British engineers) worked well – at least most of the time – and helped to transport rice and rubies, tin and teak, emeralds, oil, and cotton, as well as fruit and vegetables of all kinds to the ports along the coast, en route to many different countries worldwide.

But in a land whose population is devoutly Buddhist, as Burma is, our family was not in for an easy ride. My parents were Anglican Christians, charged to spread the Bible story as missionaries for the Society for the Propagation of the Gospel, and one can only marvel at the indomitable, deeply held beliefs which kept them going under hugely difficult circumstances. Their stipends (or pay packets) were much smaller than those enjoyed by British government employees (elite members of the Indian Civil Service) and home leave was limited to twelve months every six years or so, and this included the five week journey home by ship and the five week journey back.

Of course, all the usual tropical 'odds' were stacked against them, too, including an atrocious climate and illnesses galore, ready to pounce without notice. Cases of malaria, typhoid, plague, cholera, dengue and dysentery filled the few hospitals long before antibiotics were known. Voracious insects, carbuncles and prickly heat did their best to irritate human flesh almost beyond endurance, while earthquakes and destructive white ants caused mayhem to buildings and furniture alike. Despite all this, the family came to love the beautiful country of Burma and the friendly warmth of its people, and were heart broken to leave when illness finally made this necessary.

Once upon a time, Aunt Fan told me, thousands of years ago, a very brave Indian prince decided to leave his country and travel east across the Black Mountains to an unknown land. Somehow he made his way through the almost impenetrable jungles and dense scrub lands of western Burma, forded rivers, and battled with all sorts of beasts – crocodiles, pythons, tigers, elephants and leopards among them – before finally setting up camp a few miles to the north of Mandalay where he established a kingdom of his own, producing two sons to carry on his dynasty. This legend (as I thought it then) is now said to be true. At any rate, it is part of the written *Chronicles of the Burmese Kings*, where we are told that Abhiraja was the prince's name and Tagaung the village where he settled.[1]

Burma is a mysterious, isolated land and a country of enormous contrasts, both geographically and culturally. Because it is almost surrounded by mountains (many of them densely forested), overland access has never been easy, neither from China to the north, India to the west nor Siam (Thailand) to the east, and trade has mainly been carried on along its vast coast, which curves in a huge half circle from the Bay of Bengal to the Andaman Sea. Seven very different ethnic groups surround the central lands where the true Burmans live, each speaking its own language and enjoying its own culture. These are the Karen, Shan, Arakan, Mon, Kachin, Chin and Karenni. The whole country is drawn together by its lifeline, the mighty River Irrawaddy, running north to south from the high snows of the Himalayas to the muggy waters of the Rangoon Delta, carrying with it people and goods of many different kinds as well as stories and myths in a variety of tongues, its fertile valley producing much of the country's erstwhile wealth.

The Upper Irrawaddy Valley is the old heartland of the original Kingdoms of Burma, where local royal princes held sway over their people from time immemorial, even before the arrival of Abhiraja. Here, the climate is intensely hot under relentless blue skies, with enormous cloudbursts concentrated over just a few weeks of the year. In the Delta and coastal regions it's a different picture with steady rains for months, lush and tropical, covering everything with mildew, while in the hills it can get bitterly cold with frosty nights in winter.

The *Chronicles* tell us that the prince's elder son ventured a long way west to found the region of Arakan, while his younger boy sailed down the Irrawaddy and established his headquarters near today's town of Prome, half way between Rangoon and Mandalay, a kingdom which lasted for more than five centuries. For years without number, Upper Burma consisted of a conglomeration of these city states, each vying for precedence with its neighbour, sometimes living in relative harmony and sometimes indulging in acrimonious in-fighting. In every kingdom the monarch would reign supreme – a kind of demi-god – holding court at his royal palace, guarded by twelve huge wooden gates, each representing a sign of the zodiac and usually surrounded by a moat.

The Burmese are a very superstitious people, constantly on the look out for signs and symbols before coming to any decision, and always ready to listen to astrologers and soothsayers. So, as a child, it didn't really surprise me that the locals (although devoutly Buddhist) should also believe in spirit worship. During family walks we sometimes used to come across 'Nat Shrines' – little wooden platforms on stilts where small gifts of rice, water, and flowers were placed to placate the gods in an effort to ensure a good harvest. After all, it seemed highly likely to me that the hundreds of trees in those dark, forbidding forests surrounding us could well be alive with spirits, only too ready to cast their spooky spells on the poor people who lived and farmed nearby. It made good sense to try to please them, I thought, and in this way to get them on one's side, particularly at harvest time.

Burmese legend relates that in the fifth century B.C. when the Buddha was a young man starting on his pilgrimage, it happened that two Burmans from Rangoon were travelling to North India and there met him by chance. He was hungry, so they gave him honey and rice cakes and asked him for a small token in exchange. Straight away, he pulled eight hairs from his head and, to their astonishment and delight, presented these to them. On returning home, the hairs were buried deep below ground, the magnificent Shwedagon Pagoda in Rangoon being built above them. Today, this vast pagoda is over 300 feet high, covered in many tons of gold leaf and surrounded by a myriad of smaller shrines, their bejewelled surfaces dazzling in the sun. In my childhood, it was an enormous treat to be allowed to visit this extraordinary place of pilgrimage with its unforgettable smells of incense, cigar smoke, spices and curry, all mixed together in glorious confusion. I particularly remember the sound of all those high-pitched tinkling bells gyrating above me as they twinkled in the heat, and how my neck used to ache after staring upwards for so long.

I don't know how much truth was contained in those fascinating stories of Burma's past, recounted nightly in that ship's cabin on the high seas, but it seems probable that Theravada Buddhism didn't in fact make its way into the country until the fourth century A.D. (long after the Buddha's death in 484 B.C., apparently after he had been taken ill following a meal of rotten pork.) In the sixth century, a Chinese traveller in Burma reported of the people who lived there "that it is their custom to love life and hate killing... they know how to make astronomical calculations... they are Buddhists and have hundreds of monasteries."[2] Most members of the Burmese race that I've come to know over the years are certainly warm-hearted, gentle people, but much of their early history is one of intermittent feuding between the Burmans – the indigenous people of the plains – and the *Sawbwas* (minor kings or princes) of the numerous hill tribes.

In the ninth century, cavalry from the north swept through the Irrawaddy Delta under their leader Nanzhao, the so called "Lord of the South". He founded the magnificent and beautiful kingdom of Pagan, situated in fertile soil at the confluence of the river Irrawaddy and its tributary the Chindwin, and set about building houses and shops, pagodas and palaces on an unimaginably large scale. The kingdom prospered for nearly 500 years before it weakened, being finally overthrown by the Mongols in the late fourteenth century.

Pagan was at the height of its fame and power at the time of William the Conqueror in England (1066 and all that), and even today there are nearly 2000 pagodas to be seen, many of them ravaged by a mixture of old age and constant earthquakes but still outstanding in their battered majesty, overwhelming in size and height. I didn't have the chance to go there as a child, but I shall never forget a recent visit when we travelled by horse and cart from stupa to stupa, trotting gently along endless sandy tracks between huge fields of sesame, beans and groundnuts. No vestige of the old houses are left – some of them have been forcibly removed to New Pagan – just the vastly beautiful pagodas remain, but it doesn't take much in the way of imagination to visualise a little of its erstwhile grandeur and colossal scale. Had a Domesday Survey been made in Burma at that time, as happened in England, what an immensity of wealth would have been revealed! Paintings of the period remain on a few interior walls of the larger pagodas, as reminders of some of the activities of the time; one, I remember, vividly depicted boating and fishing, and another showed men and women planting rice.

This, too, was the period when the very first attempts were apparently being made to commit to writing what had, up to now, been only a spoken language. And so it was, in the eleventh century, in this great period of enterprise and growth, that the medieval empire of Pagan gave birth to the flowing Burmese script that is still in

Anne with her sons Thomas and Peter at Pagan in 2007.

use today. As a youngster, I was fascinated with this beautiful curly writing, with its rounded, flourishing strokes of different thicknesses, and spent many hours trying to master it, with pretty poor results. To this day, I hope it is not wrong of me to feel that the script is so beautiful and complex, that it could well be used to advantage by interior fashion designers as a basis for eye-catching curtain materials or wallpapers. At a family level, one of our treasured possessions is a circular wooden bread trencher – which I remember was given as a birthday present to my mother – with "Man doth not live by bread alone" engraved round its rim in the bold loops and curves of Burmese lettering.

But to return to the earlier narrative of conquest, it seems that one of Burma's famous and most brutal kings was Bayinnaung, who, in the second half of the sixteenth century, established the greatest and largest Burmese Empire of the time. Aided by Portuguese mercenaries, he made non-stop war on the independent towns and princedoms throughout the country and beyond. His aim was to build a kingdom to rival Pagan and he chose to set up his headquarters at Pegu, north-east

သ	a	as in *what*.
သာ	â	as in *father*.
ဣ	i	as in *police*.
ဤ	î	as in *machine*.
ဥ	u	as in *recruit*.
ဦ	û	as in *rule*.
ဧ	e	as in *grey*.
ဪ	e:	as the first *e* in *never*.
သယ်	è	as the first *e* in *everlasting*.
ဩ	aw	as in *law*.
ဪ	aw	as in *drawl*.
အံ॥သန်*	an	as un in *dun*.
သား	â:	as in *ah!*
ဩ	o	as in *holy*.
ဩက်॥ဩုက်	ôk	as in *yoke*.
ဩုံ॥ဩုန်	ôn	as in *cone*.
ဩိပ်॥ဩိတ်	ei	as *a* in *rake, rate*.
ဩိန့်॥ဩိုဝ်	ei	as in *vein*.
သစ်	it	as in *pit*.
သင်	in	as in *pin*.
သပ်॥သတ်	at	as in *what*.
သက်	et	as in *pet*.
အိုက်	aik	as *ai* in *aisle*.
အိုင်	aing	as *ine* in *Rhine*.
ဩောက်	auk	as *ou* in *out*.
ဩောင်	aung	as *oun* in *sound*.

A page from my Burmese grammar book.

of Rangoon, peopled with fugitives from the twenty subordinate kingdoms he had captured throughout the south-east. In time, he came to be accepted as a great man, ruling over much of Asia, accruing huge wealth and building palace after palace in ever-increasing magnificence.

Aunt Fan told me something of all this, I think, but of course she had to leave out many of the grisly details and failed to mention two other interesting things. The first was the extraordinary fact that when the king himself died in 1581, he had fathered close to one hundred children, so continuing for posterity a legacy of royal kinship going right back to the days of Abhiraja; the second consequence (which, fortunately, she couldn't have foreseen) was that Bayinnaung's reign of subjugation and cruelty would one day play a major part in the future history of the country, leaving as it has, a lasting template for use by the Burmese military junta of modern times. History has a habit of repeating itself, and the Burmese people have a passionate belief in continuity.

Pegu's dominance lasted for less than 200 years, for in 1757 it was taken by force by another powerful king, Alaungphaya, this time aided by French mercenaries. My aunt, I know, tried to cut out 'the bloody bits' of Burmese history, but she had to mention something of the turmoil that ensued, with its dreadful massacre of men, women and children, adding that she believed that thousands had managed to escape but omitting the fact that many others were sold into slavery. A monk wrote at that awful time that "Sons could not find their mothers, nor mothers their sons, and there was weeping throughout the land"[3]; this was only the beginning of countless years of conflict.

Not content with many other conquests besides Pegu, King Alaungphaya was now determined to extend his empire eastwards to Siam, and in 1759 started to besiege Ayutthaya, the capital city of that great country. There was a brief reprieve following the king's unexpected illness the following year, but his sons were only too ready and eager to continue the fight. On an April day in 1767, after over a year of fearsome siege, the Burmese army at last breached the walls and put the thousands of starving, disease ridden Siamese occupants to death. Ayutthaya was a densely populated city, far larger than anything of which Burma could boast and said to rival London or Paris in size; this was a huge victory, far beyond their wildest dreams. In their euphoria they destroyed the entire place, including the Grand Palace, home to five dynasties of noble Siamese kings, burning and defacing everything as they went. Despite this mighty conquest, Burma was to fail in its attempt to overrun the whole country and in due course Siam recovered its sovereignty, re-establishing a new capital at Bangkok, and determinedly building up its prosperity again. Who could then have dreamt that, 250 years later, Burma would have become the poor relation, and Thailand the country of wealth and tourism?

In my old age, I have become an avid reader of newspapers, and just the other day, drinking a cup of coffee on a chilly January morning in the year 2011, the name King Alaungphaya jumped out at me from the printed page.[4] It seems that in

1756 this Burmese king wrote to his fellow monarch, King George II of England, but the letter has only just been deciphered. All this time until then, when scholars started to peruse it, the document has lain ignored in a Hanoverian vault, discarded and unanswered, inside the very ivory tusk in which it was delivered. Inscribed on a pure gold sheet and adorned with twenty-four rubies, it was "an effusive and gushing appeal for camaraderie and trade with Britain." Written in Burmese script and praising King George as "the most meritorious and supreme master of all the parasol-bearing kings… Lord of ruby, gold, silver, copper, iron, amber and precious stone mines, Lord of white elephants, red elephants and elephants of various colours": it certainly made my day!

On a more serious note, however, the letter is an example of how the Burmese, in the late eighteenth century, were beginning to see themselves as the masters of Asia. Taking astrological advice, even the Court of Ava (based at the ancient capital city of that name) was now moved, literally piece by piece, to Amarapura, to be known in future as the 'Immortal City'.

In British India, the power of the East India Company had by now increased greatly. In the early eighteen-hundreds their Court of Directors in London was told by the Governor-General in Calcutta that war with Burma might soon be inevitable, in order "to humble the overweening pride and arrogance of the Burmese monarch"[5], who at that time was Bagyidaw, great-grandson of Alaungphaya. The Burmese king, it seems, was also attempting to make some friendly overtures to France, and this began to alarm Britain.

In due course we declared war, Aunt Fan explained, and went on to tell me a little about what happened. Apparently, it was in May 1824 that H.M.S. Liffey, at the head of a large convoy of ships of the East India Company, anchored at the main wharf on the outskirts of Rangoon – then a fishing port of only some 20, 000 people – her artillery at the ready. After some initial short-lived success, the British advance was halted by strongly defended Burmese forts – many of them underground and manned by locals who knew the territory – and the English and Indian soldiery were forced to bivouac for months, in torrential rain and with little food. By September the British were beginning to die in their thousands from malaria and dysentery, and the future looked very bleak. In fact, it was not until the spring of the following year that the decimated troops at last managed to get the upper hand, and this was only through the use of deadly new weapons imported from India. These were rockets, first invented by the Indian Army only a few years earlier, and nothing could stand up to the intensity of their devastating fire power.

This was total disaster for the proud Burmese people, for not only had they lost large areas of territory, but they had also lost face in front of the whole world, and in some ways, particularly for an Asiatic nation, this was probably the harder of the two to bear. A temporary armistice was eventually agreed, with much of southern Burma's long cherished independence being ousted from them. But even this state of affairs was not to last, for only a generation later, under a superficial pretext, a second Anglo-Burmese war was to follow and by 1852 the whole of southern Burma lay in British hands.

CHAPTER TWO

Christianity challenges Buddhism

In 1813, when Burma was still an independent country, an amazing American Baptist missionary arrived in the country saddled with the intriguing name of Dr. Adoniram Judson. Within a few years he somehow managed to teach himself Burmese and to compile a dictionary of this complex language. The Buddhists didn't care for him at all, disliking the Christian message that he brought with him, and he had a very tough time of it, spending long periods in prison. Despite all this, he managed to translate the Bible into Burmese so that it could be read in the churches he set up, an extraordinary feat for the time. In particular he befriended the Karens, one of Burma's most populous hill tribes, whose peoples had always been treated contemptuously by the Burmans of the plains.

Now the Karens, Aunt Fan told me, had a legend, known as the story of the Golden Book, and this was to help spread the Christian message in an unexpected way. The legend says that the original father of all the people of Burma had three sons. The eldest was a Karen, to whom his father gave a golden book; the second was a Burman, to whom he gave a palm-leaf book; the youngest was white, and he received a book of leather. The father sent his sons down into Burma from the north where white ants soon destroyed the palm-leaf book, and pigs devoured the leather one. Quite soon the Burman son began to quarrel with his older brother over possession of the golden book so the Karen entrusted it to the young white brother who promised to look after it, but before long he sailed away across the seas, and no more was heard of him. However, the legend refused to die, with the Karens believing that one day the white man would return, bringing with him the golden book and the sufferings of their people would cease. It was a sort of messianic hope, seemingly fulfilled later on by the coming of Dr. Judson.

King Mindon Min, the most loved of the later Burmese kings, was only five years old when Dr. Judson arrived in Burma. Mindon was said to be one of the wisest and most peaceable rulers the country had ever known, reigning from 1853 to 1878, and being able to trace his dynasty right back to Prince Abhiraja who had lived in years beyond memory. King Mindon was very open minded and sent Burmese scholars to study in many of the bustling cities of Europe, and though a practising Buddhist himself, was apparently not totally averse to Christian teaching.

It was indeed this great king who decided to move his court once more, this time from Amarapura to Mandalay, which was no more than an impoverished village then. Aunt Fan described to me how the huge teak beams of the many palaces and pagodas of the old capital would have been literally laden onto carts – drawn by oxen or bullocks – and moved, piece by piece along dirt tracks, to their new destination, gradually building it up into the city in which we had lived so recently, and that we had come to love. Rudyard Kipling's famous poem 'Come you back to Mandalay' suggests that the town has been there since time immemorial, but this is a fallacy, for it was, in fact, only built during Queen Victoria's reign in 1857, and ironically it seems that the poet never even paid a visit to Mandalay himself!

One can just imagine the panoply of the great day when King Mindon arrived at his new Mandalay palace, set behind towering walls, a mile square, and bounded on all sides by a magnificent moat. It was an auspicious day, the 16th July 1858, and even the rain seems to have held off as he was carried along by palanquin in an enormously noisy and colourful procession, accompanied by the highest officials of his kingdom and surrounded by a phalanx of bejewelled royal elephants. Entering through the main gate of the twelve, with the populace falling to their knees as he passed, what were his thoughts, one wonders now, as he seated himself high on his throne? Was my aunt right in saying that he was a man of peace, someone who would do his best to integrate what was left of the ancient kingdom of Burma into the beckoning arms of the outside world? I ponder over this now, in my dotage, but as an eight year old lying in my top bunk in the good ship *Kemmendine*, I was much more interested in the procession of elephants, lumbering along in front of the king with their brightly coloured coats adorned with rubies and emeralds shining in the sun, than I was about his motives.

It was soon after King Mindon's move to Mandalay that the first Anglican priest from the Society for the Propagation of the Gospel came into the picture. Aunt Fan told me that his name was Dr. Marks, an important figure in the life of the early

Dr. Marks (left) and the Rev. J. Tsan Baw, one of his pupils.

church in Burma, adding that she believed it was mainly because of him that my father had come out east in the first place. This piqued my curiosity, and I remember pestering her again and again to tell me more about him.

Dr. Marks, she said, was a British missionary who had already been hard at work setting up Christian schools in Burma, and as he was a strict disciplinarian, his schools flourished. It seems that he became widely trusted with many Burmese people coming to him for help and advice – among them the Thonzah Mintha, one of King Mindon Min's older sons, who had recently quarrelled with his father. Dr. Marks went out of his way to befriend the young man and advised him to return to court, where in due course, he was reconciled with the king.

"What happened next?" I asked, and this is what I was told.

The prince, it seems, lost no time in inviting Dr. Marks to visit him in Mandalay and with the blessing of his superior, the Bishop of Calcutta, the school master accepted, setting out overland on the 28th August 1868 with six of his best school boys from Rangoon. All of them had been taught to eat with knives and forks, which caused a lot of amusement and amazement as the Burmese usually eat rice with the fingers. They visited other mission schools on the way – some of them staffed by his former pupils – even celebrating Holy Communion at each, before leaving for the capital by boat.

Before setting out, Dr. Marks had been in touch with Major Sladen, the British political agent at court, who had encouraged him to come, writing that he had had many discussions with His Majesty on religious matters. The king, he said, though a devout Buddhist, was far from intolerant in matters of belief, understanding that people sometimes needed to follow their own path of faith even if it was different from the teaching of 'the enlightened one', the Buddha. Above all things, King Mindon was interested in education and might well give his backing to the setting up of a Christian school in Mandalay, having heard such good reports of Dr. Marks' work elsewhere. Indeed, he might even send his own sons there.

So, full of confidence, Dr. Marks arrived at the king's palace, the party removing their shoes before entering, where they squatted on the floor. In a letter recounting the visit, the missionary wrote[6] "in a few minutes, the king came in attended by a little boy, one of his sons. The king is a tall, stout, thoroughly Burmese looking man, about fifty-five years of age. He had on only one garment, the pulso or beautiful silk cloth covering from his waist to his feet. He reclined on a velvet carpet, near which the little prince placed the golden betel-box and water-cup and then reverently retired. As the king entered, every man bowed his head to the ground and kept it there. His Majesty, according to his usual custom, took up a pair of binocular glasses, and had a good stare at us. He then asked if I was the English *Poongyee* (or priest). When did I arrive? How old was I? And many other questions. He then asked me what requests I had to make to him, assuring me that all were granted before I spoke."

The king was as good as his word, approving Dr. Marks to work as a Christian missionary, providing land for the building of a Christian school for Burmese boys, a Christian church for worship, houses for the staff and a cemetery. To crown it all, he agreed to build them entirely at his own cost.

"He directed me to prepare the plans," the letter goes on, "adding that the school was to be built for 1,000 boys. The king said that it was his wish to place some of his own sons under our care, and he sent for nine of the young princes, fine intelligent looking lads of about ten years of age, and formally handed them over to me. He handed me a hundred gold pieces (worth £50) to buy books etc. for the school. He asked me whether I would procure machinery for him from Europe. I said that, with every desire to oblige His Majesty, I must decline all commercial or political business; that my province was simply that of a religious teacher. The interview having lasted over two hours, His Majesty concluded by inviting my boys and self to breakfast in the palace on the following day. We travelled in covered bullock carts, as it is considered very wrong for a *poongyee* to ride on horseback. We found the king in the *Hmnan nan dor* (or glass palace) attended by several of his queens and daughters. My boys prostrated themselves, as did the other Burmans, while I squatted down in a cramped position, being obliged to keep my feet out of sight. The king was seated on the highest of a flight of six steps. He began by asking me if I was comfortably housed and cared for. He reiterated his promises of yesterday, and expressed his hope that all would not be in vain. He made me tell him about each boy, and he addressed some kind words to them. I presented him with a pretty telescope, and the boys gave a lot of English toys to the young princes. We were then conducted to another apartment, where a sumptuous breakfast was served to us in the English style. Suddenly my boys all slipped off their chairs on to the ground, and when I looked up to see the cause, I found that one of the elder princes, a lad of about seventeen, had entered, having been deputed by his father to see that all was right. More than thirty different kinds of sweetmeats, all made by the queens' own hands, were offered to us. After breakfast we were conducted by one of the *woons* or governors over the royal gardens which are unlike what are generally known as gardens elsewhere. There were very few flowers, but a number of shrubs and young trees, planted in no order as far as I could discover. The place is neatly kept, and is divided into two parts by a canal of stagnant water."

I remember how uproariously Aunt Fan and I laughed when we came to this bit of the story, only stopping to hold our noses as we all but experienced the awful stench surrounding the royal gardens (a smell we had been all too familiar with in Mandalay, as I recall). I was totally gripped by the 'goings on' at the palace, feeling myself part of it all, slipping off my chair when the young prince entered the dining room, and shutting my eyes to avoid the king's terrifying stare as he examined us through his binoculars.

But, as Aunt Fan said, one should not belittle Dr. Marks' magnificent achievement, for this was a real breakthrough for Christian education. The king soon fulfilled his promise and in next to no time had started to build a splendid school, with boarding accommodation for students and staff, as well as a fine church on the English pattern, all made of solid teak from the local forests. Even the cemetery was not forgotten.

True to his word, when The Royal School opened in 1868, King Mindon enrolled several of his sons as pupils, but this is where the trouble started. Naturally, they arrived as princes, riding in state on the royal elephants and sheltered from the sun by golden parasols, but of course these had to be left behind at the school gates, despite the humiliating hullabaloo this caused. Once safely inside, Dr. Marks insisted that the lads were to be treated no differently from the other students, but again pandemonium ensued when boys kept slipping to the ground each time a prince approached. It was only Dr. Marks who was able to deal with this, as the Burmese members of his staff – ingrained since birth with the concept of the divinity of kings – also bowed their heads in homage, even when trying to teach. Of course all the

THE MANDALAY MISSION COMPOUND, CHURCH, SCHOOL AND CLERGY HOUSE
(An old wood-cut from the painting by a Burmese artist).

Woodcut of the Mandalay Mission Compound (1868).

youngsters – commoner and royal alike – took advantage of this unusual situation, and got up to all sorts of tricks, and mayhem ruled whenever the headmaster was not present.

After a few years, the princes were withdrawn, peace and order being restored once more, and the school allowed to flourish. When, eventually, Dr. Marks resigned through ill health in 1895, after serving thirty-five years in Burma, it was announced that no less than 15, 000 children had come under his influence. I remember, as a small child, being absolutely staggered by these figures, for one of my great delights was to bury my head in a story book, and I thought how wonderful it was that so many others were now able to enjoy the thrill of reading too. From that day onwards, Dr. Marks became my hero.

The Royal School survived his departure, having been built on sturdy principles, like its founder. The buildings decayed eventually, of course, but it was not until 1911 that the old wooden structure was replaced, having stood its ground for forty-three years, battered by boys, devoured by termites, and ravaged by monsoons. The rebuild was put in hand by the next generation of missionaries, including my own father and uncle, but this comes later.

Aunt Fan told me that the original Anglican place of worship in Mandalay was the fine teak building, Christ Church, in whose compound our family was destined to live later on. She explained that the church started to be used at the same time as the school, but was not consecrated until 1873, following the gift of a stone font by Queen Victoria, who gushingly expressed her gratitude to King Mindon for his great generosity. The Bishop of Calcutta performed the ceremony, the whole Anglican church in Burma remaining in that diocese for only another four years after this, before the Diocese of Rangoon was founded in 1877, with the Rev. Jonathan Holt Titcomb as the very first bishop.

Throughout my Burmese childhood, I was constantly in the presence of my parents' friends, mainly clergymen and lay-workers – British, Indian, Burmese, Karen, Chinese or of mixed race – who were valiantly building up the work of the church throughout the country, but my memory of them is often poor, confused and shadowy. To me, of course, they were elderly and remote figures, and being a little shy, I often found them intimidating, and their names confusing.

I have always been bad at recalling names and excuse myself by thinking that this dates back to my childhood, when I was expected to remember so many! In those days, etiquette demanded that gentlemen should be addressed as 'Mr' and ladies as 'Mrs' or 'Miss', followed by the surname, but usually without mention of any Christian name. Professional men, on the other hand, called their colleagues by their surnames only, without any prefix, a practice dating back to their schooldays. This seems strange to today's generation, who automatically call everyone by their first name from the moment they meet. It also presents problems of identification, because 'Miss Atwool', in Aunt Fan's diary, for example, can be one of several sisters, and 'Thursfield', in Father's letters, can be one of countless cousins. Many of these people figure in the family letters and diaries, quoted in this story. Where quotations are used in the text, the name is given as it is written, but otherwise I have tried to adhere to the fashion of the day, usually omitting first names, but adding the obligatory 'Mr', 'Mrs' or 'Miss'.[7]

CHAPTER THREE

Dark Deeds and the Threat of Civil War (1878-1879)

Aunt Fan told me that King Mindon Min was struck down with dysentery in the autumn of 1878, from which he did not recover, and the search was suddenly on for a new king. There were princes galore to choose from, apparently, and the senior Mandalay Ministers put their heads together to make a choice that would try to appease everyone. Above all, they wanted to avoid civil war if at all possible. It seems that King Mindon's chief queen had died some time ago and the Middle Palace Queen was the highest ranking of all the palace women; as she passionately desired that one of her daughters should be made queen, wife to a compliant husband, the ministers thought it prudent to go along with her plans. Prince Thibaw, just twenty years old, the son of a minor queen and a bit of a nonentity, was head over heels in love with the Middle Queen's eighteen-year-old daughter Princess Supayalat, so he was an obvious choice, and the deal was done. On 19th September 1878 the Council of State appointed him as heir.

Thibaw was one of the princes who had been at Dr. Marks' School. Here, we are led to believe, he had been made to stand in the corner for bad behaviour, and had also learned to play cricket, "being tolerably good with a bat" and later becoming an accomplished classical scholar.[8]

The beginning of the new king's reign was a time of great unhappiness, Aunt Fan said, adding that she didn't really want to talk about it, but I wanted to know what happened and pleaded with her to tell me, which eventually she did. In the end, I rather wished she hadn't, as the tale, I think you will agree, is horrendous and gave me nightmares.

Many of King Thibaw's half brothers and sisters had by now been imprisoned for some time in a dank prison, she told me, not far from the Royal Court, in an effort to prevent unrest and revolt. At least one had escaped – the prince of Nyoung

Yan – so Queen Supayalat and her minions decided that the remainder were a threat to the new establishment, and must be eliminated, and on St. Valentine's Day 1879, the executions began. In a field, near the river Irrawaddy, a huge number of King Mindon's sons and daughters were said to have been killed, strangled, or trampled by elephants (apparently, the accounts differ).

The British government was totally horrified by the massacres and extra troops were brought in, but Mandalay in Upper Burma was not as yet under their jurisdiction, and little action was taken – at least for the moment.

To change the subject, my aunt started to tell me about the Anglican Church in Mandalay, which had meanwhile been quietly gathering strength. In 1875 two new priests had arrived to take Dr. Marks' place for a couple of years (the Rev. Fairclough and the Rev. Chard), but it was in 1878 that an amazing man, the Rev. James Alfred Colbeck, first transferred from Kemmendine (Rangoon) to Mandalay, and found himself thrown unexpectedly into a period of royal mayhem. He was apparently young and vigorous, an outstanding priest and an incredibly brave character, and even as a child my father and uncle used to talk to me about him sometimes, which is why I am going to quote from some of his revealing letters that have fortunately survived.

On 16th July 1878, with great foresight (the reigning King Mindon still being in good health) Mr. Colbeck wrote as follows to his unknown correspondent:[9] "I am on the move again, the bishop has given orders for me to proceed to Mandalay. I am no coward, but yet do not at all like the idea of going to Mandalay. There are few Christians of any sort. The English can be counted on the fingers very easily. There are next to no Tamils, and altogether the 'Minister of Mandalay' has to endure a kind of banishment. Add to this the possibilities for the king giving trouble, and the continual rebellions which take place. Mandalay is a good centre for a mission, but not yet. The bishop fears I shall get obnoxious to the Burmese Government and be put into prison the first month. I don't know why exactly, but if I were put in prison for Christ's sake both you and I ought to feel it an honour."

On 30th July he wrote that he had started from Kemmendine on the 18th at 6.30 a.m., and after a long journey reached Prome at 7.30 p.m., staying the night at the Travellers' Bungalow there. The next day he took ship on the Irrawaddy "and rapidly steamed up past Thayetmyo, and then left the territory of the Empress of India (Queen Victoria) and entered that of the Empire of Burmah… after being two days within Upper Burmah, during a squall of rain and wind, the steamer got aground on a sand-bank, and there we stuck helpless for a whole day. We reached Mandalay, the Royal Golden City, on Saturday evening at 7, but it was some time before I could land. I am now well pleased that I have been sent here, and believe I shall be happy. It seems quite natural for me to be here again, and there are numbers of faces which I remember. I won't lead you into Mandalay politics because I know so little about them yet, and I am ordered to beware of politics. As for seeing the king, I do not yet know. It is very ungracious to take possession of the splendid Clergy House, Church etc. and not to be ready and willing to pay respects to the monarch who built it. I am ready and willing to pay my respects to the king, but there are obstacles in the way of free action."

By 7th August Mr. Colbeck was getting impatient, and wrote: "Mandalay is just as ever a place of plots and counter-plots. I do not think there is as much good feeling towards foreigners as there used to be. Cholera is bad here, in fact, in all parts of Burmah, more or less. Rain was wanted much, but during the last week, beautiful refreshing showers have fallen, so we ought to be thankful."

By September 18th, following King Mindon's sudden illness, matters at Court were coming to a head, and Mr. Colbeck's letters continue:

"When I wrote, I was expecting and watching for the arrival of refugee princes escaping from an expected massacre; we did not know whether the king was alive or dead, and expected to hear a wild outburst of confusion every moment. I stayed up till the next morning at three a.m., and then turned in till six; nothing happened. Next day, according to secret information received, a 'Lady of the Palace' came dressed as a bazaar woman, and shortly after came about a dozen others; they were more than I had bargained for, but I had to take them in and secrete them as well as possible. A few minutes after them came in a common coolie, as I thought. I got up and said, 'Who are you?' He said, 'I am Prince Nyoung Yan – save me'. He was terribly agitated, had escaped from a house in which he was confined, and his uncle had been cut down – not killed – in opening a way for the prince to escape. This made me a party of twelve: the prince and his wife, two daughters (princesses), one son (prince), foster mother and her daughter and attendants.

Do not blame me for risking my own safety, for after all it is something to be an Englishman, and more to be a priest. My house is even by Buddhists regarded as sacred, and not lightly to be disturbed. We knew search was being made for the fugitives, and so as soon as dusk came, we dressed up our Prince Nyoung Yan as a Tamil servant, and as it fortunately came on to rain I smuggled him into the residency compound, right under the noses of the Burmese guard at the gate. He carried a lamp and held an umbrella over me as it was raining, and I treated him in character, i.e. spoke to him as a servant etc. until the coast was clear. We did capitally. Prince Nyoung Yan did his part well, and we could afford to laugh at it, were it not that he is still in some danger. He might be proclaimed king tomorrow, or if one of his half-brothers was proclaimed, he would know that Upper Burmah is no longer safe for him. I could not take any more in that night…

Next evening I went to dinner with the British Resident. This was a bona fide engagement, as it was dark of course I needed a light, so one of the prince's children became my servant, and a sweet but sad little princess of ten years, dressed as a boy, followed me, carrying books for me. This is just in Burmese style. Priests get boys to carry books etc. for them, so we got through the guard again; I thought they were going to stop us long before we got to the gate, but walked boldly on, and the guard cleared out of my way, so Princess Tay Tain Lat got in safely to her father. Shortly after I got home at about one o'clock, two of the guard strolled into our compound with drawn swords. I heard their footsteps but did not know who they were, so I challenged them, 'Who's there?'

Answer: 'Guard.'

'What do you want?'

Answer: 'Things are very unquiet, we have come to see that all is quiet here.'

I replied, 'Very good, the best place to watch is at the gate.'

They went, and then I breathed freely again. I thought they must have got some idea of my little family. Next morning I sent Princess Tay Tain Gyee to the post office, which is inside the Residency compound, dressed up as a boy. One of my own Christian boys from Kemmendine went with her and brought back a note from Mr. Shaw, the British Resident, saying she had got in safely. The postmaster came to breakfast with me, and as he was going back to his office, I said he might as well take a boy with a box of books etc. He said 'all right,' and got safely in by another gate, also guarded. This 'boy', dressed as such, was the foster sister of the prince, and a brave little woman she was. It was she who had come first of all to prepare the way for the whole family. If she had been apprehended she would have been beaten to death very likely.

I have not time to tell how the rest got in, but at night I went again to dinner, and needing a light took the old grandmother, i.e. prince's mother-in-law, as my old man and lantern bearer, and the little princelet followed me as a shadow. We were nearly discovered because my old man, though she looked very nice, was only an old woman after all, and had poor eyes. I stumbled over her and nearly tumbled on the top of three of the guard, who were sitting down by the side of the road. Perhaps this incident got us off, the light dazzled me and them too, and the old man mended his ways so that at last we too got safely in. I can tell you I was very thankful when the last got into a place of safety, for the Burmese officers will not dare to take them out of the Residency by force. I fancy there must have been some of the prince's men in the guard, or they would hardly have allowed so many to slip through. Once or twice the fellows seemed on the point of rushing at us as they paced up and down before the gate, but they had received no orders to stop Europeans, and of course Europeans generally have a servant to carry the lamp, so that the servant goes where the master goes. Next day the old *Dine Goung* (the Sergeant), in conversation with the headmaster, said he was afraid all was not right at the English *Hypoongyee's* house, and he wanted to search it. 'You are quite at liberty to do so,' was the reply, for all the birds had flown. He did not come to do it. I got better sleep that night, six hours instead of three, and did not trouble my head to look narrowly at everybody that came near the gate.

I heard yesterday that all the princes in the Palace except two, Prince Thibaw and Prince Mine Tone, were to be starved to death. This is not confirmed today, but they are under close confinement and being badly treated." On 28ᵗʰ September, Mr. Colbeck wrote, "Between sixty and seventy princes and their relatives are now in chains, badly treated and in terror of their lives. I had another batch of refugees here yesterday, but managed to get them all safely into the British Residency Compound. One other batch is expected, and then I shall have done, I hope. The various reports of the manner in which the two princes, Nyoung Yan and his younger brother Nyoung Oke, got into the Residency, are very amusing to those who know exactly how it all happened, and their multitude is a great safeguard to us. There are people in our compound who know nothing of our having had so many people here. It was good our house is so large. There is no trade going on now, people crowd out of Mandalay by every steamer. The British Government has sent up a steamer to be ready to take us down if need be." On 12ᵗʰ October there was this brief sentence: "The Royal Funeral has taken place, and Prince Thibaw declared king. I went with the British Resident and party."

A letter dated 16ᵗʰ November tells us that "the two refugee princes have now got safely away from Mandalay on board a British steamer, so that we may fairly say they are safe from molestation. There was a great struggle before everything was settled, and time after time there were alarms of a forcible capture, which would have meant war between the Indian Government and Burmah to result perhaps in the annexation of the latter – a thing which I do not wish to happen just now – I do want a little corner in the east to be independent."

By the end of March, church work had become almost impossible. "You will hardly expect to hear much missionary news in this letter, but we are not dead in this work either; we were hoping to baptise eight or ten adults at Easter, besides five or six children, but they have become scattered here and there, and no one can come into our compound now without fear of punishment, nor will any stranger be at all pleased if I attempt to enter his house, as it would bring suspicion upon him. This state of things is of course hardly what one expected, when we first heard that one of our schoolboys, number twenty-seven, was to become king."

On 5th June Mr. Colbeck says "I have just been writing a letter to the Nyoung Yan Prince in Calcutta, to tell him of the state of his poor old mother and sister here. They have been once at least ordered out to execution, but have been spared hitherto. They are now closely confined, and have two chains on each foot. The princess is only about sixteen years of age. She wrote saying that the irons had chafed the flesh raw… of course I do not go to the palace myself, and it is amusing to hear the devices of the women who manage to convey our messages. Today the princess sent us a letter written in pencil upon a strip of cotton cloth, which was wrapped up with some sewing work supposed to be for a jacket. Often enough the small notes come out wrapped up in a Burmese cheroot or cigar. Things are so close in the palace now that it is hard to hear anything and prove its truth, so whether more executions have taken place or not is quite uncertain. It is true, however, that the young king is drinking heavily, and his wives, mother, and mother-in-law are not happy together." There are also references to the fact that Prince Nyoung Yan was now sending money to Mr. Colbeck, which he was managing to smuggle into the prison to help keep them alive.

On 11th June he writes of "a poor woman who sought refuge here with her little child of six months old, sick with smallpox. She had been kept in prison and chains for ten months, and this child was born during that time; pity or fear at last moved the authorities to let her out, and so she came here for shelter. We have had eight smallpox cases in our compound, and no one is left to get it, I think, so that we fear the less to receive the poor little stranger. There is a plague of smallpox amongst the children of Mandalay. Few are vaccinated, and the weather is too hot to allow of its being properly done now, so that death after death occurs. What a terribly loathsome disease it is; it looks as though every part of the body were rotten and corrupt, and could never be sound again. I think English anti-vaccinationists need only step over to Burmah to be convinced of the general utility of vaccination."

Mr. Colbeck's letter of 11th October 1879 shows him a free man at last, writing aboard the steamship *Panthay*, moored at Prome in British Burma. "We have rather ignominiously run away from Mandalay… crossed the frontier yesterday about noon, nearly having a fight for it… we have lost a great deal of property, and all came away with nothing. Our Christians have mostly come away, and what is to be done with us all I don't know."

Later, writing from St John's College, Rangoon, he assures his correspondent of his safety, but adds "I am longing to get back to Mandalay… we went together to church, and offered praise and thanksgiving for our safe preservation."

He explains how they got away at the viceroy's insistence, for they were utterly defenceless. "I did not wish to leave but Mr. St. Barbe, the acting Resident, told me that if I stayed, having been so mixed up in the troubles, I should probably bring on immediately what the Indian Government were not yet prepared for, and of course the Burmese Government bare me but little love for what I had done." On Sunday 5th October Mr. Colbeck celebrated evensong as usual, and at 6 a.m. the following morning most members of the small Christian community crept in silence to the awaiting steamer and eventually were on their way.

"About 3.30 on Monday morning, I went into church, dismantled the altar, took away cross and candlesticks, altar cloth, service books, registers etc. I put the altar slab under the floor of the church, and then with some sadness left it, praying soon to be permitted to come back." On 9th October 1879, he wrote thankfully, "I am no longer at the mercy of King Thibaw".

The Rev. James Alfred Colbeck was not destined to remain in Rangoon for long on this occasion. After the sudden evacuation of the Anglican Mission from Mandalay, he was sent to work in the relative safety of Moulmein, far to the east, on the seaboard bordering Siam. Here, for six years between 1879 and 1885 he consolidated and reorganized the mission, building the Church of St Augustine in the process. Upper Burma remained in turmoil throughout this time, with *dacoits* (bandits) doing their best to plague the countryside, murdering anyone and everyone who opposed them, burning and destroying whole villages in the process.

It was an immensely distressing period and recovery was slow and painstaking, as my father was to discover when he arrived on the scene some years later, thrust into the middle of this period of great unrest. By the time of his marriage, however, many years in the future, the political situation had stabilised under British domination, and we children were brought up in an era of relative safety and calm.

CHAPTER FOUR

The Looting of Mandalay Palace and the Arrival of Christmas Puddings (1885-1888)

During our years in Burma I never went to school; my little brother Douglas and I were taught at home by my mother, who was a qualified teacher. She always made our lessons interesting and exciting, never losing patience as she tried to answer my constant interruptions of "why?" and "what?" and "how?" Sometimes, I remember, Mother called me 'the elephant's child', just like the character of that name in one of our favourite books, Kipling's *Just So Stories,* "who was full of 'satiable curtiosity, and that means he asked ever so many questions".

Anne and Douglas (1929)

When stumped for an answer, she would turn to the bookcase, saying "let's find out", for on these shelves lived one of the family's proudest possessions: a complete set of the Encyclopaedia Britannica. Of course, we children would then 'help' to find the right page, learning our letters in the process. The volumes were enormous, bound in black leather, tooled in gold, and filled with reams of lightweight India paper. Today, the leather has lightened to a faded, darkish green, but the books still remain with our family.

From these pages, we learnt that the first Anglo-Burmese war had taken place in 1823/26 and the second in 1852/53, so it was almost inevitable – considering the massacres that had gone on since Thibaw came to the throne – that the British should annexe Upper Burma in due course. This they did in 1885/86 following seven years of unrest, economic decline and constant banditry, and Burma, with its proud history of independent kingship, was now to be no more than an adjunct of India, a poor relation, administered from Calcutta.

King Thibaw and Queen Supayalat were ignominiously removed from the palace together with their whole court, and taken without ceremony, bumping along by bullock cart over pot-holed roads to a waiting steamer, destined to sail away into permanent exile in India. What a truly humiliating experience for king and country used to the full panoply of royalty with its elephants and all its sartorial magnificence, and what a short-sighted manoeuvre by the conquerors. Had a Burman prince (perhaps Nyoung Yan or a member of his family) been reinstated as a new titular head, the country's history might have been very different.

Many people will have read Amitav Ghosh's novel *The Glass Palace* (first published in 2001)[10] with its vivid depiction of these tempestuous times, as he draws the picture of Thibaw's royal banishment and seeks to examine the whole complex question of empire. His sensitive writing makes the period come alive in a very convincing way, but in Britain, at this period, all these happenings were side-shows, almost non-events, and soon to be forgotten. In fact, Burma was to play little part in the national psyche until its significance was thrust upon us in the agonies of the Second World War, nearly half a century later.

We children, of course – like the British public – were blissfully unaware of the impact that these political events were having on the beautiful country that had become our home, being fully engrossed with family life and what today would be called our 'home schooling.' Mother, in addition to teaching us the three 'Rs', often used to add a few simple lessons of her own on the early church in Burma, and I have included some of these stories here.

I remember, she told us, that the original bishop of Rangoon, Bishop Titcomb, had been a canon of Winchester Cathedral in England, which had led, later on, to the creation of a very special bond between Winchester and Mandalay. The next bishop, appointed in 1882, was John Miller Strachan. He was a doctor as well as a clergyman, and from then on medical work began to be important in the life of the S.P.G. in Burma. It was also thanks to Bishop Strachan that the indefatigable Rev. James Colbeck was able to fulfil his dream of returning to Mandalay, once British rule had been established there.

On 18th December 1885 Mr. Colbeck wrote a triumphant letter[11] on board the steam ship *Thooreah*, bound for the once royal city, in which he notes that, "The bishop called me to the work… he wishes me to go up at once and get possession of the church, clergy house and schools in Mandalay, so here I am… the *Thooreah* is the first trading steamer since the outbreak of the war, but we do not expect any opposition from the Burmese as our troops have taken all the ports along the river, and gunboats patrol the line of communication… we have no news as to the church, whether it is safe or in ruins. I rather expect to find all being used as barracks for the soldiers, and if so, cannot say much till other shelter is provided for them."

In early January 1885, he was in camp with the Hampshire Regiment, east of Mandalay, and his letter shows how greatly things had changed since the king's dethronement. "I am here to do the chaplain's work, as he has gone out for a few days with one of the flying columns. Last Sunday, I preached at the parade service in the palace from the steps of the throne. It was an interesting and novel spectacle. Civil and military officers, gunners and infantry, the soldiers all armed, and standing through the whole service. It seemed singular to find oneself preaching in such a place, and to such a congregation; and yet it did not distract me, all seemed too real for fancy to build up. Truth stranger than fiction once more; and what perhaps added to it, was the roar or cry of an elephant somewhere near.

I want the country to become quiet, and hope the British Government will place my little friend Tait Tin Oo Zun on the throne. He is the son of the Nyoung Yan, whom you will remember. The father died in Calcutta last April. The mother and sister of the Nyoung Yan have been saved. They sent for me as soon as they knew I had come up, and I have had a pleasant interview with them.

When I came up to Mandalay this time I lived for a while in the house of a

Mussulman gentleman named Moola Ismail. He was collector of taxes under Thibaw, and is immensely rich. His house is more like a fort than a dwelling, and he has, I am told, seventy-five servants living in the place, and thirty wives of his own somewhere… I did not stay longer than I could help, as the church, clergy house, and school will not get into order unless one is on the spot. They are very little damaged and can soon be put all right, at little cost. Just now, however, that part of the town has a bad character, and there are no troops quartered close, and it is detached from other European houses, so it was considered hardly safe.

My follower and I got a lot of spears and *dahs* (swords) from the loot of the palace, and two guns, so we took up our quarters and slept there. We shut up all we could, and laid the arms ready for use close beside us, and after commending ourselves to God the Father's care and protection, lay down to sleep. What with rats, bugs and firing guns about us, it was a difficult matter to get off quietly. Once I awoke with a start – a gun was fired off close to us. I jumped up and looked out of the window, but could see nothing.

It is amusing to see what shifts we have to put up with. Regimental messes you know are often grand and showy in time of peace, but when I came in yesterday, the Colonel said 'Mr. Colbeck, have you got a plate, knife, spoon and fork?' They have one each, and none over, unless an officer is sent away on duty, and then even he may take his away with him."

On January 5th 1886, he wrote as follows: "I have left the camp again and come to my own place. It is better so, as I can superintend what is going on. The church looks just what it did seven years ago, except that all the furniture is gone, and it wants cleaning and renovating owing to the long neglect; of all the curious situations for writing, my present one is the most curious I have ever had. I am in the cock-loft – I don't know what other name to call it – in the clergy house, with Mark Dooroosawmy, my faithful companion. The loft is about twelve feet square and twenty feet from the ground, like a belfry chamber, and we have shut up the one door downwards with a heavy trap-door, so as not to be surprised before we know it. I am sitting on the floor, legs under me, writing on a chair, note paper on a book propped up by a box of percussion caps. Under me is a spear which used to belong to some sergeant or other non-commissioned officer in Thibaw's army, while close at hand is a naked *dah* or sword, and a loaded gun, also lately the property of one of his braves. We protect ourselves a little in this way, but our surer trust is in our God, to whom we trustfully commit ourselves.

Great destruction of property has been going on in the palace: beautiful mirrors, lamps, and candelabras smashed, beautiful mosaic walls and inlaid doors disfigured, partly by accident, partly wilful, partly by our people, partly by Burmans, but of course this is inevitable where there are thousands of soldiers going about for 'loot'."

On a much happier note, in February 1886 Mr. Colbeck writes: "I have charge now of the Royal Library in the palace, and am to set to work cataloguing as soon as possible… my dear old teacher, Dr. Rost, of the India Library, London, will doubtless be very glad to hear we have saved the Palace Library. It was being sold bit by bit for prize money, but I suggested to General Prendergast that it would be a graceful act on the part of the army to make a present to our universities at home, instead of making mincemeat of the books. He at once agreed. Whether London India Library, Oxford, Cambridge, or all three will receive the offer, is not yet settled. Strange as it may seem, the books will be of more value to learning and science in London than in Mandalay or Rangoon. The old king would not allow even copies to be made of his books. I picked up a pretty gold book – palm leaves, and written with an iron stylus – and found it was a book of meditation and devotion, belonging to the Princess of May Doo, who became Queen May Doo, one of the wives of King Bah Gyee Daw, who fought against us in the first Burmese war. The book is dated Burmese era, 1194, i.e. A.D. 1833. Another book was a part of an illustrated life of Gaudama.

The Viceroy is to be here next Friday… Lady Dufferin comes [with him], and two or three other ladies. The palace is undergoing great alterations for them, though they are to be here only three or four days. But it is right to show respect to our Empress in the person of the Viceroy; the Burmese will think all the more of him, of the Empress, and of us, if we do the grand [thing] now.

On Monday, 15th February 1886, there was a grand sight. All the officers and gentlemen, English, French, Italian, German and American, and a number of the native gentry, Burmese, Chinese and Mussulmans, went in procession before the Viceroy, each as his name was called out passed before him and made a bow which he returned. Some of the Burmans seemed frightened, and some went past without paying any salute (not from unwillingness, but from bewilderment); but they were quickly called back again. I thought some would have liked better to be sitting down in their old style, but that is not our English custom. The Chinese did their bowing very well, all their heads were nicely shaved and their cues (or pigtails) were let down behind their backs, their mark of respect.

When the native officers of the Indian army came forward there was a very interesting little ceremony – the English officer commanding each regiment introduced his native officers – *Subedars* and *Jemadars* – each marched up to the Viceroy, with turban on, saluted with the right hand in military style, and held his sword so as to let the Viceroy touch the hilt with his right hand. This custom, as you know, means that the officer will serve the Viceroy faithfully, and only bear and wield the sword in his cause. Lord Dufferin had a very grand uniform; a helmet with gold ornaments and white plumes; scarlet tunic, with sparkling stars, crosses, orders and decorations. He looked and stood like a king, smiling upon his many visitors: 'Now the Viceroy has come and gone. All Burmans are British subjects, right up to Mogaung, and I hope they will soon be peaceful and prosperous'."

In October 1886, Mr. Colbeck writes about the help he is asked to give to the 'poor queens and princesses.' "There were some thirty or forty queens, great and small. So long as the old king lived, they were well cared for, and had each of them state allowances… when the king's illness became very severe, several of them quietly committed their savings into the hands of persons they thought they could trust, and when, after the long, hard time of imprisonment in Thibaw's reign, the British Government was established here, and the royal ladies set at liberty and granted small pensions, they plucked up courage to ask the person to whom they had entrusted their property to give it back again, but with little good result… they come to me for advice and help, for some of them I have helped to get back their landed property. [For this] I have had several presents offered to me or to the church, but I have declined them.

If any one finds fault with a missionary for helping in this way, I shall answer 'consider the topsy-turviness of Mandalay just now – the people hardly know whether they are Burmese or British subjects – and whether they are on their heads or their feet; and in particular, these queens and princesses are not more accustomed to the ways of the world than a flock of good sisters of charity from a convent would be.'"

On November 22nd 1886 comes this letter: "Reports have got about that we are to be attacked in the clergy house, and that the design is to hurt me. I don't know what I have done to cause this, perhaps it is all nonsense. We had a guard two nights last week but nothing happened… two more chaplains have come, so my calls to outside work are less, and are likely to be less."

In December, he is bidden "to distribute a number of Christmas puddings. The Bishop and Mrs Strachan have had a hundred made in Rangoon, and are sending them about to young officers on detachment duty, far away from regimental messes, so that these young fellows will not feel utterly forgotten on Christmas Day." This humorous entry foreshadows later comments in my father's letters about the wonderful plum puddings sent by his sisters for Christmas. They were obviously of immense importance, even in tropical heat!

Two months later, the Bishop came to Mandalay to inspect The Royal School amongst other things. "I must tell you about our welcome. We made our arrangements beforehand and drilled the boys into order. Telegram at 9 o'clock, Friday morning, 4th February, told that the bishop's steamer was near, so off 'H' trotted, and our mounted boys, some thirty-five or forty in number, under the command of their teachers, forming quite a bright cavalcade. I expected to have to drive the bishop up, so I borrowed a horse and trap, one of the few in the station at present, and with a smartly dressed footman – livery black, with scarlet facings and slashes – hurried down to the shore, startling the people in the road, who looked a bit astonished to see the quiet English *Hypoongyee* driving so furiously at the head of a mounted troop of dashing young Burmans… the bishop was amused, astonished, and pleased with his novel bodyguard, and said he had never heard of the like to meet a bishop before… when we came over the bridge near the clergy house, we saw the whole of the boys of the school drawn up in two files along the front road, with banners and flags at the gates, on the trees of the compound, and on the high church tower… [later] we marched to the church, everybody, choir and clergy vested. The bishop sat in his throne to the north side of the altar, and we sang 'All People that on Earth do Dwell,' said the Lord's Prayer and sang again, 'God Save the Queen,' all in Burmese. The boys formed outside the church, gave three cheers, then at the word, the riding boys mounted again and followed us in the trap to the palace, where the bishop thanked them for their courtesy, and they saluted and returned."

By August, Mr. Colbeck had been hard at work studying Buddhism and its statistics in Mandalay. He writes, "In all, there are, I suppose, at least 50,000 monks wearing the yellow robe, is not our task a great one to fight against this host? What but Divine help could give us even the faintest prospect of eventual success or present advantage?" Nevertheless, he struggled on, and in November was at Madaya, about seventeen miles from Mandalay, "Where we are building a small mission house and house for a native catechist. The house is up and roof on, it only wants the walls now.

"I have been now for more than a year one of the government examiners, at the central board in Mandalay. All the young officers, in fact everybody entering government service for revenue, law, police, or forest service, has to come before the committee at least twice. This has given me a good insight into what is required for the examinations, and I have determined to bring out a book to help the candidates. If it had been done a year ago hundreds of copies would have been sold, which would no doubt have proved helpful. It would also perhaps open the way for a bigger book on the Burmese language to be done when I return (D.V.) from furlough."

Sadly and unexpectedly, Mr. Colbeck died from malaria early in 1888, and was buried in King Mindon's cemetery in Mandalay. Others priests followed him in due course, but Christian work there – right in the heartland of Buddhist belief – has always had periods of ebb and flow, and Mandalay went through a very bad patch without the charismatic Mr. Colbeck at its head.

CHAPTER FIVE

The Start of the Winchester Brotherhood (1899-1913)

I have quoted Mr. Colbeck's letters at length because he was such an inspirational figure to my father, who arrived in Mandalay in 1906 – less than twenty years after Colbeck's untimely death – to work for the Winchester Brotherhood. This had just been founded, based in Mandalay, and when I was old enough to understand, my parents explained to me how it had begun.

The very first bishop of Rangoon, they told me – Bishop Titcomb – had retired to England early through ill health but, wanting to keep up his link with Burma in a practical way, had encouraged the people of the Winchester diocese to set up a fund to send missionaries to Mandalay to continue Mr. Colbeck's abandoned work. Just as Buddhist monasteries were filled with unmarried men much revered for their celibacy by the Burmese populace, so the new Brotherhood was to be run by unmarried British clergy who would try to bring Christianity to Mandalay and the whole of Upper Burma, a district nearly as large as Great Britain itself.

The second man in charge of the Rangoon diocese, Bishop Strachan – 'the Doctor Bishop' as he was always called – had retired in 1903 and was followed by Bishop Knight, a scholar of Pembroke College, Cambridge, where he had been awarded a first class theological tripos (or degree). This bishop gave his full backing to the new scheme linking Winchester with Mandalay, his scholarship and enthusiasm inspiring my father to be one of the original people to offer his services to the mission, headed by Mr. Fyffe – later a great family friend.

The start of the Brotherhood must have been disheartening in the extreme. Mr. Jerwood was the first candidate to join Mr. Fyffe from England; he reached Mandalay in December 1905, only to die the following March and to take his place beside Mr. Colbeck in the Christian cemetery. The next man was my father, Charles Garrad, who arrived in December 1906, only to succumb to a very bad bout of typhoid and to be out of action for eight months, becoming so much a physical wreck in the process as nearly to be sent home. The fourth was Mr. Edmonds, who initially worked for two years as Riverine Chaplain (serving many isolated villages on the Irrawaddy) before throwing in his lot with Mr. Fyffe and the others, while the fifth was Mr. Beloe, who had earlier spent a short period as chaplain to the English Church in Mandalay. My uncle, William Garrad (Father's younger brother) was to join the merry band a little later on. All these missionaries had gained good theological degrees at Britain's leading universities.

I have often wondered what persuaded my gentle father to leave his safe, secluded life of learning at Cambridge for the chaotic, demanding and sometimes dangerous life of Burma. That he was a devoted man of God, there is no doubt, but why did he choose to use his many talents in this particular way? He had taken a double first in theology at Cambridge, and at thirty years of age was not only a fellow of Clare College, but also vice-principal of the clergy training school there (known today as Westcott House). Looking back, I think that he had hoped to become Dean of Clare one day (for he loved learning and had proved to himself that he could teach) but, being already afflicted to some degree with the insidious family trait of deafness, had decided that this was not realistic. But why the mission field?

Father was the fourth son and the seventh child of a Suffolk farming family – a strapping six foot in height, no good at sport, but practical with his hands and painstaking in all he did – a lover of wildlife and country pursuits like walking and cycling, and immensely studious, with a great love of life and a subtle sense of humour. In his time at Cambridge, he had won just about every prize obtainable in Latin, Greek, Hebrew and Theology, and the whole research field surely lay before him, just waiting for exploration. But I believe that he was also something of a dreamer at a time when Victorian expansion worldwide was 'the done thing', offering, as it did, all sorts of exciting and exotic opportunities for service abroad. David Livingstone's late missionary adventures and travels in Africa were still the talk of the town, and Bishop Knight's persuasive academic influence probably tipped the balance in the end.

Recently, I came across a moving little letter written by my grandfather to my father Charles at the time of his ordination in 1899. Grandfather William Garrad was a farmer of substance, blind since the age of sixteen, who had taught himself to type and to master braille, a man of many parts who was also churchwarden and choirmaster at Bures St. Mary's church, playing the organ by touch. He had been a

Blind Grandfather William Garrad.

widower since 1885 when my grandmother died, following the birth of their twelfth child. The letter is typed in capital letters and reads:

"SATURDAY MORNING. DECEMBER 16TH. 1899.

MY DEAR CHARLIE

OUR BEST WISHES AND PRAYERS WILL ATTEND YOU TOMORROW. MAY GOD'S BLESSING REST ON YOUR ORDINATION AND HELP YOU IN THE GOOD WORK YOU ARE UNDERTAKING. I WAS VERY PLEASED WITH YOUR LETTER. IT IS OF COURSE A PLEASURE AS WELL AS A DUTY TO DO WHAT I CAN FOR MY CHILDREN, AND I AM MORE THAN REWARDED IN THE RESULT. I SHOULD MUCH LIKE TO BE PRESENT IN PERSON WITH YOU TOMORROW, BUT I THINK IT WILL BE BETTER TO COME IN THE SPRING.

BELIEVE ME YOUR VERY LOVING FATHER

WILLIAM GARRAD"

Sometimes, my grandfather's fingers started off on the wrong typewriter keys, and the notes he sent to his family (some of which are among my treasured possessions) can be a little difficult to fathom. If, for example, he had begun this particular letter on the F instead of the D, it would have read "FRST VJST;OR" instead of "DEAR CHARLIE," and several such missives have been kept by their recipients (usually his children) as mementoes, with the deciphered message written in pencil underneath!

Grandfather's letters typed to Charlie in Burma bear no blemishes of this kind and once the worrying health scare was over are full of questions as to his work and lifestyle. Typhoid had made an indelible mark on my father, however, leaving him very thin, very deaf, and with a scarcity of what had once been a head of abundant, wavy brown hair. Indeed, his sister Fan, on meeting him later, wrote in her diary, "I barely recognised him."

Be that as it may, he and his colleagues turned to their work in the new brotherhood with enthusiasm, and all sorts of projects were set in hand. Their first priority was to see The Royal School reinstated as a place of learning, for it had fallen on bad times. There were a hundred names on the register but the daily attendance was a good deal less, and of the eight teachers only two were qualified enough to draw a government salary grant. Mr. Fyffe was fortunate in getting Ernest Hart out from England (always known to his friends as 'Honest Heart') and under his headship, from 1905 to 1913, the school grew and prospered greatly.

In 1909 Bishop Knight resigned, returning to England to take up the wardenship of St. Augustine's College, Canterbury, and this left a temporary vacuum. Soon, however, and apparently with unanimous approval, the bishopric of Rangoon was offered to, and accepted by, Mr. Fyffe, of the Winchester Brotherhood, with my father taking his place as head.

The Royal School was still in the wooden building put up by King Mindon in 1869 and was getting old. The corrugated iron roof radiated so much heat that it is said that Mr. Hart had to wear his *topee* (sun helmet) indoors, all day long! The place was really untenable but no one liked to say so, until one day an inspector remarked on it. After that, funds started to be collected for a re-build. So, instead of concentrating on spreading the gospel, on which he had hoped to spend most of his energies, Father found himself faced with the practicalities of an enormous building project, which was perhaps not quite what he had intended.

It is at this juncture in 1910 that William Garrad joined the party, coming out to Mandalay as the newest Winchester member. He was my father's brother, younger by five years, and, like him, a graduate of Clare College, Cambridge, having taken a good honours degree in theology, winning several prizes in the process. It seems that for some time he had been thinking of joining Charlie in Burma, and in 1908 had written to him from Holbeck, where he was a curate, asking for his advice. He had already talked matters over with some of his superiors in England, and was also concerned about leaving his blind father, who was getting old, and to whom he was much attached. "I am very happy in the work at Holbeck", he writes, "and it will certainly be a wrench to leave, if it comes to that, but in about six months I shall ask the vicar (that is if my sentiments still continue as they are now) to write to Father to tell him that I had wished to go abroad when at the clergy school… [after that] I shall probably run down to Bures and have a good talk with Father and then interview your bishop before he leaves England. Please don't say anything about it to anybody but pray quietly over it. It seems so difficult to me to distinguish between a call to work abroad and a desire to be with you.

Is it right that I should offer myself only for work in Burma? I ought to be ready to go anywhere and do anything, and to leave it to others as to where I am sent. I think I am ready to do the latter, and yet I want to be with you: so I must consider it carefully. By the bye, is the climate really very awful? George [their youngest brother who had been badly ill in India] says that his complaint was not due to the climate and that I could be inoculated against what you had. So at present I am simply going to ruminate, but shall be pleased to hear any advice you can give me: you have always been more or less my spiritual adviser, and I attach a good deal of importance to what you will have to say."

Sadly Father's reply is not among my stash of old letters, but it must have been positive, and what an enormous contribution Wiliam Garrad was to make in so many different ways to the church in Burma, and by way of a small start, to the re-building of The Royal School. Like his brother, he was six foot tall, a practical countryman with a combination of great physical energy and charm, and most importantly of all his health was good, and he wasn't deaf.

With my Uncle Will's arrival, I'm told that it only took a mere eighteen months before the new school buildings were up and ready for occupation. These were no less than three storeys high, and soon proved to be a huge boon to both teachers and scholars, so that when Mr. Hart moved to Moulmein in 1913 he left behind an establishment with a good reputation, ready to be built up into something considerably greater still. Mr. John Neal then came out from England to be superintendent and during eighteen years of service worked wonders, despite a plethora of problems including snakes, strikes and seasonal setbacks. During his time, the school quadrupled, with – at its zenith – 400 names on the books, and a boarding house of sixty boys, when extra rooms had to be built to hold everybody. Bishop Fyffe opened other schools, too, elsewhere in Burma, for Christian education lay at the heart of all the church's work.

Church services formed the bulk of the missionaries 'task', Father told me, and two locally ordained priests who did much to help were *Saya* (teacher) George, the Burman, who he said was an outstanding man, and Rev. Asirvatham, a Tamil priest, who was (to quote my uncle's words!) "a first class plodder." There were many Tamils among the local congregation at Christ Church, men who had come from India as shop-keepers, clerks and railway workers, and who formed a large part of the Christian community, and they needed services in their own language.

All this time, my father had been working away at learning Burmese – struggling to read, write and speak it, hampered though he must have been by his deafness. (Later on, of course, he was highly amused by my childish fascination with the twirls and circles of the script, and I still have the 'how to do it' book he gave me.) He had spent most of his last few months in England learning the language, as well as time aboard the steamship *Martaban* on his voyage out, and the long months recovering from illness, so that when his brother finally arrived in Mandalay, Charlie was already reasonably fluent, able to conduct services in Burmese, and even – though with some trepidation perhaps – able to preach a short sermon in the vernacular, if need be. William did his best to follow suit, and literary work began to be an important part of the brotherhood's activities.

The stock of Burmese prayer books was nearly exhausted and the old edition was pronounced too faulty for a reprint, so a new translation had to be made. Mr. Whitehead of Kemmendine, Rangoon, was responsible for the original rough draft, and Father, ably assisted by *Saya* George, was given the job of putting this into shape.

Another side of the work needing development was the preaching of the gospel, often in far flung places. Most of this went unrewarded – people were uninterested, even hostile sometimes, for Buddhism was the national faith – but occasionally, often due to the influence of one single person, the mission bore fruit. One such success was at the little village of Bootalet, miles away up country, where long ago two brothers, having been inspired by a solitary missionary's talk, sold a bullock, and with the proceeds made their way to Mandalay to learn more. Here they became Christians, and eventually persuaded Bishop Fyffe and *Saya* George to visit their village. Though the journey involved sixteen tedious hours on a train, followed by walking on rough paths and wading through streams, not to mention a whole day tossed around in a bullock cart, it proved well worth while. In due course a tiny but strong Christian community was set up there, together with a well-used bamboo church which the parishioners built themselves. Indeed, one of the highlights of my father's year (as well as that of my uncle's) was an annual pilgrimage to Bootalet, forging unforgettable friendships with these simple, unlettered people, and sharing with them the very mystery of faith itself.

Originally, I was told, there had been only one place of Christian worship in

Old Christ Church, Mandalay (1920s).

The Winchester Ladies and Schoolchildren in 1910

Mandalay – the wonderful old wooden Christ Church – but in 1902, a second church, St. Mary's, was built near the palace, in order to serve the British and European congregations, and in memory of Queen Victoria, who had died the preceding year. It was agreed that members of the Winchester Brotherhood would take services at St. Mary's when the government chaplain was away, so this added considerably to their duties and to their influence. Because of the Queen's enormous world-wide prestige, many non-Christians gave gifts to the church in her honour, among them "a reredos from the Hindus, the chancel screen from the Mohammedans (Muslims), the processional cross from the Buddhists and a nave carpet from the Parsees."

Until now, when mention has been made of the work of the church, the emphasis has been on the part played by the clergy, but Father was also keen to tell me about the invaluable contribution of the ladies. Indeed, he emphasised that my mother – of whom he was very proud – had come out in 1920 to be the Principal of the Blind School in Rangoon, having been just one among an increasing number of valiant teachers and nurses working tirelessly alongside their menfolk.

With hindsight, 1908 was to become a defining date in the history of women's work in Upper Burma, for it was then that an amazing lady called Miss Kathleen Gabriel Patch arrived in Mandalay to start the women's branch of the Winchester Brotherhood. Miss Patch was by training a nurse, and though at first she was to open a successful Burmese school and boarding house, her great longing was to found a children's hospital in Mandalay. It took her thirteen years to achieve her goal, but achieve it she did, and her memorable story will be told later.

Father took his first furlough home in 1912, and what rejoicing there must have been in the old family home at Brook House, Bures, on the borders of Suffolk and Essex. He'd been away for six long years and had aged a great deal in the process, rather more than his brothers and sisters left behind in England, who seemed to him hardly older than before he went. This was, of course, due partly to the after effects of the typhoid he'd suffered when he first arrived, but also because of Mandalay's atrocious climate, where the heat and humidity of the monsoon were sometimes almost more than his frail body could bear.

At home to greet him were his old, blind, widowed father, his eldest brother John and five of his six unmarried sisters: Mary, Edith, Katie, Daisy and Bessie. John, in his mid-forties, was running the family business of farming and malting, while Mary, just eighteen months younger, was in charge of the household, with the help of a resident cook, parlourmaid and housemaid. This she ran with frightening efficiency, my father being more than a little in awe of her, I think. "What would Mary say?" was always his slightly tongue-in-cheek comment whenever any of us misbehaved ourselves in later life! Round the corner in the centre of the village in a lovely old house with the quaint name of 'The Secretaries', lived eighty-five year old Great-Aunt Lizzie Day, my grandfather William's widowed sister, and her companion, my beloved Aunt Fan (four years older than Father, and soon to join him in Burma). Charlie's other brothers were scattered – Frank a doctor in Harrogate; Robert a parson in Horsforth, Yorkshire; Will, now in Burma; and farmer George, lecturing at Wye Agricultural College in Kent.

The holiday months passed all too swiftly but Father made the most of every day, working with the men on the farm, tramping over the countryside, visiting old friends and family and, of course, helping out in local churches where needed, and preaching about his work. It doesn't sound exactly restful, but it was a wonderful way of regaining both health and energy.

Uncle Will had been deputising for Father in Mandalay during this time, and was delighted to welcome him back, finding Charlie a new man on return. The Bishop, wanting to expand the work of the church, now asked if William Garrad, by this time a fluent speaker of Burmese himself, would like to base himself in a small town named Myittha about two and half hours by train south of Mandalay, where there were already two or three Christians. There had been a church and school there many years previously, but the whole place had burnt down in a fire in 1897 and had not been re-developed since.

The challenge, therefore, was to build up a new, outlying Christian settlement and, as Myittha was reasonably close to the town, also to keep in close touch with the heart of things at Mandalay. William seems to have jumped at the chance, and during his time there a considerable congregation came into being, together with the erection of a new church and school. Indeed, the Divinity School itself moved from Kemmendine, Rangoon, to Myittha in 1916, with my uncle becoming its head after the war, alternating this post from time to time with Mr. Edmonds. It was at the Divinity School that all the Burmese catechists in the country were trained as priests, so this was a pivotal post in the diocese. Later this school moved back to Kemmendine, being finally installed at Holy Cross, Rangoon, where it was to remain. Will was to give much of his life to work at Myittha during the period 1912-35, though afterwards the mission station fell on hard times.

CHAPTER SIX

The Aftermath of the First World War and Aunt Fan's Epic Journey East (1914-1920)

The horrors of the Great War of 1914-18 were not felt immediately in far away Burma, but it wasn't long before some of the younger clergy felt they should join up. Uncle Will, who had taken his first home leave in 1915, became a temporary chaplain to the forces from 1916-19, and for most of this time was stationed at the Cumballa War Hospital in Bombay. Here he ministered to many severely wounded and dying men, and these experiences made a strong and lasting impression on him.

Rev. W.R. Garrad in Bombay (1918).

Another chaplaincy was served by his great friend, Francis Edmonds, and a third priest, Mr. Dunkley also volunteered, so the band of S.P.G. missionaries in Mandalay became seriously depleted as all had been members of the Winchester Brotherhood. This meant that Father's work more than doubled, and I remember him talking later on about this period as a specially strenuous and demanding time in his ministry, being grieved that all translation work – in which he was particularly interested – had to be put on hold for such a long time. It was tough enough just to keep going.

Meanwhile, back in Britain, almost every household was mourning a family member or friend who had been killed or wounded in the conflict, though the Garrads were left largely unscathed. Frank, the Harrogate doctor, had served abroad in the Royal Army Medical Corps, but had survived, while the Bures coterie of ladies had spent their time knitting socks for soldiers, serving in canteens and so on, in a gallant attempt to help the war effort. Old Great-Aunt Lizzie at The Secretaries didn't quite live out the conflict, celebrating her ninetieth birthday on the 23rd March 1917 and dying just a month later. Her dutiful companion Aunt Fan, with her task as 'carer' finished, simply up-sticked and went back to live with the family in the old farmhouse, hardly daring to wonder to herself whether she could now fulfil her secret dream of joining her brothers in Burma. Many a time, after all, she'd discussed this with them in private, when they were home on leave.

By 1919, after she had moved to Kent (where she had now taken up the role of housekeeper to her youngest brother George) Aunt Fan began to keep a diary, maintaining the habit for the next thirty years or so, and what a treasure trove these funny little battered books have proved to be. I made their discovery in 1958 after her death, when I was asked to help clear out her belongings, and found them tied up with twine in a box under her bed. My whoop of joy at this unexpected treasure trove startled little Aunt Bessie, her youngest sister, who was with me, I remember, and who couldn't understand in the least why I was so excited.

On 9th April 1919 is this riveting entry in the very first diary: "Heard from Charlie that he would like me to go to Mandalay, so I wrote to him."

On 13th April: "Had a letter from Bishop Knight."

On 17th: "Went to S.P.G. House to ask about passage to Burma."

On 19th: "I cabled to Charlie that I was coming to Burma in October." This was certainly somebody who didn't waste much time!

Aunt Fan was now forty-seven years old, and suffered from a slightly curved spine (almost certainly the medical condition of scoliosis), though she and everyone else paid no regard to it at all. She was slight of build, barely five foot in height, her stoop making her appear shorter still, and had been accustomed to a reasonably prosperous lifestyle. Great-Aunt Lizzie, with whom she had lived for many years, was the widowed 'relict' of Dr. Edmund Day, a Mayfair doctor, and there were three resident servants to 'do' for them. In addition, they had a brougham, a light four-wheeled horse-drawn carriage, and in earlier days had been known to ride around the village delivering gifts of once-brewed tea-leaves – still, apparently, a relative delicacy in Victorian times – to 'grateful parishioners'! Having said all this, Fan herself was a most calm and competent person; skilled in first aid, knowledgeable about the scriptures, able to read and write braille fluently and a fine pianist and organist, who often gave music lessons to local pupils.

The story of her attempts to get to the Far East could well make a book in itself, for she was thwarted at almost every turn.

On 28th April: "Thick snow. Went to London by train and met Edith (her sister, a qualified nurse) at Dr. Russell Wells to be examined for going to Burma."

On 31st May: "Went to Canterbury to see Miss Knight. She told me all about my outfit for Burma."

On 15th June: "Played with the Burmese bows and arrows on the lawn". (This last entry was from Bures, and one does wonder what the sisters' idea of Burmese life could possibly have been!)

On 18th June: "Went to town for the day to the Rangoon meeting… called at S.P.G. House and saw Miss Saunders."

On 21st July: "Looked at tin-lined trunks" (at least she knew about the menace of wood-boring termites or white ants) "and went to Harrods & Pontings."

On 22nd July: "I did a lot of sewing for Burma."

On 26th July, there was great news: "I had a letter from Miss Saunders telling me to be ready to sail for Burma on 20th Sept." A flurry of activity followed.

On 28th July: "Sister Katie and I went to Blake's together and chose an evening dress for Burma."

On 5th August: "Miss Phillips and her sister came to tea with me and we discussed music teaching. I put a new lining in my coat."

On 9th August (staying in Harrogate, to say goodbye to her brother Frank and his wife Maud): "I bought a new coat and skirt and hat ready for Burma."

On 11/12th August: "Shopping. I ordered a canvas sack for Burma and got a sunshade."

On 14th August, on a goodbye visit to Bingley, Yorks, where she was visiting her brother Robert and his family, came this unexpected entry: "Heard that the *'Bhamo'* had been cancelled by the government, and my passage was cancelled." Fan duly went back to Kent, somewhat crestfallen.

On 26th Aug: "Took my muslin dress back to Blakes to be altered. Saw Miss Mace who showed me a parting present she had got ready."

28th August brought a little cheer: "Sewed a lot. Had a letter from Bishop Knight asking me if I should like to travel by the Bibby line."

On 29th August: "Went to London for the day and enquired at S.P.G. House about my passage for Burma, but could not bring me much hope of one." Many visits to London follow, for she certainly did not intend to give up.

On the 7th November came this great entry: "A telegram arrived to tell me I had a passage to Burma via Trieste."

On 8th Nov: "I had a letter from Miss Saunders about my passage, and we consulted Dr. Pallett (the family doctor) about inoculations."

On 10th Nov: "I went to S.P.G. House and then bought some typhoid vaccine."

On 11th Nov: "Inoculated against typhoid. It only made my arm a little stiff. Anniversary of Armistice. We observed two minutes' silence at 11 o'clock."

On 17th Nov: "Started my packing for Burma."

On 19th Nov: "I was inoculated again. It made my arm ache."

On 21st Nov: "Sister Katie and I went to my dismissal service at the S.P.G."

On 22nd Nov: "I went to the French, Swiss and Italian legations to get my passport visas."

On 24th Nov: "We had a private celebration of Holy Communion for Father at 11 o'clock and George and all of us sisters were there. George and I started at 12.04 (from Bures) for me to begin my journey to Burma. G. took the bags to the hotel and I went to S.P.G. House and heard we were not to start for a week! G. had taken tickets for Chu Chin Chow, so we went there in the evening."

On 25th Nov: "George and I parted after breakfast. I missed the early train home at Liverpool St., so I took a bus to Bermondsey and went to see Miss Dunkley (a Burma missionary) at the Medical Mission. Got home at 4.18. Mary and Bessie met me at the station and I had such a welcome home."

On 1st Dec: "Telegraphed to S.P.G. and was told to go for my ticket. Left home at 12.17 that day. Stayed the night with Mac (from S.P.G.). George appeared in the evening and Mac gave us both supper."

On 2nd Dec: "Mac came to see me off at eight at Charing Cross. George was there. Very wet. Seven of us went from S.P.G. Very rough crossing. Did not arrive at Paris till 9.30 p.m., two hours late and two of our party got separated. Very relieved to find the others had arrived."

On 3rd Dec: "Went to see the Louvre. Stayed at hotel in the afternoon and had a tea party in my bedroom. Left the hotel at 8 p.m. Spent the night in the train for Lausanne. Very hot carriage and rather full. Had to turn out in the cold at 5.30 a.m. to show our passports."

On 4th Dec: "Very late at Lausanne. Had bothers getting our luggage examined. Had a tram ride up the hill to Chailly.

On 5th Dec: "Breakfast at 7.45 a.m. and started for Milan. Glorious day and most lovely views."

On 6th Dec: "Sightseeing. Went to Cook's office about the luggage; it was sent on in advance. Went to the church of Santa Maria della Gratia and saw the famous picture of 'The Last Supper' by da Vinci."

On 7th Dec: "Started at 6 a.m. for Trieste and did not arrive till 9.0 p.m. Our luggage was missing. Had to go straight to bed, very tired and hungry."

On 8th Dec: "Our ship sailed at 8 a.m. and arrived at Venice at 5 p.m. but did not go close to land."

On 9th Dec: "We went ashore in the morning and went to see St. Marks. Did a little shopping in case our luggage was not found, and by the afternoon it was still missing. Miss Leatherdale bought a big roll of stuff (with which to make clothes). We were all seasick in the evening."

The voyage goes on and on in much the same way, with endless hot hours of sewing and brief visits to bazaars in the various ports of call in an attempt to replace some, at least, of their lost wardrobe, for the capacious trunks of all seven of the lady missionaries were missing. They were often seasick, but even so managed to enjoy new sights and smells and had a few adventures into the bargain.

On 20th Dec: "Three of us slept on deck; two men invaded us with their bedclothes in the dark; they decked out a lifeboat and slept there."

On 23rd Dec: "Slept on deck after great consultations; no Arabs invaded us but we got covered with smuts." They seemed to have enjoyed Christmas, particularly the several Christian services being held on board. Aunt Fan received a present of eau de cologne from the crew, and gave her fellow missionaries a bottle of ginger ale each!

At last on 29th December they arrived at Bombay, after eight days travelling overland across Europe and three weeks at sea. The entry reads, "Very groggy in the morning, all of us. Packing was difficult, until we got into Bombay harbour. Arrived at 11 a.m., but could not land until nearly 5 p.m. Mr Kimble from S.P.G. met us, we four Burma ones went to the missionary hostel for the night."

On 30th Dec: "Had *Chota Hazri* for the first time; the others all came and sat round my bed." This was always the first meal of the day, a snack taken at about 6.30 a.m. before a more substantial breakfast (or brunch) – often of curry and rice – later in the morning. "Went out at 9 a.m. Found post office and telegraph office and went to Cook's about our lost luggage. Breakfast at 11 a.m. Rested on our beds and had tea at 3 p.m. Went shopping and bought *topees* (sun helmets) and some muslin dresses. Packed up, had supper at 8 p.m. and started for Calcutta at 9 p.m. Had a very disturbed night as we had no bolt on the door and the train rocked very much."

On 31st Dec: "*Chota Hazri* at 7 a.m., breakfast at 11 a.m. Very exciting as we asked for breakfast for two, knowing it would be enough for four. A pyramid of plates for a table d'hote meal arrived, tied up in a cloth. We read, and looked out of the windows, fascinating views of native villages. We said evensong together, and played bridge in the evening and got very hungry as supper was very late. The guard put bolts on our doors."

A day later, on 1st January 1920, they arrived in Calcutta. "Slept better and enjoyed our day in the train. Arrived at Calcutta at 5 p.m. Had a great trouble to get two *gharris* (horse and carts); an Englishman helped us. We went to the Y.W.C.A. boarding house at 31 Free School Street. Had rather a shock when we saw our quarters. All Eurasians except Miss Thomas, the head. She lent us a sheet and a towel each. Used Indian bathrooms for first time. Three of us slept together and Miss Roscoe had to sleep with a Eurasian nurse (Anglo-Burmese or Anglo-Indian). Felt rather horrified at first."

On 2nd Jan: "Sent our clothes to the *dhobi* (washerwoman) and then went to Cook's to find that the boat was to sail a day sooner than we expected. Had to get our clothes back from the *dhobi* rough dried. They let us have a brazier in our bathroom and a flat iron so we ironed a blouse each. Went to see the cathedral after tea."

On 3rd Jan: "Got up at 5 a.m. and started at 6 for the docks in two taxis. We went on board the *Aronda* for Rangoon and started at 7.15. a.m. We were delighted with the boat and travelled first class."

On 5th Jan: "Arrived at Rangoon in the afternoon. Mr. Purser, Miss England,

Miss Colbatch Clark and Miss Sellwood were on the wharf and my brother Charlie came very soon. I hardly knew him. Mr. Park was also there with a motor. We all went to tea at Bishopscourt. Mr. and Mrs. Price were living there with the bishop while Mrs. Fyffe was in England. I slept there, and Charlie stayed at Mr. Park's, but came to dinner that evening. C and I had a little walk to the pagoda after tea. Slept under a mosquito net for the first time."

The next day was 6th January, Epiphany. "Got up at 5.30 a.m. for there was a celebration in the cathedral, and we new workers were thanked for by name. Later I bought three dresses in the bazaar. Charlie came to tea, and then Mrs. Price drove me to the lakes in her pony cart and C cycled there, and we had a punt. After dinner we motored to St. Mary's School for compline and address, the first service of a two day retreat that Bishop Fyffe was taking."

After a three day rest in Rangoon, Charlie and his sister left for Mandalay on 9th January by the midday train and shared the railway carriage for the night. "C. tucked me up with his mosquito net. At 5.15 a.m. the next day the train stopped. We found that an engine had been derailed and we must get out and into another train, which was a very long time in starting. We were five hours late and arrived at 12 midday instead of 7 a.m. Found Will waiting at Christ Church for us and we had breakfast together. Looked at the church, had a rest, and after tea we called on Miss Patch. Charles and Will both came to see me to bed, and changed my mattress. They called it a *'chupattie!'*

On 11th January the service at Christ Church was at 9.15 a.m., when Charles Garrad celebrated and *Saya* George (the Burmese priest) assisted. Aunt Fan went with them and commented in her diary afterwards, "I felt in a perfectly new world, and realised for the first time how I had begun a new life."

It had been suggested before leaving England, apparently, that Fan should spend her first few weeks housekeeping for her brothers while she acclimatised herself to the strangeness of the Orient, before going on to work at one of the Burmese blind schools. My aunt wasn't formally qualified in any way but she could write and read braille fluently, even possessing a braille typewriter, and, perhaps most importantly of all, had first hand knowledge of the problems encountered by the blind, like her own father. She was also a good pianist, and music plays an important part in communicating with the visually handicapped.

One of the strengths of the S.P.G., it has always seemed to me, has been its age-old insistence on trying to show God's love for the world in practical ways, like caring for the sick and needy. From a small start, in Burma, there was considerable emphasis on working with the blind, in teaching them a skill like basketry, weaving or pottery, and in helping them to find employment later on, for there was no governmental provision. By 1912, for instance, there was a flourishing blind school in Moulmein, with Mr. Atwool at the helm, and two years later Mr. Purser started an elementary school for blind children, while he was the superintendent of St. Michael's, Kemmendine, Rangoon.

In 1917, with the arrival of a very special padre from England, the Rev. William Henry Jackson, much more was about to be achieved. I remember Father Jackson well, partly (horrid child that I was) because he once gave me a present of a most beautiful Burmese doll, but mostly because he was such an unusual character, a total original. By training and upbringing he was very English, a young Oxford graduate just like many of the other missionaries, but with two great differences, the first being that he was totally blind, and the second that once arrived in the country he decided to live as a Burman, in other words to go native. Having come out at his own request, as an unpaid volunteer, he was free to do much as he liked, though, on the whole he seems to have worked really well with his more conventional colleagues,

Father Jackson and blind students at Kemmendine (about 1928).

who were employees of the S.P.G. (and some of the B.C.M.S. – the Bible Churchmen's Missionary Society) and so were more obliged to toe the line.

I can see him now, walking barefoot everywhere, wearing the ubiquitous '*longyi*' (a cloth sheet wrapped round the lower body as a skirt, and tied at the waist with a special knot) and '*aingyi*' (or shirt). He ate rice with his fingers (which I was forbidden to do) and even denied himself the comfort of a mosquito net at night. He spoke Burmese fluently, though a little ungrammatically, his personality being such that he was a huge success with children of all nationalities both blind and sighted, and was always great fun to be with, ready to play whacky games and laugh uproariously at jokes even when he became ill with cancer.

I remember being very upset when he died; it was 1931 and he was very special to me, a seven-year-old. In my possession today is a copy of a wonderful letter about him, written to his parents. It is from Sir Alexander Paterson, the great prison reformer who had been greatly helped by the blind padre on a visit to Burma six years earlier. Sir Alexander wrote "Your son gave me the finest description of the working of the mind of a Burmese boy that I was able to obtain anywhere in Burma… how strange it was that a blind missionary knew more of the character of the people than all the others in the province."

Though Aunt Fan did work with Father Jackson occasionally, most of her time was destined to be spent on the staff of St. Mary's School, Mandalay, where the children were sighted. Here she taught scripture and music, did playground duty, helped matron endlessly with the children's clothes, played the piano for singing and dancing, assisted the head with keeping the accounts, and cared for any boarders who were sick, even sharing her sleeping quarters with them, to ensure that they were well looked after. "Tommy Newson was feverish. The doctor isolated him in my bedroom," is a typical diary entry.

On 13th Jan. 1920, while she was living at Christ Church, she paid her very first visit to the school, and wrote "I went to St. Mary's School at 9 a.m., and stayed till 4 p.m. Mr. Anderson (the principal) introduced me to everyone but I felt very strange and awkward and there was hardly anything to do. Georgie Lovat was a new little boarder and was crying, so I tried to amuse him. Charlie and I cycled round after tea and left visiting cards in people's boxes." Fan got on much better the next day and only two days later was to write "St. Mary's as usual. Played for the kindergarten songs and gave scripture lesson on Christmas. Did a lot of writing for Mr Anderson."

St. Mary's School Staff, Mandalay (Aunt Fan centre right) (1922).

With my Uncle Will, Mr. Edmonds and Mr. Dunkley back at Christ Church after war service, the bishop now felt that Father could at last be spared to do full time Bible translation work, through the sponsorship of the Bible Society. He – with others – had already put several books of the Old Testament into Burmese, during a precious few days here and there, snatched from other duties, and the Book of Psalms – all one hundred and fifty of them – was already in print. But first, Charlie needed a rest, after serving the Winchester Brotherhood almost single-handedly throughout the war.

So, no sooner had Aunt Fan arrived in Burma to be with her brothers, than one of them was to be whisked away to England, or so she thought. In fact, this didn't happen till later in the year, because Charlie, with a load of work to finish off, and scrupulously conscientious as always, didn't manage to leave until the end of May. He was so busy, anyway, that Fan was to see little of him, and had to find her own way in this strange new world.

On 16th January she went to stay with Miss Patch, a close friendship soon developing between them. The diary entry reads "Went across from St Mary's at tea-time to Miss Patch's and had a delicious tea with her. Saw her give Gigi (her 'adopted' Burmese daughter) a bath and then she and I cycled to the fort and left some notes. Played the piano and saw all her little Burmese girls and then Mr. Anderson came to call. Went to bed early with Burmese children sleeping everywhere. Miss Patch was surrounded with them."

Four days later they had a new experience: "Garden Party at Lady Craddock's (the wife of the Lieutenant Governor). Everybody went. The Burmese princesses were there, in lovely dresses."

25th January Sunday: "I played the organ at St. Mary's church both morning and evening."

26th January: "Mr Anderson offered me the post of organist with a salary and also offered me a salary at the school." (Shortly after this Mr. Anderson was to retire as head, and Miss Cook was to replace him).

11th February: "Prize giving entertainment in the evening. I had to sit on the platform with Mr and Mrs Anderson, Miss Cook and the Rev. Dunkley. Mr. Anderson made a farewell speech to the children; he also welcomed Miss Cook back, and gave me a welcome too. I played the piano for the kindergarten children's song." It was at this time that she started giving music lessons to private pupils, sometimes as many as five in one day.

Illness was never far away, as these random extracts testify:

On 9th Feb: "I did not feel at all well. Took castor oil." (This was Fan's remedy for almost everything.)

On 13th Feb: "Went to see Major Harries at the hospital. He ordered me to bed for two days with nothing but arrowroot."

On 1st March: "One of Joshua's children died of plague." (Joshua was the Tamil priest).

On 4th March: "Seven children had mumps at St. Mary's, and the big dormitory on Mrs. Rayner's side (she was matron) was given up to them. The little boys slept in the empty dormitory; great excitement over the movement of their things."

On 11th March: "My cabin trunk came! Aired my clothes all over my bedroom!"

The school closed at the end of March, and on Easter Monday, 5th April, we're told that "Miss Patch, Gigi and I came to Maymyo. I got up at 4.15 a.m. and went to Miss Patch's at 5. We had a bullock cart for the luggage and cycled (to the station) ourselves. Had *Chota Hazri* in the train. Miss Watson (another missionary teacher on holiday) met us at the station and we cycled to Ratter Cottage. Had a lovely bedroom and breakfast was waiting for us. After tea Miss Watson and I cycled to call on Miss Seeley and met the Archdeacon (Mr Seeley, her father, who lived in Maymyo) coming to call on us. We turned back and then I went to the station to meet Will. He slept at Asirvatham's (the local Tamil priest) and had meals at Ratter Cottage."

On 8th April: "Will and I started at 8 a.m. for a week's tour." Travelling by train, on foot and by bullock cart, sleeping sometimes in the Circuit House or in the train, and occasionally with friends, they visited many places around Lashio, taking Holy Communion to small, scattered groups of Christians, Burmese, Tamil and English alike, with Aunt Fan playing hymns on whatever was available, be it a tiny American organ, perhaps, or a harmonium. But it wasn't all work, for Will was to play tennis with the Bulkeleys (very senior, much respected members of the Burma Education Service) even having to borrow his host's shoes for the occasion! Fan comments, "We went to dinner at the Bulkeleys in the evening and had raspberry tart; walked home with our hurricane lantern."

On 24th May: "We came back from Maymyo. Miss Patch and the children by the 9.40 a.m. train, Miss Watson by the 2.40 p.m., and I came down with Mr. and Mrs. Park (he was chaplain at Maymyo) in their motor. Reached Christ Church at 11a.m. Had a great welcome and a most exciting ride."

On 29th May, Father was doing his final packing before going on leave. The diary reads, "Very hot day. Miss Patch and Miss Cook gave a party in C.'s honour. We had Charlie, Will, Mr. Neal (head of the Royal School) and Mr. Edmonds (C.'s fellow missionary, later to be priest and organist at Rangoon Cathedral). Lovely cold dinner with iced things. Miss Patch had made a garland of mango fruit and written an address. Had music afterwards and Mr. Edmonds was in great form."

On 2nd June: "The school's sixth birthday. We played games with the children in the evening and Miss Cook treated us to lemonade and curry puffs. It was cooler and we thought rain was coming, but it went away again."

There were constant problems with school fees and the keeping of accounts, and these often blew out of proportion in the very hot weather, particularly with the arrival of a new young priest, Mr. Delahay, who had yet to learn the virtues of tolerance when dealing with members of the overstretched female staff. This diary snippet is just one of many in the middle of June: "Mr. Delahay had an outburst with Miss Cook while I was out about the need of reducing our staff and economy;

she was rather upset and went and consulted Miss Patch. I was upset too."

All the entries from Mandalay at this season of the year centre on the appallingly hot climate, so it is not surprising that during the time that Aunt Fan spent at St. Mary's School an annual pattern was established of spending six weeks or so in Maymyo during the Easter holidays, in order to avoid the overpowering heat of the plains. The hill station, particularly for the English, was the great mecca for the gathering of the clans during this period, providing a wonderful, cool setting for much needed relaxation, with opportunities for picnics, swimming, tennis parties and even croquet. The place had originally been established as a rest station for the military by an English officer, Major May, the suffix "myo" meaning town. Today it has reverted to its Burmese name of Pyin Oo Lwin.

By July 1920, both climate and tempers in Mandalay had cooled down somewhat and missionaries were once again on the move. The diary entry for 25th says "Mr. Jackson, the blind padre, preached at the evening service. The children were very thrilled." Two days later, "Mr. Jackson gave an address to the children in the scripture hour and brought three blind children with their books etc." This must have borne fruit, for Miss Whitmarsh came to Mandalay shortly afterwards, "looking for a site for a blind school." Events moved quickly, for Aunt Fan writes on 5th November, "Went to make my first call on Miss Whitmarsh and saw the blind children who had just arrived."

Three months before this on 8th August, Trinity Sunday, with William Garrad in charge, the annual Christ Church Festival had taken place, a hugely stirring event for all concerned, and what stamina it shows from the participants! "There was no 8 a.m. service at St Mary's; we all went to Christ Church. We sat near Miss Patch at the harmonium; had wonderful music composed by Mr. Edmonds and *Saya* George. Two processional hymns with banners. All the congregation stayed all day and had two meals of rice and curry. All the padres came to St Mary's in the evening."

So, day in, day out, week in, week out, the diaries continue to chronicle the minutiae of the life of both school and church, as Aunt Fan saw it, and it's often difficult to sift the wheat from the chaff.

CHAPTER SEVEN

Romance in the Air (1921-22)

Perhaps the greatest understatement in the whole of Aunt Fan's diary is that of 1st January 1921, when Father returned to Mandalay from his furlough at home, and she went to meet him at the railway station. It's a simple one line entry, "C. looked ever so well and jolly". What's significant about that, one might ask, for surely, isn't this just what one hopes for after home leave? On this occasion, however, there was a hidden meaning lurking beneath the surface. Believe it or not, Charlie, for the first time in his life, had fallen in love.

Being a man of rigorous discipline, however, my father always managed to keep his emotions tightly under control and even now found it quite impossible to explain to his sister the magnitude of what had occurred on his voyage home. Indeed, it was only bit by bit that he was able to come to terms with it himself and he was determined, above all things, that his private life should remain that way – completely private.

Travelling with him, on board ship, he explained, had been an attractive young English woman on her first trip to the east, destined, to his astonishment, to become principal of St. Raphael's Blind School for Girls in Insein, near Rangoon, under the auspices of the S.P.G. Of course he had felt it his duty to befriend her and to tell her something of the life that lay before her, and she had seemed to welcome this, wanting to find out all she could about Burma, the 'exotic land' that was soon to be her home. In their conversations together, he had discovered that her name was Miss Marjory Rawson, a qualified teacher and fellow Christian, and, at thirty-five years of age, ten years his junior. She was small and slight – about five foot two inches in height he thought – with light brown hair and blue eyes. Yes indeed, it had been a pleasant voyage back.

More than this he didn't tell his sister, but Aunt Fan was a very perceptive person and sensed her brother's untold secret. Never once, however, in all the diary entries, does she reveal her hidden knowledge, only she herself knowing what really lay behind such innocuous seeming entries as, "Charlie went to Rangoon" or "Charlie visited Shwebo".

Now, under the sponsorship of the Bible Society, together with Mr. Sherratt (a Wesleyan minister) and Rev. George Kya Bin (of Christ Church), Father was about to start full time on his life's work, moving to the cool climate of the hill station at Maymyo to do so, while Father Edmonds was to take over as head of the Winchester Brotherhood with Will Garrad following him two years later.

Two January entries for 1921 follow. On 15th Jan: "Charlie went to Maymyo to start work for the Bible Society," and on 19th Jan: "Found a letter from Charlie with a cablegram from home to say that Father (Mr. William Garrad of Bures) died last Sunday 16th." What a sad start for them this must have been, so far from home, for they were a devoted family.

William Sherratt was the hardworking head of the Burma Bible Society, being secretary to the translation group throughout. What sort of a man was he, I wondered, my father's close collaborator and colleague for nearly four years? By chance, I was able to see his portrait when I visited Rangoon in November 2007, hanging, as it does, on an upstairs wall of Bible Society Headquarters alongside other directors of the past. It's not a particularly good painting, but shows a strong face, with a determined jaw and something of a twinkle in the eye, so I feel that Father was probably in capable hands.

And what about *Saya* George, as he was known, or Rev. George Kya Bin, to give him his full title? What sort of character was he? Once again I was unexpectedly to find the answer on my recent Burma visit, when, on a particularly memorable Sunday, I was driven with all three sons by horse and cart to a Holy Communion service at All Saints' Church, Maymyo, in whose font I had been christened all those years ago. Here, among many other fellow communicants, I was introduced to no less a person than the granddaughter of George Kya Bin himself, the Bible translator. An intriguing conversation with this charming Burmese lady was to follow, taking my thoughts back to my early childhood, and to all that Father used to tell me about his splendid colleague, whom I had once met as a toddler. It was an unforgettable occasion, and to crown it all, as, with some reluctance, I tore myself away and said goodbye, she was to hand me a wonderful present – a short biography of *Saya* George himself.

Saya George and his wife (late 1920s).

George Kya Bin was already an elderly man when he started to translate the Bible with my father, having been born "on the 5th waxing day of the month of Tabodwe (January) in the year 1219, Burmese Era", which is to say by our calculations, 1858 a.d. His parents were U Moe and Daw Min Thuy, devout Buddhists, who were residents of a village called Kya Bin just a few miles away from the royal city of Mandalay, capital of the last two Burmese kings. In true traditional manner, the baby boy was, with due ceremony, given the name of Kya Bin, and at the tender age of five was put in the charge of a *Sayadaw* 'Reverend Master' in a monastery. Here he proved himself "not only above the average in intelligence but extraordinarily eager to learn," being sent at the age of eight to the Khin-m-gau Monastery in Mandalay. From here he passed all of His Majesty's examinations so outstandingly well, that he came to the attention of King Mindon himself , "and the young man was honoured by being carried on the gilded palanquin (used only by royalty) all over the royal city as a mark of respect for learning and achievement."

When Kya Bin left the monastery he was appointed to the service of His Majesty the King, and was quite soon appointed permanent clerk of the Privy Council. Following King Thibaw's acccssion, he was transferred to the Middle Queen's household, and later, although only eighteen years of age, served the monarch himself as Governor of the Royal Barns or Granary. What memories this brought back to me of Aunt Fan's tales on board ship, and of Mr. Colbeck's letters, even evoking echoes of the Old Testament story of Joseph and his coat of many colours.

In 1885 (or the Burmese Era 1247) the year of Thibaw's dethronement, the British government, probably to ensure some sort of continuity, is said to have offered him the post of sub-divisional officer, but Kya Bin became ill and took six months' leave of absence and soon afterwards married Sarah Ma Ma Gyi, a Christian lady. It was through his wife that he came into contact with the Rev. Colbeck himself, and the two of them had long discussions together on the relative merits and beliefs of Buddhism and Christianity. Through these meetings he was, in due course, converted to his wife's religion, being baptised with the new name of George, and becoming a voluntary church worker.

His family was horrified and did everything possible to make Kya Bin return to his old faith and to his government work, even disinheriting him in the process, but he procrastinated. His eyes had begun to give trouble, and after losing his sight totally, he and his wife used to kneel side by side, literally and figuratively, beseeching the Holy Father to help him come to a decision. Once he had made up his mind to remain God's faithful worker, his eyesight was miraculously restored, and his work with the foreign missionaries in Mandalay took on new zeal and purpose.

His task, at first, was to go around the town and local villages preaching the gospel, and he travelled many miles on foot and by bullock cart. Few were inclined to listen in the urban areas, for Mandalay itself is the Buddhist heartland, but in the outlying countryside he made many converts. He also helped to teach the Burmese language to the English missionaries, giving them greater understanding of the intricacies of the Buddhist faith as he did so, and making a valuable contribution to the music of the church, writing both melodies and lyrics for the hymns, which he apparently used to sing with gusto. "He was a learned man with a faithful heart and a good voice", consecrating himself in prayer before every piece of work he undertook.

Later, *Saya* George became ordained into the priesthood, working with the members of the Winchester Brotherhood – who both respected and loved him – his crowning achievement being the help he was to give in the huge task of Bible translation. His first hand knowledge of 'correct' Burmese, as spoken at the old Court of Ava was a great asset, as was his deep understanding of Pali and the workings of the Burmese mind, so different from that of the European. He died aged seventy-seven in 1933. "We thank God for his faithful servant" was the concluding sentence in the book.

Father didn't talk to me much about 'the translation years' as he called this period of his life, but when, in his retirement, visiting clergy came to the house to reminisce, I would try to stay unobtrusively in a corner and listen. For most of the time, it seems that the three of them (William Sherratt, Charles Garrad and *Saya* George) worked in a circular bamboo hut with a leaky palm roof in the grounds of Mr. Sherratt's house in Maymyo, sometimes skipping meals and putting in a ten or twelve hour day in their total determination to complete the task in their few years of secondment to the Bible Society. Although these conditions were far from ideal, they were quiet and peaceful and the three of them learned to make the most of them, only having to carry out intensive and sometimes urgent roof repairs during the monsoon.

Judson's century old translation was still the version of the Bible in current use, but a native Christian scholar had, some years back, produced a good translation of the New Testament from modern English into Burmese, so this is what they had to work on. With his scrupulous scholarship, however, Father insisted on going right back to original sources, to the Greek of the New Testament and the Hebrew of the Old, and what a task this proved to be.

At first, they tried to liaise with the American Baptists, who were beginning to revise Judson's work, but this just didn't work. The Baptists thought the Anglicans far too finicky in their search for precise wording, and the Anglicans thought the Baptists far too sloppy, and there was a complete stale mate. It appears that Father's temper sometimes got the better of him over some contretemps or other, when he would pound the table with his fist in rage or walk out of the room in disgust, his growing deafness adding to the difficulties of communication.

He was at his happiest when working alone, I think, but the three of them formed a harmonious trio on the whole, though Father often despaired of Sherratt's 'peculiar punctuation'. Father must have been an extremely difficult man to work with – perfectionists always are – but he managed to clarify many difficult Biblical texts in such a way that more than once people were heard to exclaim in astonishment, "So that's what that Bible passage means... I never understood it before."

All this time, of course, Father – unknown to his colleagues – was struggling with his inner emotions, and this probably didn't help his temper on occasion. His letters from this period have not survived, but letters there were, going backwards and forwards between Maymyo and far away Rangoon, and on rare occasions he was able to visit Marjory as he now dared to call her, for they were at last on first name terms.

Missionaries visited each others' outstations from time to time, and Aunt Fan's diary entry for 29th March 1921, written in Mandalay, is really rather amusing, but must have been a great disappointment to Charlie. It reads, "Miss Patch thought Miss Rawson was coming and made her a fruit salad, and then found it was a mistake, so she brought us the fruit salad instead; I had to eat Miss Cook's share as well as my own as Miss C. was not well". This was followed on 30th March by, "Miss Patch arrived with more fruit salad, for again Miss Rawson did not come!" (There was, in fact, nothing sinister in this, for it transpires that one of Marjory's blind school children had become ill, so she couldn't get away.)

At this time, Aunt Fan, it seems, was wondering whether or not she should offer her services to work with the blind, being particularly interested in the new blind school in Mandalay. On 1st February, she attended the reception for its opening, recording that "Mr. Purser and Father Jackson came up from Rangoon on purpose for it." On 2nd February, she visited Miss Whitmarsh (the principal) "and found her just sending for a doctor for one of the children. The little child died while I was there." The diaries are full of these tragic events, malaria being the main killer.

Meanwhile, Fan's great friend, Miss Patch, had been busily making arrangements for the setting up of the long awaited children's hospital in Mandalay. During her furlough in England in the Great War, she had managed to collect sufficient money with which to found the hospital and endow a doctor, and now at last things were coming to fruition. The building was almost finished and her pride in her septic tank and her English bath was immense – both novelties in Mandalay. Aunt Fan joined her on many shopping expeditions, helping to choose beds and bedding, material for the curtains, toys and so on, and was almost as much involved as Miss Patch herself. Thanks to hard work from the Winchester Brotherhood and especially from Uncle Will, money for the project had also been given by S.P.G.

On 8th August 1921 the great day dawned when the children's hospital was to be dedicated. Aunt Fan writes, "We all went round in procession and the bishop

Miss Patch and patients (about 1922).

offered prayers in every room. All our children went too." Three weeks later, on 27th August, "Miss Patch had her first two patients in the hospital, and opened the outpatients department." The highlight was, of course, the opening itself, held on 31st August. "We had a whole holiday for the opening of the Children's Hospital at 5 p.m. The bishop made a long speech; Miss Patch and Miss Butt were given their K.I.H. medals, and then the Lieutenant Governor declared the hospital open, in a short speech. Our Girl Guides and Boy Scouts lined the entrance. Afterwards we all talked to everybody, and then Charlie, Will and I went to Miss Watson's new boat, and sat on the moat in the twilight." The next day, 1st September, "Miss Rawson and Miss Linstead came to call on us." Had they, one wonders, been at the opening too?

The 'new boat' was to prove a great attraction, moored on the Irrawaddy, near Christ Church, and provided much needed recreation. On 24th September, "After tea, Miss Cook (principal of St. Mary's School), Miss Hurdon, Miss Scott-Moncrieff (nurses on the staff of the Children's Hospital) and I had a row in the boat. Most exciting, going under the bridges." A month later, on 29th October, "Will, Mr. Caldicott, Miss Cook and I went in the boat; very lovely evening. Miss Hurdon joined us later; we also gave Mrs. Laidlaw a row."

Operating Theatre at Children's Hospital, Mandalay (early 1920s).
Miss Scott-Moncrieff (left) and Miss Patch (matron).

But life on the whole was hard work. On 27th November, "Miss Lauchlin came and inspected our girls." These occasions were taken very seriously and much preparation went on beforehand, particularly when someone as senior as Miss L. was involved. She was, after all, the principal of the biggest and best S.P.G. girls' school in the country, St. Mary's High School, Latter Street, Rangoon, and her standards were second to none. A fortnight later, there were worries of another kind for on 15th December, "Our cook died suddenly in the night. *Ayah* told us in the morning and gave us a great shock."

The next diary entry of note concerns the long awaited arrival of the Prince of Wales, the future King Edward VIII, all the way from England. On the 5th January 1921 she wrote, "The Prince of Wales arrived at 4.30 p.m. I sat on the school stand at the fort with the school children." The following day on the 6th January: "Saw the Prince at parade, polo, at home and at the Shan Chiefs' camp." On 7th January: "Saw the Prince go on the state barge, and all the native boats. He was so handsome and charming, and seems to have made a huge impression on everyone."

Father missed this great occasion, wisely coming down to Mandalay from Maymyo for a holiday a little later, when all the fuss was over. As usual he came down by bike, but instead of returning by train managed to cycle the whole way up as well. He must have been very fit for it's a long drawn out climb, steeply uphill for nearly forty miles. Obviously his friendship with Miss Rawson was doing wonders for his physique.

Miss Patch, on the other hand, had become seriously ill, perhaps through overwork, and Aunt Fan was very worried.

On 9th February: "Miss Patch was taken to the General Hospital."

On 12th February: "We prayed for Miss Patch in church."

On 21st February: "Miss Patch had a relapse."

On 26th February: "Miss Patch was very weak and wandering, but a little better." Entries like this follow day by day and though it was to be another five weeks before Fan was even allowed to see her, Miss Patch did make a full recovery eventually, and was able to return as matron to her beloved children's hospital.

Cars were a novelty on the Burma roads in the early 1920s, and were always giving trouble. Two brief diary entries give a flavour of this: "We went for a drive in a taxi. The tyre burst and we were a long time before we could get home," and another: "Mr… met Charlie at the store with the motor, but had forgotten to take any petrol." Short journeys were made by cycle or *gharri*, while long journeys were mainly taken by train. These, however, could prove hazardous, particularly during the monsoon when there were frequent mud slides. One diary entry puts the problem very neatly: "The bishop could not come on account of the breach on the railway." On another occasion, in March: "The train could not run. Heat buckled the railway line."

On 17th April Charlie took a few days off to meet Miss Rawson (who was on holiday) though the diary is very circumspect, noting only, "C. went to Kalaw by afternoon train, and took a tent." Ten days later, now back in Maymyo, there is this brief entry: "C. had a letter from Kalaw at tea time. He was sad." On 5th May "We sent a telegram to Kalaw". I was pleased to read the 'we' in this entry, for it must mean that Father had at last felt able to unburden his heart to his sister, and she was always a great encourager.

Looking back, I'm convinced that it was Aunt Fan who now persuaded him to pursue his suit by going down to the blind school in Insein, for it was just a month later, on the 9th June, that my aunt wrote, "C. is going to Rangoon for a fortnight". In fact, it didn't take nearly this long for the deed to be done, as only five days later came the wonderful news: "Had a telegram to say that C. was engaged to Marjory Rawson."

Perhaps, at last, it's time to talk a little about Marjory, so far only a shadowy character in this story, who in due course of time was to become my much loved mother. She was the second of five children, four girls and a boy, who had all started life as members of a very happy family, living in a comfortable Victorian vicarage in Ince, Cheshire, where their father was the parson. Tragedy was to strike, however, when the Rev. Edward Rawson suddenly died from pneumonia at the early age of forty, leaving a distraught young widow, a large family, and little or no money. Marjory was less than six years old at the time, and missed her father greatly, remembering the years that followed as most unhappy, constantly moving from one lot of unsatisfactory lodgings to another until rescued by "Uncle Evie", her mother's bachelor brother. This kindly man, the Rev. Evelyn K. Douglas, lived in what seemed to her to be a palatial house in Cheveley, near Newmarket, where he 'reigned' as rector, and was to give them a good home for several years, even teaching them to play cricket, at which they excelled.

After a somewhat strict education as a boarder at St. Margaret's, Bushey (where there were many clergy orphans), Marjory had a year at a French school, followed by a spell in Germany, and became a proficient linguist. Returning to England, she first taught German to a young lady in Richmond, Yorkshire, before finding a niche with a family near Guildford, where she was governess to Mr. Arthur Wood's motherless daughter Frances and her friend Susan Randolph, both nine or ten years old. This would have been an exceedingly happy time – Marjory keeping in close touch with them throughout her life and even asking Frances to be Godmother to her youngest child – except for two tragic events. The first was the illness of her mother, whom Marjory did much to care for with the help of nurses, until her death from cancer in 1912, while the second was the news that her only brother, Second Lieutenant Edward Douglas Rawson, South Staffordshire Regiment, had been killed in action in France. (Marjory was his next of kin, and we are the proud custodians of his World War I medals to this day.)

These were bitter blows that left her feeling distraught and lonely. Her youngest sister had been 'adopted' by strangers after her father's death to ease the financial burden; another sister lived miles away in South Africa, and there was minimal contact with the eldest, who had married an actor and was immersed in theatrical life, but the Wood family were wonderfully supportive, and saw her through the crisis.

For a short while, she joined the Red Cross, deciding – once peace was established – to study for the Cambridge Teaching Diploma at St. Mary's College, Paddington, before offering her services to the educational department of the S.P.G. as a teacher. At first she asked to be sent to India as her mother and many members of her family had been born there, her grandfather (Stuart Douglas) having been a partner in an East India Company trading between Liverpool and Calcutta. It was at this juncture that the Bishop of Rangoon (Rt. Rev. Fyffe) intervened, desperately needing qualified staff for his S.P.G. schools and asking if she would re-consider and come to Burma instead. At this juncture, Mother knew absolutely nothing about Burma, even having to look up its location on the map, I'm told, but it didn't take her long to change her mind.

Was it fate, or the bishop, I used to wonder, who had originally brought my parents together on the high seas, giving them time to get to know each other away from prying eyes? On the face of it, they were perhaps an ill-matched pair, for he was scholarly and introverted while she was vivacious and outgoing, but underneath they had an enormous amount in common, both being gentle, caring people. In addition, they shared two vitally important things: the first a deeply held Christian faith, and the second a strange sense of loneliness (largely hidden from the world), going way back to their childhood experiences of loss. After all, Father was only nine when his much-loved mother died, while Mother was even younger when her father's life came to an end, and this had left its mark on both of them. At last they had each other, and could learn to love and be loved in a way they had never experienced before.

CHAPTER EIGHT

A Mosquito-Proof Room for the New Baby (1922-1925)

Once the S.P.G. community had got over the shock of Charlie and Marjory's unexpected engagement, and after the couple had taken a brief holiday in Maymyo with Fan playing gooseberry as chaperone, life seems to have reverted to its usual routine. All the padres went down to the Diocesan Council in Rangoon, while Marjory and Fan took up the threads again at their different schools. Marjory felt very torn; she loved her blind children dearly but knew that she would have to leave them soon, as British women were not normally permitted to carry on teaching in those days, once they had married.

Miss Garrad (aka Aunt Fan) at St Mary's school, Mandalay, didn't have this worry, but she was concerned about her piano pupils. In due course, the fateful day arrived when the music exam was to be held, the climax of all her hard work. As usual, the diary has a terse one liner: "They all passed, but no honours." On a lighter note, the whole school was to have a half-holiday on 26th July. "All the children went to see *The Kid* by Charlie Chaplin. I went too, and Miss Cook came and saw us all safely there. There were ninety-six children and five teachers." (This was at the 'Bioscope', of which Mandalay was justly proud, where moving pictures were shown on a large screen, a forerunner of the cinema).

On 25th August the Bishop wrote out of the blue, asking Fan to go to the blind school at Insein, on the outskirts of Rangoon (Marjory's old school) and letters went backwards and forwards between them, while on 6th September Father Jackson came to see her to try to get her to agree. The diaries, however, give no hint of her decision, and life went on much as usual.

A municipal garden party was given in honour of the Lieutenant Governor, Sir Reginald and Lady Craddock on 18th October, and attended by Miss Cook. On the 20th is this delicious entry: "Miss C and I went to Lady Craddock's farewell garden party. *Very* dull one." Continuing in this vein, one of Fan's duties was to play for the Burmese children's country dancing classes, the gallant teacher being none other than Miss Leapingwell!

In late October the diarist, perhaps a little concerned about her future, was unwell for a week or more. On 24th October she wrote, "Very little temperature, but I stayed in bed." On 26th October: "Had a rash on my face and hands, so I took castor oil and stayed in bed all day." Dengue fever (a serious condition carried by mosquitoes) struck down Miss Cook and several of the children in November. A diary entry says: "I took Rosie Lewis and Archie Lyddy to the hospital with dengue in the afternoon; I had four more little ones ill." Slightly later, "Father Edmonds had dengue and could not appear. I had to play the organ at Christ Church for him at the evening service." (Aunt Fan herself was the regular organist at the English church, St. Mary's.)

There's a puzzling entry on 10th December: "Took Sunday School for the last time". Nothing more follows by way of explanation until the 22nd when everything is clarified. "Started at 1.15 for Insein." (So she *had* decided to change course after all). On 23rd December: "Arrived at Rangoon at 8 a.m. and Marjory met us and brought us to Insein. The blind children all came out to greet us." Christmas was spent in Rangoon, and visits were made to the blind school to meet Rose Davidson, a delightful young Anglo-Burmese lady who was a senior teacher there. But Fan felt totally out of her depth in this strange environment, the final diary entry in 1922 reading as follows: "The Blind School, Sunday 31st December. Marjory stayed the night in Rangoon. I felt frightened of my life here. Rose Davidson was away too."

Two days later on 2nd January 1923, while Aunt Fan was establishing herself at St. Raphael's School, Marjory (its former principal) went off on her very last jungle tour. This one was led by Mr. Purser (the senior Rangoon cleric) and was to last a week, the mission team visiting outlying Christians in their own homes, taking them Holy Communion and giving talks in the open air, sometimes illustrated by lantern slides. In her absence Fan was struggling manfully with her new post, mournfully writing in her diary "I went to Rangoon with the boy to meet Miss Woods, my successor at St. Mary's."

Charlie and Marjory's wedding was to be on Candlemas Day, 2nd February, in Rangoon Cathedral. The diary is full of all the details of last minute shopping arrangements, cake ordering and so on, in which Fan was very involved, while on

15th January the bride-to-be herself left for Maymyo, returning a short while later, and her 'trousseau of clothes' arrived on the 31st.

A few days after this on 19th January, just as she was beginning to settle down, we read: "Mr Jackson telephoned for me to go and see him. He wanted to tell me that the school was to move to Moulmein and that the Poultons were appointed as principals". So, taking everything in her stride as usual, only four days later Fan was to set off by train for Moulmein where she was shown round the well-established blind school there by Mr. Atwool, the priest in charge of the missionary station. She spent three days there in all, writing on 27th January: "Inspected the school once more and came home after tea. Had a carriage all to myself. Tried to learn the Lord's Prayer in Burmese."

Charlie arrived in Rangoon from Maymyo on 1st February and Marjory went to

ကောင်းကင်ဘုံ၌ ရှိတော်မူသော ကျွန်တော်တို့အဘ၊ နာမတော်ကိုရို သေခြင်း၊ နိုင်ငံတော်တည်ထောင်ခြင်း၊ အလိုတော်ပြည့်စုံခြင်းများသည် ကောင်းကင်ဘုံ၌ကဲ့သို့ မြေကြီးပေါ်မှာ စုလင်ပါစေသော။ အသက်မွေး လောက်သော အစာကို ယနေ့ ပေးသနားတော်မူပါ။ ကျွန်တော်တို့အား ပြစ်မှားသူတို့အပေါ်တွင် ကိုယ်တိုင်ဖြေလွှတ်ကြသကဲ့သို့ ကျွန်တော်တို့၏ အပြစ်များကို ဖြေလွှတ်တော်မူပါ။ အပြစ်သွေးဆောင်ရာသို့ မလိုက်မပါ စေဘဲအဆိုးမှလည်းကယ်နှုတ်တော်မူပါ။ အာမင်။

ဘုန်းကြီး။ နာမတော်၏ဘုန်းတော်အလို့ငှါကျွန်တော်တို့၏ချို့တဲ့ခြင်း များကို ထောက်ရှုတော်မူ၍ ခံထိုက်သောဒုက္ခများကို ပယ်ရှားတော်မူပါ၊ အာဘဘုရား။ ကျွန်တော်တို့သည် ပုပန်ခြင်းအမျိုးမျိုး သင့်ရောက်သော အခါမဟာကရုဏာတော်ကိုအားကိုးခိုလှုံကြလျက် ဘုန်းတော်ဂုဏ်တော် ထင်ရှားစေရန် အသက်ထက်ဆုံးသန့်ရှင်းစင်ကြယ်ခြင်း၌ကျင်လည်၍ အမှု တော်ကိုဆောင်ရွက်ရကြစေခြင်း၎င်၊ အရှင်သခင်ယေရှုခရစ်၏ ရွှေမျက်နှာ တော်ကိုထောက်ထား၍မစသနားတော်မူပါဘုရား။ အာမင်။

The Lord's Prayer in Burmese Script.

meet him. "She came back to tea and to pack her things and then she slept the night at the Johnsons." (Mr. James Johnson held a senior post with the Burmese railways, and his wife was to act as Marjory's right hand throughout). "C and I had dinner there." (Uncle Will missed all the excitement, being at home on furlough at the time).

The diary entry for the wedding day itself is, as usual, brief and to the point. "C. and M.'s wedding! We all went to 7 a.m. celebration. Then we arranged the presents at Bishopscourt, went shopping and had a very late breakfast. Mrs. J. dressed the bride and acted hostess at Bishopscourt. We saw them off at the station after dinner."

Fortunately, *The Rangoon Gazette* was a little more expansive. Under the heading GARRAD-RAWSON WEDDING, it reads: "The Cathedral Church of the Holy Trinity was the scene of a very pretty wedding which took place on Friday, February 2nd, in the presence of a large congregation, the bridegroom being the Rev. C.E. Garrad, son of the late Mr. William Garrad, Bures, Suffolk, and the bride Miss Marjory Rawson, daughter of the late Rev. E.O. Rawson. Punctually at four o'clock the bride arrived on the arm of Mr. J. Johnson, Burma Railways, who gave her away, the bridegroom being attended by the Rev. F.R. Edmonds of the Winchester Mission, Mandalay, as best man. The service was taken by the Bishop of Rangoon, who gave the address, and he was assisted by the Rev. N.K. Anderson, Chaplain of the Cathedral. Mr L.G. Constable officiating at the organ played Mendelssohn's 'Wedding March' at the close of the service, the singing of the hymns 'O Perfect Love' and 'Thine For Ever' being led by a choir consisting of the girls of the Diocesan School. The bride looked charming in her simple dress of ivory crepe – the veil of white tulle with wreath of orange and myrtle, and girdle embroidered in pearls to match the true lovers' knot on her full court train. The train was of satin draped with ivory georgette and had been worn by her mother and sister at their weddings. She was attended by Miss Sally Compton, who made a most graceful and efficient little train bearer, and the bridesmaids were four Burmese girls, the daughters of Burmese priests and catechists. The little trainbearer's dress was of white embroidered voile and her veil was held in position by a wreath of dainty pink rosebuds. The bridesmaids made a pretty picture in their lace veils, white muslin *aingyis* and silk *longyis*, two pink and two blue. The bride's going-away dress was of French mauve voile and she wore a hat of white crepe trimmed with black and white wheat-ears."

Charles and Marjory's Wedding (2 Feb 1923).

Bride and Bridesmaids (2 Feb 1923).

"After the wedding ceremony, the Bishop of Rangoon held a largely attended reception at Bishopscourt. In the absence of Mrs. Fyffe, Mrs. J. Johnson acted as hostess. The toast of the happy couple was proposed by General Sir Vere Fane, who was present at the ceremony with Lady Fane. He alluded to the various activities in which they had both been engaged, and wished them every happiness in their married life. Mr. Garrad suitably responded. The cake was supplied by the Vienna Café. The girls of St. Raphael's Blind School, who owe so much to their Principal, were all present at the Cathedral and at the reception, and threw rose petals as the bridal pair passed through the hall on their way to the motor waiting for them. They left the same evening by the Prome mail for Pagan." A long list follows of the wedding presents, including this quaint entry, which perhaps says it all "Bridegroom to bride, Thackeray's works; bride to bridegroom, suit case."

Once safely married, my parents no longer feature as the central figures in the diaries, which now concentrate on the many complex problems of work with the blind.

On 7th March, Aunt Fan wrote "Father Jackson came to breakfast and we discussed many things. We settled to close the school next week." (This was St. Raphael's, Insein, of which Marjory had been principal.) On 11th March: "Mr Jackson had a boy ill with smallpox." The following day, to avoid spreading infection, "Father Jackson came and baptized two of the little ones in my sitting room. It was baptism by immersion, and we used our big tub. It was a very impressive, strange service."

Over the next week, some of the blind children were escorted to their homes up and down the country by Rose Davidson and some by Fan herself, a few of the little ones remaining with them. There was confusion all round as to where to take the remaining pupils before the move to Moulmein could materialise, so, eventually, on 22nd March, "The girls and I went to Shwebo, we travelled second class and had a very hot journey. Miss Linstead took care of us. We went to church and talked to Mr Stockings, and I saw all the weaving looms."[12]

The entry for 1st April reads, "Easter Sunday. We took the four children to Kemmendine. Rose came back with us for breakfast. We ate two of our chickens. I had my last Holy Week talk. The four children, Ruth and I went to Moulmein in the evening. All slept in my first class carriage." The next day, "I had *chota hazri* with the Atwools, and Ma Lucy (the Burmese headmistress of the Moulmein Blind School) had breakfast and tea with me, and gave me a bed to lie down on and a bath. I travelled back in the evening."

Fan was to spend the next month on holiday in Maymyo visiting Charlie and Marjory, and many of her other friends, but first she had to get to Rangoon in a hurry to meet her brother, Will, whose boat was due to dock at any moment. Travelling on the aptly named *S.S. Burma*, he duly arrived back from furlough on the morning of 9th April, and, to her surprise, Fan found that Mr. Purser and Mr. Jackson were on the quayside too. Were they also waiting for Will? No, not really, for among the many passengers arriving from England were none other than Mr. and Mrs. Poulton, en route for the blind school at Moulmein.

Goodbyes over, Will and Fan were soon on their way to Maymyo by rail, where they received a big welcome in the cool of the hills. Will made it quite obvious that he much approved of his new sister-in-law, but he had to get back to work almost at once, while Fan was to enjoy a whole blissful month away from the scorching heat.

It was 9th May when Fan returned to Moulmein, having stayed the night before at the children's hospital, Mandalay, where she was delighted to meet her old friend Mrs West, the recently married Miss Scott-Moncrieff of days gone by.

Life was tough going at the blind school. On 18th May she wrote, "The insects were dreadful." On 31st May, "Very heavy rain in the night. The roof leaked badly and we had to put baths and basins to catch the water." And, a month later, "The little ones helped me rub away the mould off the walls." There were good times, too, such as the day when "I watched the elephants at work in the timber yards."

Fan was now struggling harder than ever to improve her Burmese, as none of her pupils here spoke English, as they had done at St. Mary's. She was a great story-teller, but usually had to have an interpreter to help her, until this triumphant diary entry on 9th July: "Told the children a story in Burmese for the first time – the first half of *Thumbelina*" – and a few days later, "Told the story of *The Town Mouse* in Burmese."

On 14th July she had a nasty experience. "At 4 a.m. I was wakened by the dogs barking and found a man in my room. He ran down the stairs. We called the servants but we could do nothing. In the morning I found my cabin trunk was stolen. The police inspector came and made enquiries." On the 28th, "In the afternoon there was a small cyclone half a mile away. The rain came in everywhere. Mr. Atwool came back from Rangoon and came twice to see me. The police sent a messenger twice with some of my stolen clothes for me to identify; they had caught two thieves. The teachers were very excited. They brought my old stockings and an old coat." On 6th August: "Tremendous rain all the morning. The house was full of water. Rose had one class up in my room."

Suddenly on 8th August, "Had a telegram in the evening from the bishop asking me to go to Mandalay." Five days later, on 13th August, "Packed up to leave Moulmein, and then was stopped at the last minute by the police. I had been to the bank and shopping with Mr. and Mrs. Poulton. The boy had given me a special dinner to eat in the train!" The next day: "Had to give evidence in the police court. Mr Adamson tried the case and I saw the two prisoners but did not hear the result." Years later, Aunt Fan was still able to recount her horror at this court experience, as it was only the most raggedy remains of her old clothes that had been found, the good ones having almost certainly been sold. Time after time she was asked, "Is this stocking yours?" or "Is this pair of knickers yours?" as some luckless garment was held up for all to see, and she would have to repeat her shame-faced answer, "Yes, I'm afraid it is".

On 15th August 1923 she wrote: "Left Moulmein in the afternoon. Mr. and Mrs. Atwool came to the jetty to see me start, and Rose, Ruth and Ma Saw Kyan and four girls came right across to Martaban." She arrived at Mandalay on 17th August and was met by Miss Upperton, the new headmistress of St. Mary's. No explanation of why she had been recalled so suddenly is given in the diaries, but the name of Miss Woods (her successor) is nowhere to be found, so presumably there was now a vacuum which had to be filled quickly. Whatever the reason, Fan slipped back happily and quietly into her former role – part teacher and part general factotum – and all was well.

Months passed, with Charlie and Marjory enjoying married life in their very first home, Weybridge, in Maymyo, and Will, now head of the Winchester Brotherhood, overseeing the mission work at Mandalay, Myittha and Madaya.

There was much illness about, and in January the children's hospital was particularly busy with little blind Raphael dying of fever, when Father Jackson had to be sent for. Many people suffered with suppurating boils which needed to be lanced, Uncle Will enduring a particularly nasty one in late January 1924. At that time, too, plague raised its ugly head again and Fan's diary entry on 29th January is significant: "I went with Will to see some Burmese people near the shore. Some of them were camping out because of the plague, and they knew one little boy called Roy who had died from it." On 18th February: "Miss Upperton took four of the little ones to be inoculated for plague, and the *mali* and *paniwallah* too" (these were the guard and water carrier at the school). On 15th March the thermometer in Mandalay reached 100 degrees Fahrenheit, and the next day "Miss Stevens came to say that their dog had gone mad and that the whole family had to go to Rangoon for treatment." Rabies was a constant concern, and, as I well remember from my childhood, there were stray dogs everywhere.

The staff at St Mary's must have been thankful when the school closed in early April, and they could make their way to cooler climes. On 7th April, when Fan reached Maymyo she wrote in her diary, "Found Marjory on a long chair in the garden. M. had to keep her feet up nearly all the time. After tea I cycled to the town to look for patterns of baby clothes." So the secret was out, and how fortunate it was that my mother was able to spend her pregnancy away from the unbearable heat of the plains.

Fan returned to Mandalay on the 29th May, and it was still ninety-nine degrees at tea time! Plans were now being made for Charlie and Marjory, with a baby on the way, to move to a larger house, so Fan went back to Maymyo by the midday train on 7th June, when she wrote, "Very lovely to get back to the cool. I felt as if I had been boiled and washed out." The next day, "Mr. Sherratt came to dinner, and we discussed the move to Lansdowne." This was the large, teak house where the Sherratts had been living for several years, they being now prepared to move to something smaller and more convenient. On 11th June is this entry: "After tea we walked to Lansdowne and Mrs Sherratt took us all over the house, to see what would be wanted."

On 13th June 1924: "The last meeting of the Bible Society's Committee was held." Fan had ordered a cake from the Vienna Café for the occasion, and wrote, "I iced it in my bedroom in the afternoon and in the evening Marjory put a Burmese inscription on it, ready for the Bible Committee's tea. I carried the iced cake to Lansdowne before breakfast and asked Miss Ross to put it on the Committee's tea table for a surprise. We went to dinner in the evening to celebrate the event".

It's excellent news that there was a celebratory cake and dinner, but other than this, the diary pages give no mention of the successful completion of the Bible translation itself. What a tremendous task it had been, spanning nearly four years of total dedication, and what an overwhelming sense of relief they must now have felt. And yet, lingering in the background, was surely a sense of anxiety, for would the new wording be acceptable in the eyes of those steeped in the old Judson version? They would just have to wait and see.

Domestic arrangements being in the forefront of Fan's mind, on 23rd June she wrote, "I went to Lansdowne before breakfast and took the little boy, and we swept and cleaned the shelves in the storeroom. I got covered with dirt. Went to the town first and bought a scrubbing brush. C. went to Lansdowne after tea to arrange his study and I went to the station to meet Will." On 24th June: "Went to Lansdowne before breakfast and moved all Mr. Sherratt's things out of the small store room, and the sweeper cleared it out. After breakfast, Charlie, Will and I all went again and they arranged some makeshift shelves for me in the store room, and moved a lot of heavy things. Then Will went back to Mandalay by the 2.40 train. Marjory, C. and I walked to Lansdowne after tea and M. liked it much better than before." On 25th June: "Went to Lansdowne before and after breakfast. The sweeper cleaned C.'s study and the little boy and I cleaned things in the back premises, and his father white washed the store room. In the evening, we all three went to Lansdowne and settled that we would move at once. We left all the packing till the morning and played bridge as usual."

On 26th June 1924 Aunt Fan wrote: "Moved to Lansdowne. C. and I worked violently at the packing. The 'bus' did not come till 1.30 and we had to send it back at 3. We had two bullock carts. We had tea at Weybridge, and then Miss Coton and the Girl Guides came and carried all sorts of things for us and we all went across. We got fairly straight somehow and would have been quite happy only M. got bitten with lice."

A fortnight later, "We went and looked at the maternity ward at the hospital," and soon afterwards "I rode down the town to get a parcel from the post office – Baby's dresses from M's sister." Finally, on 21st July 1924, "C. went to the hospital at 5.30 a.m. and heard that a baby girl had been born at 3.30. She only weighed 4lb 6oz. Marjory was wonderful." That baby was me!

Charlie busied himself meanwhile making a 'mosquito-proof room' that would enclose three beds – one for the parents, one for the *ayah* (nursemaid) and one for the infant – and Fan was sewing sandbags to weigh the netting down. On 1st August, "C. put up the 'mosquito-proof room' in his bedroom ready for Marjory", but she wasn't allowed home till the 6th and then had to be carried upstairs. Luckily, I quickly put on weight and Mother regained her strength, and everybody breathed a sigh of relief.

European women having babies in Burma were not always so fortunate, as the diary sadly relates. It was only a few months later that Mrs. West (Fan's former nursing friend, Miss Scott-Moncrieff) was not to survive childbirth, the baby dying too. This is Fan's poignant diary entry: "Miss Patch went to the funeral and brought back the cradle that Mrs. West had got ready. She showed me all the baby clothes, which Mr. West had said she was to take for the children at the hospital."

My christening at All Saints' Church, Maymyo, was on Monday 25th August 1924. The godparents present were Aunt Fan and Uncle Will, Mother standing proxy for her youngest sister Heather Rawson. My new godmother wrote, "I ironed Baby's robe and did the flowers and we all arranged the drawing room. The christening was at 4 p.m. Very nice service; I gave Baby to Charlie. We had eight visitors to tea afterwards. The cake came from the Vienna café. Baby weighed 6 lb 5 oz."

Father, throughout his time in Maymyo, had always been ready to play his part in helping out the local clergy, where needed, when people were ill or away on leave. Three churches, in particular, were specifically mentioned in the diaries.

The biggest and best was All Saints, a beautiful brick building which had been consecrated by Bishop Fyffe in 1914, taking the place of a much-loved hut, erected in 1902. It forms a memorial to the soldiers and civilians who have died during service in Burma. It was designed by Mr Seton Morris, consulting architect to the government, and the work of building (1912-14) was supervised by the Public Works Department Engineer, in both cases as a labour of love.

Since then many gifts have been donated to the church, including the reredos given by the Indian Civil Service, the font and appointments of the Baptistry by the Forest Department, and the marble flooring of the sanctuary by the Burma Rifles. The tower was added later in 1927 and the beautiful Pre-Raphaelite window restored in the early 21st century by David Knowles, with funds raised by Brigadier and Mrs. van Orton, generously supported by Burma Star veterans and others. A huge service of dedication was held on 13th November 2005, under the auspices of Remembrance Travel, led by the Bishop of Mandalay, in the presence of Viscount and Lady Slim, Ms Vicky Bowman (H.M. Ambassador to Burma) and seventy Ghurkas who had stayed behind in Burma at the end of the war. 'FEED MY LAMBS' – the text in the window – has now given birth to the Burma Children's Fund (a national charity) whose goal is to improve the lives of all children in Burma. The window is illustrated on the rear cover of this book.

The second church in Maymyo (at which Father also assisted) was the Garrison Church, serving a constantly changing population, for troops were always on the move, being sent here, there and everywhere in an effort to keep the peace wherever troubles arose. At this period, the political situation in Burma was reasonably stable, but *dacoits* were always causing problems which had to be kept under control. Father

All Saints' Church, Maymyo (2007).

enjoyed his contact with the British and Indian soldiery, but found his deafness a considerable drawback.

The third was St. Michael's, attached to the school of the same name. This had been started in a very small way by the Sisters of the Church in 1902, their buildings being erected the following year. Sister Lois was its founder and principal, and saw the school grow to a considerable size, ably assisted by Sister Amy, Sister Harriet and others. Aunt Fan was on very friendly terms with the sisters, often mentioning them in the diaries and on several occasions either Charles or Will Garrad was glad of a bed there, when unexpected duties brought them up from Mandalay in a hurry.

Later there was to be a fourth church, St. Matthew's, dedicated by Bishop Tubbs in 1928. This was an enterprise of the Indian congregation, who thoroughly appreciated the welcome always given to them at All Saints' Church but found difficulty about the times that could be made available for services in the Tamil language.

The diaries show that Fan, somewhat reluctantly, left Maymyo on 1st September, to return to St. Mary's, Mandalay, where she was given a heart warming welcome. School life went on much as usual until an earthquake on 20th November gave them all a shock, but little damage was done and no one was hurt. Meanwhile, Charlie, it appears, was still continuing his work with Mr Sherratt, as they were to do for many months to come, making minor adjustments to the Biblical text and correcting proofs. Everybody had a few days off at Christmas which we all celebrated together at our house called Lansdowne, and I – the new and precious baby – was the centre of attention.

Lansdowne, I think, must then have belonged to the S.P.G., for over the years we lived in Burma many people besides ourselves were to enjoy its spacious rooms and gardens, and after our moves to other mission stations we often returned there for occasional short stay holidays. It is now the property of the Chinese Baptists, being used by them as a Bible College, as my family and I discovered when we made our pilgrimage to Burma in 2007.

On this occasion, armed simply with a faded black and white photograph of the house taken in the 1920s, the four of us decided to hunt it down. In this, we were ably aided and abetted by a valiant English friend who lives in Maymyo – Mr. Chris Harrison – with his elderly car and out-dated map, plus various enthusiastic hangers-on, including a young Burman on a motorbike that had seen better days, all claiming to know the way in sign language. The detective work involved was worthy of Sherlock Holmes himself as we forged our way along a myriad of dusty tracks, following one wrong turning after another, until eureka! There the house was in all its glory, looking exactly the same as it had done eighty years ago. Indeed, the old teak building had hardly changed at all except that it was now in very much better condition, having recently been given a coat of paint. To prove this we took another photograph from the same spot as the original, and they were almost identical. Finally, to cap it all a charming Chinese teacher was kind enough to take us round, explaining everything in perfect English, while a multi-lingual group of her fascinated students buzzed around us, keen to ask questions about 'the old days'. It was a truly memorable day.

Within a fortnight of that happy Christmas we spent at Lansdowne in 1924, two sad happenings occurred at St. Mary's School. A much loved member of staff, Miss Atwool, died on the 30th January, and Aunt Fan rushed down to Mandalay for the funeral the following day. The bishop arrived by the early train and celebrated Communion, and Rev. Atwool from Moulmein – her brother – arrived just in time at 3 p.m. Fan wrote in her diary, "I went in a motor lorry with Miss Patch and all the children. We carried the flowers with us. The bishop took the service, and Joshua and *Saya* Peter each said a prayer at the end and we sang the 'Nunc Dimittis' in Burmese. Miss Fleck (another teacher) had lined the grave with flowers." This whole occasion must have been very traumatic for Fan, Miss Atwool being her particular friend, for later she noted "Mrs. Blakeston and I cycled to the cemetery and put some flowers on her grave." Only ten days after this, Mr. Frank Garrood (the husband of the matron of St. Mary's School) was to die in the General Hospital, and it was Uncle Will this time who took his funeral.

In April 1925, Charlie was asked by the bishop to postpone his furlough to England in order to finalise the translation work and Aunt Fan spent the school holidays with our family at Lansdowne, returning to her work in Mandalay at the

Lansdowne, Maymyo in 1924.

end of May. In June, she had to say goodbye to Miss Patch, who was leaving her much loved Alexandra Children's Hospital for the last time, her place being taken by Miss Avice Cam, always affectionately known as 'the Camel'. Will, meanwhile, was hard at work putting up new clergy houses in the Christ Church compound, and in July there was such a heavy storm of rain one afternoon that the S.P.G. school room at St. Mary's was invaded by goats taking shelter! Fortunately they were shooed away before the arrival of the new head mistress, Miss Seeley, who was about to take over from Miss Upperton. The huge Christ Church festival took place on 9th August, in the presence of the bishop and all the clergy, with Aunt Fan, in some trepidation, at the organ. "I was very thankful to be able to play *Saya* George's hymn" was her comment.

In the autumn, Fan was troubled with a truly horrible carbuncle. On 12th September she wrote, "Dr. Blakeston cut my carbuncle. I lay down on the operating table while she and Miss Cam did it." On 16th September: "Went to the hospital in a *gharri* and saw Dr. Guilbert, and Nurse King dressed the carbuncle for me. Will did it the other times." On 21st and 23rd September, "Went to the hospital and had

Lansdowne, Maymyo in 2007.

a lot of stuff taken out". My aunt had, by now, borne the brunt of six long years in Mandalay and Moulmein, without furlough, and it was high time for her to have a rest. As our family would be going back to England soon, it was agreed that she should join us and the diary is full of entries about all the final preparations and general packing up. Having a baby to cope with more than doubled the amount of luggage needed.

On 26th September: "The Tamils gave a farewell meeting to Charles and Marjory. They were garlanded, and there was a garland for Baby too."

On 3rd October: "Left Maymyo by 9.30 a.m. train. The lorry came for our luggage and forgot to bring a cover, and our things got wet on the way to the station. It poured in torrents. We found Charlie in a great muddle; the paraffin stove had upset all over the floor of the carriage and everything was damp with the rain. Miss Cam travelled down with us. The Thursfields, Rev. Asirvatham, *Saya* George and his wife and others were all at the station in the rain. At Mandalay we had another big reception and Will had tea ready for us. Miss Seeley, the teachers and lots of people were there. We had all our meals in the train."

On 4th October: "We slept well. Arrived at Rangoon at 8.45, but were not nearly ready to get out of the train and had to do up the luggage in a hurry." Our family stayed with Mr. and Mrs. Park, who were kindness itself.

On 6th October: "Charlie and I went to early service. After breakfast, Marjory and I went shopping in Mrs. Fyffe's car and went to Bishopscourt to wish them goodbye. Mr. Park and Sheila went with us to the wharf at 1.30 ready for our boat. We did not wait at all, but went straight into the launch. We had to say goodbye to *Ayah* and were very sad. We were very busy all the rest of the day arranging our cabins on the *Chindwin*. I had a two berth cabin to myself opposite Marjory and Charles."

CHAPTER NINE

From Maymyo to Moulmein via the Metropolis (1925-1927)

The journey started badly. "Baby had prickly heat and was cross. Charlie had to go to bed with a temperature of nearly 103." It was even worse the following day: "Marjory was seasick. We had the doctor for C., and he was put into another cabin. Baby was unbearably cross and upset." When Father's carbuncle burst a few days later, he quickly got better and it seems that I began to enjoy my new surroundings a little too much, toddling about everywhere I shouldn't so that the grown-ups had to have eyes in the backs of their heads. The voyage lasted a month, and must have seemed infinitely longer, for Mother was not a good sailor and was six months pregnant into the bargain.

We landed at Plymouth on 4th November and found our way to London en route for the Garrad family home at Bures, where people flocked to greet Charlie's new bride and to make a huge fuss of me, her baby. Later we all went to stay at Reigate, with Aunt Agatha Macfarlane (Mother's younger sister), before moving to a house at nearby Cranleigh, which Father had rented for the duration of his leave. A nanny was quickly found for me and everybody was able to relax, make new friends and settle down to English life. The only trouble was the cold weather, which must have been something of a shock after the tropics, particularly when it snowed as it did that winter.

On 26th January 1926 the dairy reads, "Mrs. Willis brought us the news at 8.30 a.m. that John Douglas had arrived, and that all was well." He had been born at 5 a.m. at a nearby nursing home. "Charlie went to Reigate, cycling as far as Shelford, and got back at 7.45, very happy." I'm told I wasn't allowed to see my brother till the 5th February when we all went to visit him, while Father continued to cycle there and back every day, relaying us with news of everything that happened.

Mother and Baby made great progress and a very sociable time was had by all, as, once back in Cranleigh, friends and relations poured in to see the newly arrived son and heir. At long last, I find myself being called by my own name of 'Anne' in the diaries, Douglas now having supplanted me as 'Baby'. But why did our parents choose to call us by the second of our two Christian names, I wonder? By rights, he should have been 'John' and I should have been 'Margaret', for these were our first names, duly entered on our birth certificates and still in use by us today on official records, when visiting the doctor or hospital, for instance. This has always been a real nuisance – an unnecessary complication – and at times of stress it can even be difficult to remember one's double identity!

But on the day of Douglas' christening, nothing was further from everyone's thoughts. Uncle John Garrad, Charlie's eldest brother, arrived at supper time on 6th March, to be one of the godfathers, the christening taking place the very next day, which was a Sunday. "Marjory iced the cake. Baby's service was at 4 p.m. Mr. Cunningham christened Baby. John, Mr. A. Wood and Mrs. Macfarlane were godparents. Tea party afterwards: Mrs. Woods (the bishop's wife); Mr. A. Wood and Frances (Mother's much loved ex-pupil and her father in whose home she had lived as a governess years ago); Mr. and Mrs. Macfarlane (Mother's sister and brother-in-law); Miss G. Douglas (Mother's maternal aunt); Meg (our cousin, Agatha Macfarlane's daughter); Mrs. Willis (the local doctor's wife) and Wendy (her daughter) and Mr. and Mrs. Cunningham (the vicar and his wife)." Quite a gathering.

Aunt Fan made the most of her time in England, visiting her Suffolk home whenever she could be spared from looking after us. She was at Bures for her fifty-fourth birthday when she wrote in the diary, "Edith and I went to early service. I had a birthday egg, an enormous hen's egg with Burmese drawings on it." She was planning to visit other family members but the general strike prevented it for sometime. On 4th May 1926, "The great strike began; miners and railwaymen. There were no trains at all. The only news we got was on the wireless." On 12th May, "Heard that the general strike was called off!" But two days later, "The railwaymen still did not work." On the 17th, "Most of the trains began to run again." One of the after effects was a lasting shortage of fuel, and a later diary entry reads, "I tried to do cooking in the morning but it was very difficult with the limited coal."

On 23rd July our household was in a muddle and Aunt Fan was urgently sent for: "Had a telegram at 11.45 asking me to go to Cranleigh as Nanny was in hospital. I started at 2.45 and arrived at 7.30. Went by tube to Waterloo and felt very brave at going on the escalator with luggage in both hands. Charlie met me at Cranleigh. Marjory was looking very tired. Aunt B. (another of Mother's maternal aunts) was staying there and I slept with Anne in the top room. Marjory was having pain and sickness and the doctor didn't know what was the matter with her." As usual, Fan's practical abilities came to the fore and things soon calmed down, with plans being made for a return to Burma in the late autumn.

There were so many people to see before we left, so many visits to the doctor and dentist to be made, and so many clothes to be bought, that time just raced by. At Bures on 3rd September Fan had the first of two further inoculations for enteric (typhoid) and "My arm began to swell at bedtime." The next day is this poignant entry: "I drew Burmese inscriptions on a cross that Deaves (the local carpenter) made for me to take to Burma for Catherine's grave." (This, I think, was the Miss Atwool who had died nearly two years ago in Mandalay.)

On 30th September 1926: "Started from Bures by the 2.40 train for Burma." On 1st October: "We left Euston at 11.50. Agatha and Heather (two of Mother's sisters) and Bessie (Charlie's youngest sister) and Nanny saw us off. We got to Birkenhead at 4.30 p.m. and soon got on the *Chindwin*. We had tea and got the babies to bed as soon as possible. Anne and I had a cabin together."

Once again the voyage was to last a month and this time it seems to have been a slightly less eventful journey, though Fan herself was to feel unwell, on and off, and we children were a handful. The plan was to go straight from Rangoon to Moulmein, where Father, at the Bishop's request, was now to take care of St. Augustine's Mission while the Rev. Atwool went on furlough. It was decided that Aunt Fan would go with us, to help with the family, rather than return to her previous work at St. Mary's School, Mandalay.

On 2nd November: "Arrived at Rangoon at 1 p.m. Bishop Fyffe and Mrs. Bulkeley met us." On 3rd November: "Po Yin came as our boy". On 4th November: "We put the babies to bed at Bishopscourt for a little while, had an early dinner and then took the babies out of bed and went to the train for Moulmein. Mr. Purser came to the station with us." On 5th November: "Arrived at Moulmein at 7 a.m. We had quite a good night. Mr. and Mrs. Atwool and Mr. Clack were on the wharf to meet us and Mr. Tresham with a motor. Mrs. A. came to the house with us, and everything was ready for us. Had a very busy day unpacking and settling and people kept coming to see Charlie. We went to the blind school and had a great reception."

As on so many occasions, the family had a rather unfortunate start. On 9th November: "Charlie had boils and could not sit comfortably. He turned faint in morning church and had to come out. We had Colonel Guilbert to see him (the army doctor)." On 10th November: "Charlie was rather better but could not leave the house." On 12th November: "C. was a little better but not fit to go to the Chinese School" (one of several schools run by S.P.G. and for which Father had overall responsibility). Fortunately he recovered, once the wretched boil had burst, and was soon able to find his feet.

Meanwhile, Fan, of course, felt on home ground, showing everyone around, and soon a very capable Burmese lady named Ma Jessie was engaged as our *ayah* or nurse. On 17th November: "Ma Jessie pushed the pram for a very hot walk." On 18th November: "Had a great struggle with Anne on the way home as she would not ride in the pram."

Christmas services were celebrated in church with great enthusiasm, but home life was difficult, as Ma Jessie was unwell and had to go hospital. Po Yin was a wonderful help, particularly at meal times, but no one had thought to explain the strange intricacies of English cuisine to him before he served dinner, so Fan notes in great amusement, "Po Yin handed the mince pies with the roast duck!"

Until now domestic details have tended to dominate this tale, because Aunt Fan's diaries have been the only source of reference, but once the new year of 1927 starts, Father's letters become available, and make a great addition to the narrative. There can have been few missionaries who wrote home every week without fail, as he did, so this must stand as an archive of considerable interest and importance for this period.

To set the scene, there were two churches in Moulmein, St. Augustine's (originally built by Mr. Colbeck) where Father was the priest in charge, and the English-speaking church St. Matthew's, which had Mr. Clack as chaplain at this period.

On 2nd January 1927, Father wrote from St. Augustine's Mission, Moulmein, to his sister Bess at Bures. "Will is here and seems nicely well, though certainly not fat. We have really got him for a week which is great. He brought with him our silver and plate, the dinner-service, the tea-service, glasses, our sewing-machine, two baths containing all sorts of things, two boxes also full of very miscellaneous articles, and even a few pictures! No, I'm sorry, he didn't bring all that; he brought a lot, and other things came by goods train and actually arrived yesterday, including the chesterfield, (or sofa) and now we begin to feel as if we were living in our own house.

"I have been out nearly all the week – went on Monday to Thaton (thirty-five miles away by train) and stayed there two days, which proved only just long enough, then thirty miles further along the line to Kyaikhto for one night, and then fifteen miles further to Moatpalin for one night, and finally I got back home on Friday evening."

Father's 'parish' covered a huge area, these three towns lying in line, one after the other, along the northern coastline of the Gulf of Martaban (traversing, in fact, almost half the distance to Rangoon) while Thanbyuzayat, nearly forty miles away to the south, was his furthest port of call in that direction.

The next week he wrote home again, this time to his oldest sister Mary. "I don't think I have ever mentioned how good the Christmas plum-pudding was, just as it always is." (What a pungent comment, and how much it must have pleased the sisters at home! The home-made Bures plum-puddings are a greatly valued, comforting feature throughout the whole Burma saga, never failing to be thanked for in Christmas letters home.)

On 16th January he wrote: "Nobody could wish for a prettier spot than Moulmein. The sun-rise in particular (about 6 a.m.) is glorious every day. First there is the Southern Cross standing out bold and clear, then a rosy flush on the mountains, and then the bright day. I have had a jungle trip this week. Most of Monday I spent very comfortably on a river-steamer, going up the Salween, all exceedingly beautiful. We reached our port (so to speak) at 8.30 in the evening, and then had five miles of road to traverse to Kappali. Some of the Kappali people were at the riverside with a bullock cart, so I put into it my kit and my cook, and walked with the Karen school-master, who speaks Burmese, and who (unlike most Burmans) walks at four miles an hour. It was a beautiful moonlight night. We went to bed as soon as we got in. Tuesday began with Holy Communion – fourteen Karen communicants and one Chinaman. I think all the confirmed people there are. I chatted with them a while both while they were gathering and after, and then spent an hour in the little school, with which I was disappointed. I doubt whether the school-master is the right man, in spite of his good walking. Then I was told that the Chinaman wanted to give me breakfast in his village, three miles away. It was a very long three miles, I should think actually between four and five miles, but it was a nice cool day and nice country.

There is however one objection to jungle-walks that is new to me. I was wearing white trousers and arrived in an awful mess, not only from dust (to which I am thoroughly used) but from black grease. Our Mandalay bullock carts all have wooden axles; they are not often greased, and when they are the grease does not come out beyond the hub of the wheel. But here they use iron axles, very long, projecting six inches beyond the hub of the wheel on either side, and they grease them a lot. The result is that the bushes along the cart track all get greasy and make presents of their blackness to passers-by! Well, I found my breakfast at the Chinaman's house a bigger thing than I had expected. I thought it was to be only I and two *Sayas*, (teachers) but nearly all the Christians of Kappali came along too, and all were fed. Then there had to be prayers and preaching, which I welcomed gladly. What with the walk there, the walk back, the meal and the service there, and the waiting while food was being prepared, 10.30 a.m. to 5.15 p.m. had gone out of my one day at Kappali! Yet I don't know that I could have spent it better. Then we had Evensong, read by the Karen deacon and a sermon from me, preached in Burmese, and translated into Karen, and not long after that we all went to bed. On Wednesday we started off at daylight, and got into the boat again, and at 4.30 p.m. we were back in Moulmein."

On 23rd January: "I went out to Thanbyuzayat on Monday (thirty-five miles, two and a half hours by train), and stayed one night. Our mission there is a very poor affair – practically no Christians but the catechist's family and the school teachers. The catechist is a nice boy, but he is not man enough to tackle the Buddhists (it needs a good deal of ability before a man can do that) and I cannot see that he has anything else to do. The position at Thaton is similar, only there are a few Christians there, and the catechist has at least a congregation to preach to on Sundays. What surprised me at Thanbyuzayat was the delightful English people living there. They are all occupied with a rubber plantation."

Father then describes how he was trying to put up a map on his study wall. "I had finished the bottom half, and was perched on a rather high but very small stool working away at the top half, when the stool turned over and I came down such a flop! Marjory rendered first aid, but I had to get a *gharry* and drive down to the hospital and have two stitches put in. The map is looking at me reproachfully, hanging in a graceful fold. The incident upset a little household plan. Marjory, Fan and Anne were all going to drive down into the town and do some shopping, and Anne was going to buy a birthday present for Douglas out of the contents of her money-box; but it all had to be abandoned."

A week later, "My leg is progressing well. I had the stitches out this morning and though it is still raw and sore it will soon be healed. I haven't attempted a bicycle since the fall but I am surprised to find how much I can get about without serious discomfort. I went to Thaton for my monthly visit, Thursday to Saturday."

The schools in Moulmein feature heavily both in Father's letters and Fan's diaries, all having opened their doors on 3rd January for the new term. There are so many of them, that it is sometimes difficult to know which is which! He had no less than six under his jurisdiction.[13]

Miss Fairclough, who was for forty years a missionary at Moulmein, was head of St. Matthew's Girls' School, and was a frequent visitor at the Mission House where we all lived, while both Mother and Aunt Fan helped out with voluntary teaching, as required. My aunt, for example, wrote in her diary on 7th January: "Taught English and the children were all very fidgety. Ma Lucy had not been well enough to come to school for four days."

Writing home on 6th February, Father said: "We are rather proud of ourselves at St. Augustine's School just now, because we won the Midgets Cup in the annual inter-school sports. 'Midgets' are the smallest boys. There are four classes of boys – Seniors, Juniors, Junior-Juniors and Midgets. In the two older classes we have no

Father on his bike (1928).

chance at all against the high schools, being only a middle school ourselves, but in the two younger classes we have as good a chance as anybody else."

On 14th February there is a tragic tale in the weekly letter home. "Rev. and Mrs. Menzies came and stayed a couple of nights with us during the week. They had been making a tour amongst the Karens of my district and had been quite encouraged by what they found. But on the last day of the tour a most horrible thing happened. The marriage of our school-master at Kappali was just beginning, when the floor of the church (a school – call it what you like – the building in which I slept on my visit of a month ago) fell right out and everybody dropped down six feet. The worst thing of all was that there were some children playing underneath. One was killed on the spot, and two others were so badly cut that Mrs. Menzies is doubtful whether they can get well, since their parents will not listen to the suggestion of bringing them to the hospital. The people who fell with the floor did not suffer so badly, but one man had got a blow which they feared might have serious effects. I gather there were eighty to a hundred of them, mostly non-Christians, and there had never been anything like that number in the building before. The whole floor did not go, but all the western end – about two-thirds of the whole. Mr. Menzies was left standing in his place, the deacon Daw Mwa, the bride and bridegroom, the bridesmaids and best man. The rest all went down together. The building is still there, and most of it sound; it was the floor that was not sufficiently supported. But I believe it will all have to be pulled down and rebuilt elsewhere. I am told that no non-Christian Karen would ever enter it if repaired where it stands. *Saya* Tun Win, my best catechist, is going there on Wednesday, to see whether there is anything to be done and give us later news. I should have sent him before only he has been away elsewhere."

On 20th February 1927: "We have had our Harvest Festival today, a little late – it is true – but not as late as it will sound to you. Harvest comes after Christmas here. The things that were brought – fruit, vegetables, flowers, and four live chickens – made three really nice hampers, which we sent to the General Hospital, the American Baptist Women's Hospital and the Leper Home."

"Last night there was a dance at the Club, to bid farewell to Mr. and Mrs. Anderson. Mr Anderson is the Commissioner, the highest government officer in about one-sixth part of Burma. He is a splendid person, always at church on Sunday evening, so simple and nice and friendly. His wife is no less splendid. We shall miss them both greatly.

"I seem to have spent most of the last week at the Chinese School. There are various puzzles there. The most urgent one concerns accommodation. I dare not go on using any part of the old building as it is; it would be asking for another disaster like that at Kappali. Probably we shall pull it right down and build something or other afresh, partly with the old materials. The latest news from Kappali is that the injured people are all doing well. I am exceedingly glad to hear that. The schoolmaster however has had to go. Apparently the villagers have no doubt at all that he and his bride had offended the spirits, and not a single heathen child would come again to the school while he was there. It remains to be seen whether we shall get the children again with another teacher and another school. I expect that before long I had better pay them another visit myself, but Karen is their language, and the only person whom I can understand with ease is the deacon, who speaks Burmese excellently."

Language problems were always a huge issue in this multi-tongued country, and the next letter says, "I have started to try to learn Tamil. It seems essential here. I have no hope of ever learning to speak it usefully, but it ought to be possible to manage to read the church service intelligibly, and that would be something... do you remember what happened to Edmonds when he started at Tamil? He gave the blessing in Tamil one day, and a Tamil gentleman was overheard saying to a companion as he left church: 'Why on earth did Father Edmonds say the blessing in Latin today?'"

CHAPTER TEN

Burmese Buses, Buildings, Bibles, Babies, Baptisms and Bishops (1927)

At this period, Father was anxiously awaiting the publication of the new translation of the Bible on which he had worked so hard. Writing home on 27th February 1927, he said, "I have been to Thaton again, and met Mr. Sherratt there. He has seen, in proof, the last chapter of *Revelation*, and hopes that the Burmese Bible may be published in another month. I hope it will, as I am wanting it badly; the old one seems so hopeless."

Meanwhile, the rest of our family, it seems, were planning a holiday to the seaside, and a fortnight later, Father found himself left on his own at Moulmein. On 14th March, feeling very lonely, he wrote to his sister Bess, "I am in desolation. Marjory, Fan, Anne and Douglas, not to mention Ma Jessie (the *ayah*) all left me at 7.25 this morning. I meant to have gone too, but there are bits of business here that made it difficult, and my intention now is to go Monday to Tuesday next week. They went in a taxi, and beyond a suitcase slung on to each side, there were no encumbrances worth mentioning. The luggage went by motor-bus. We have funny little buses here, many of them really Ford cars with a different carriage. Our bus cost only half as much as the taxi, because on the return journey it will be able to do its ordinary work as a bus and get fares. Well, we filled it with luggage, and we tied luggage on all round it, until the general effect was something like Tweedledee in his armour and it started ten minutes ahead of the taxi. On the box were the driver, and Po Yin the butler ('the boy' as Fan calls him, which is probably nearer the truth) and Ko Bein who is Ma Lucy's husband and wanted to be useful; on the step behind was the *mali*. They should all be in Amherst by now; I hope they are. Oh – you will be puzzled by this early departure to Amherst. Having occasion to visit Thanbyuzayat (forty miles away) last week, I went on to Amherst (fifteen miles further) in order to hire a house for April, and found that I could not get one. A house was available for the rest of March without rent, lent by Mrs Curtice of Thanbyuzayat, but nothing could be had in April. So we determined that the family must go immediately.

Apart from any desire for a change, they simply had to get out while a new roof is being put on this house, and fortunately I was able to arrange for the roof to be done at once. This morning at 7 a.m., a band of Chinamen arrived, who have now laid bare half the roof and at 7.25 the family got out! I have quite forgotten all about house-keeping, but the cook stays with me and probably will do it all without my needing to bother."

A week later, Father wrote, "I am feeling disappointed. I had planned to go to Amherst tomorrow for a night, but it proves impossible. I have to go to Kappali instead. A faithful old Chinaman in the neighbourhood is bad with dysentery, and urgently desires Holy Communion. That means three days – three days for one private Communion! The house is hateful at present. Sometimes I go downstairs, because there I have sufficient protection from the sun, but generally it seems easier to stay upstairs, wearing a *topee* because the ceiling boards are not sufficient protection from the sun. All the shingles (wooden) are off; and very poor things they prove to be; no wonder, as they are forty years old. In another week we shall probably have new ones on; just a few are already in place at the edge."

On 27th March: "I paid my visit up the Salween at the beginning of the week. Shwegwun (where the boat stops) and Kappali (where the church is) and Chon-Mago (where the Chinaman lives) form an equilateral triangle, each five or six miles from the others. We got to Shwegwun at 8.30 in the evening, and tramped off at once to Chon-Mago, my luggage in a bullock cart, and my cook too, but I preferred to walk. I could not do much there, but after sleeping the night I celebrated Holy Communion, for which the sick man was longing. I stayed there for breakfast and then went on to Kappali. To my surprise I found the Christian men very busy repairing the church, and by sunset they had it all complete. Their labour was freely given. I found another group (who however will have to be paid) working away at the sawing of the timber for the new school. Apparently they have made up their minds that the old building had better continue for worship (as the Christians are not afraid of it) and for the accommodation of wandering missionaries, though a new building is essential for heathen school-children. After dark we had evensong in the church, and then I slept there. The next morning at daybreak I was off again for Shwegwun, this time in the bullock cart, as my escort was in a hurry and would not let me walk. We went fast, and didn't we just get a jolting!"

Bullock Cart.

He adds, rather wistfully, "I get letters from Amherst every day; they sound very happy. I am longing to pay them a visit, and possibly I may manage it towards the end of the week, but tomorrow I go to Thaton". Fan's diaries reveal that we were indeed having a lovely time, bathing in the sea twice a day, before breakfast and after tea, and missing Father badly.

He goes on, "This house has made great progress. It has most of its shingles on now, and I have not any longer to wear a *topee* indoors. There is an awful row all the time – hammer, hammer, hammer, all over the roof. Apparently there was really some danger early this evening, while I was out, of its all being burnt down. I am devoutly glad that it wasn't. Two petrol lamps of an unfamiliar type were presented to us a month ago, and one of them blazed right up as it was hanging in the verandah. The cook seems to have acted splendidly. He got a bit of something to protect his hands, and then lifted the lamp off the hook and hurled it over the railing. Even then he must have managed cleverly not to let it set light to the piles of old shingles that are lying around. He threw earth over it, but I am still puzzled as to why the blazing petrol did not get hold in the few seconds that it must have taken him to run downstairs. Ma Lucy saw the blaze from her house 150 yards away, and came running to see what was happening; she was still out of breath when I came in and she told me all about it. The cook himself took it very calmly."

Father managed to escape to Amherst the following week, just for one night. "We spent all the time after tea on the beach, and had a bathe in the beautifully warm water. The hermit-crabs on the beach are great fun, as also are the ordinary crabs, which I am sure run faster than any English crab. They simply scoot over the ground. Unfortunately I was in rather a miserable plight myself, having a most particularly painful boil under my arm, but the bathe apparently did it a lot of good; at any rate it began to discharge freely directly after it, and now it only bothers me in that it has to have frequent dressings. The cook does the bandaging for me at this end, and he is (to my surprise) very good at it; so far his bandages have all kept in place."

By the 24th April 1927, the men had finished the work on the house, having replaced the supporting pillars as well as the roof. "They have also made progress at the school, and are now earth-oiling the roof of the church. That is the worst of a wooden roof; it has to be smeared with thick oil every year, and I (not knowing the climate) have left it rather late; if one of these heavy storms comes before the oil has had time to sink in, it just washes it all off! This year I must hope for luck, and next year I must start earlier."

Fortunately, Father was to pay several more visits to the family before we came back to our renovated home in early May, after seven whole weeks away. He wrote after one trip "We had a long bathe in the evening, including Anne, who now loves it and doesn't make a bit of fuss over a mouthful of water. The waves are quite considerable, and being warm are very nice indeed."

On 8th May: "I think we have got a lot of useful things done this week – three new teachers found for the two boys' schools, a next door house to be hired for the Chinese School until we can supply it with yet another building, and plans prepared for the said new building. There may be hitches yet; not all of these things are quite settled, but they look like working out. Also I have some hope that Mr. Tresham (the headmaster) will take the boarder-boys off my hands for six months, after which there may be another missionary to do it."

Throughout this time, it seems that the boarders of St. Augustine's Burmese Boys' School (about twelve in number) had been sleeping at the Mission House, where Father was meant to keep an eye on them, and he felt it was high time for this to end, particularly as he was so often away, when his wife was expected to cope. A cable had recently arrived at the Mission addressed to the absent Mr. Atwool (for whom Father was deputising) announcing the forthcoming arrival of a new young missionary, Arthur Dilworth by name, but without any further details, and Father was already planning how best to make use of this much-needed extra pair of hands.

"The Burmese Bible is out at last!" is the welcome news in his letter of 15th May 1927. "I wonder whether people will take kindly to it. We had a tiny ceremony this morning in church, putting a copy on the lectern." This incredibly brief entry is all there is, sandwiched between long descriptions of white ants and Indian baptisms.

"Such a mess of white ants' wings swept into a heap on the verandah! (No! since the sweeping, it is not much of a mess, but it is a heap.) They came out in swarms a little before dinner, but we managed to keep them out of the house fairly by putting two bright petrol-lamps on the verandah and having only a dim oil lamp inside. After an hour or two, they stopped, more or less, but it seems a very crawly night still.

At the other church I had some baptisms this morning – two Telugu lime-diggers from thirty miles away, a Punjabi sweeper of Moulmein and his Telegu wife, and a young brother of the wife. I think they are all promising people, but it is very difficult to know about people with whom one cannot converse except through an interpreter."

A fortnight later is this comment: "The white ants of Moulmein seem to be keepers of Sunday. We had a plague last Sunday evening, then a free week, and now another plague tonight. They do not do any damage at this stage, when they come out with wings, but they are very unpleasant.

The schools are just re-opening (22nd May). Have I told you that Mr Tresham (headmaster of the boys' school) is taking over the boarders? It is splendid I think. They will have excellent discipline, which they badly need, and I shall be free… we have three new teachers on the staff here, and two (with possibly a third to follow) at the Chinese School. The new ones are three Burmese Buddhists, one Christian Indian (Baptist), and an Anglo-Indian girl of our own church. I do wish we could staff our schools with Christians."

Adverse remarks about my behaviour follow. "Douglas is such a bonny little boy. He walks about now, with abrupt sittings-down very frequently, and is awfully pleased with himself. Anne is rather troubling us. She is charming when she is good, perfectly delightful, but at other times she is contrary and passionate beyond words. We are fairly puzzled as to what to do. As the result Fan is rather tired, but that will soon pass if only Anne will behave herself." A short time later, he was to write, "Anne has been much better lately, very much better, and we are hoping that the worst occasions were partly due to 'wriggly worrums' inside." (Aunt Fan, in her diary, goes on to relate something of the doctor's de-worming treatment for this irritating condition, so perhaps I may be forgiven!) On 10th July the tables were turned. "Anne has been very good lately; Douglas has been the naughty one in the last few days, and by turns he has been angelic."

Throughout this time, Fan's diaries give particularly lurid accounts of the difficulties of child rearing in the tropics. Both Douglas and I were constantly having fever and dysentery, causing many sleepless nights for everyone, including Sabetta (our *ayah*) but the local army doctors seem to have been supportive throughout, which must have been a considerable comfort. In addition, I was causing parental concern over a 'lazy eye', which meant that I was squinting badly, and there were several visits to the Rangoon oculist to deal with this. As a result, I had to wear spectacles, with the 'good eye' covered up for three hours a day, and it was all rather trying and ineffectual. In compensation, I was given a doll's pram, which I insisted on taking everywhere I went, this wretched toy proving to be an even bigger nuisance than the specs themselves!

Marjory and Charles Garrad with their children Anne and Douglas (1928).

Father was now much involved with an important matter called 'The Constitution of the Church of India' and had to go to a council meeting at Rangoon to discuss it. He wrote home, "As a matter of fact I don't feel any certainty that I shall be at the council. Between us and Rangoon there is a long bridge across the River Sittang; it is in a very bad way, and it is exceedingly likely that it may have to be closed and all the traffic stopped when the floods come. But I can't count on that. I only hope that it won't happen while I am in Rangoon, so that I can't get back again."

On 25th July 1927: "The Diocesan Council is just on the point of beginning, and I have come to Rangoon for it." Two weeks later he was back in Moulmein. "The council was disappointing. It seemed more muddly than usual. But the bishop spoke very well, both in his charge to the clergy and in his sermon at the Jubilee Service. He seemed much better than I had expected. He told us definitely that he is retiring very soon. I don't look forward to a new man; I prefer the old. In this country we see much more of our bishop than is the case in England, and it makes all the difference in the world what sort of man we have.

I had to go to court on Friday. A man had stolen two brass vases from the church, and (strange to say) the police had caught him! I fear he is feeling sore, as he was ordered a beating. He is a Telugu coolie, living somewhere near. I was summoned for 10 a.m. on Friday; having been to court before, I turned up about midday; by 1 p.m. or so they had decided which magistrate was to try the case, and at 2.20 it was actually called. I got home about 3.30, bringing with me the two vases, and also three rupees which the government gave me for my time. The wretched culprit didn't get home that night; he had to wait for his beating till the next day. Thursday I spent almost equally unprofitably. I called for the school registers, expecting to spend an hour over them, and they took me eight and a quarter hours! Monday to Wednesday I was at Thaton. Yesterday (Saturday) I went to Martaban in the morning to give Holy Communion to an old couple; this took four hours; then I baptised a woman, and was just on the point of trying to marry her when it was discovered that the wedding ring was missing. However it was not a very serious matter; both bride and bridegroom went off together to the bazaar, and came back with a cheap little brass ring with a bit of glass in it. They were married with that, but I don't think they regard it as the real wedding ring. I think it is to be replaced by a nice gold ring. I should have preferred of course to have had the permanent ring at the time, but they had come in on purpose from the jungle, and I was very glad to find that they had no sort of objection to this procedure.

We are wondering whether the bishop is going to stay with us when he comes to Moulmein next month. I wrote and asked him, but my letter reached Bishopscourt just after he had left for Port Blair and Car Nicobar. However, I feel sure that he would rather come here than go and stay with the Commissioner or some other great person; and Marjory has bought a shaving-glass for him, so he *must* come. It is possible also that we may have a visit from the Bishop of Singapore, as he is apparently paying a visit to Burma on his way home and lands at Moulmein; he will be much more formidable, as his wife and daughter will be with him."

On 18th Sept 1927: "The retired Bishop of Singapore has been here, with his wife and little girl. Generally he was very nice indeed, but there were times when he lapsed into the episcopal vein and wanted to arrange things for us more than we liked. In the schools he was exceedingly good with the teachers, as also with an old sick teacher (a Buddhist) whom I took him to see at home, because he wanted to see Burmans. He heard that I had a weekly Hindustani meeting, and at once said, 'Can't you put it a day earlier, and let me speak?' Before Singapore he was in Delhi, and knows that language well. It was an immense success. The wife was very trying. Marjory did no end for her, but the only thing she could remember was Douglas' cries at night. Of course they would be trying to an elderly woman, tired out, but we thought she might have covered up her annoyance. The little girl (an adopted daughter aged seven) played very happily with Anne.

Now we are expecting our own bishop. He will sleep downstairs, where he will not hear Douglas at night. Besides, Douglas isn't as bad as all that, though he does wake up when he ought not to wake, and having waked is very naughty.

The Bishop arrives at midday on Tuesday; the Commissioner is very kindly sending his car to take me to the jetty and bring the bishop up. Two other cars we can borrow once or twice. I wish it were not going to be his last visit. I shall miss him more than I dare to think about. We have no idea who will succeed him. I hope they will send us someone quite fresh from England."

On 25th September: "The Bishop's visit was very pleasant. He was so nice and appreciative of all our efforts. He managed to get about too, in spite of his bad knees. At the confirmation there was the trouble that one has grown to expect with native people, three candidates lacking at the proper time, although they were instructed to come half an hour early. I held everything up for ten minutes, and then very reluctantly gave the word for the bell to be rung and came across to the house to fetch the bishop. Then the three candidates turned up, and the number was complete after all – only nineteen this time, speaking four different languages. The Burmese were the largest element, so the service was held in Burmese throughout, except that the question was read also in Tamil and Telugu, and the hymns were sung in Tamil as well as Burmese."

On 24th October: "Next week I have to go to Rangoon again, to preach at the ordination of a Karen, and to conduct two quiet days beforehand for him and a recently ordained deacon. I would rather have stayed quietly at home, where I find plenty to do, but I can't possibly refuse, especially as it is the last request I am ever likely to receive from our present Bishop."

In due course, Father stayed with Bishop Fyffe in Rangoon (just a week before he left) having taken the two quiet days, and having preached two sermons, one at the ordination itself and the other in St John's College Chapel. "We hate losing the Bishop, and he hates going, but he needs an easier sphere of work. I don't suppose that we shall know anything about his successor for months. We all expect him to be somebody new from England, somebody of whom we have never heard. I wish he could be chosen and announced quickly, even if he could not come at once. In the interval it is rather embarrassing. I know that St. Augustine's is expecting me to return to Moulmein this week in knee-breeches, and the Archdeacon tells me that his friends are treating him in the same sort of way. Marjory's attitude is more or less this: 'Well we aren't likely to have the chance again. Let's make the most of it while it lasts. Let's enjoy being bishop for a few weeks!'"

On 20th November: "The great excitement is that Mr. Arthur Dilworth is here, and we like him very much. Both the children have taken a great fancy to him. He has been working at Burmese on the way out, and I think that quite quickly he will be starting to use it. He strikes me as a nice sensible fellow, anxious to be useful." A little later Fan wrote that "Mr. Dilworth unpacked his Christmas parcel from home and found that the ants were attacking his cake." Despite this, Christmas was spent happily, and Father wrote "I had several presents from home, including a share in a plum pudding such as only Bures can produce!"

"The communicants were 121, which is a small number, I know, but the whole number on our communicants' roll when I made it up three months ago (for the whole district) was only 197, and nineteen have been confirmed since them. People have been most astonishingly kind in giving presents to Anne and Douglas, and they had so many as to be overwhelmed… Marjory has gone up the Salween today with Miss Fairclough to pay a visit to Mr. West and his Karens. They won't be back till Thursday. Marjory hates leaving the family, but she is very keen to see Kappali and its people, and the River Salween is extraordinarily beautiful." And so ended the Garrad family's first full year in Moulmein.

CHAPTER ELEVEN

From Moulmein to Mandalay and Thoughts about I. T. (1928)

As the first day of 1928 dawned, there was much speculation as to who was to be the new bishop. Writing home on 1st January, Father was to say, "I am glad that you all sat on Mr. Davies a few weeks ago when he wanted to make me Bishop of Rangoon. I am *not* a candidate. You see, we get worn out early in this country, and I am getting near the limit. Also, seeing that a bishop spends half his time either talking with people or presiding over meetings, he needs to be able to hear." Father was not yet fifty-three years old, but he had already been in Burma for nearly a quarter of a century, and his deafness was a real trial. Time and again in his letters home he emphasises how much he hates committees, simply because he cannot hear, and of course there were no amplifiers then, fitting snugly inside the ear. It was an immense handicap.

On 15th January he wrote that the chaplain of St. Matthew's Church, Mr. Clack, had just left. "He will be much missed. He is a very quiet, unobtrusive man, who has won everybody's respect by his diligence in doing his work. But he has not got people to church, in spite of it all. I am not at all looking forward to having his work to do. Of course we can only attempt parts of it."

Then, on 29th comes a news item of some importance. "We have got our orders (more or less) for July – Mandalay again. The archdeacon came here yesterday from Rangoon, on purpose for a talk. It was very good of him as it involves travelling the whole of two nights to get eight hours here. He propounded all the various possibilities, with the pros and cons of each, and would have let me choose any one of them, but it seemed so clear that Mandalay is the right place for a time that I could not ask for any other. It is only for a year, at least I hope so; I refused to entertain the suggestion for more than a single year. I think Will will be pleased. I have just written to him, asking whether he can hold out until August. Mr Atwool is due back here about the second week of July, and my idea is to take the family up to Maymyo and have two or three weeks' holiday with them there and then go on to Mandalay."

Uncle Will was due for furlough and of course it made sense for his brother to replace him during his time away, but what a lot of heart-searching this was to cause. In his letters home, Father goes on to explain in some detail how excruciating he finds the Mandalay climate, and there is now the added worry as to how his wife and children will cope. Maybe, he explains, he could get a separate house in Maymyo for the family, while he lives in Mandalay, visiting them from time to time, but Marjory would have none of it. The whole clan would stay together, she insisted, coping with whatever the weather had to throw at them. "I don't myself think it will work," wrote Father, "but Marjory seems determined to try it." Finally, in mid February, he summed up the dilemma neatly: "As Mandalay is only to last one year, it would be a pity to magnify it by anticipating its troubles five months ahead." So life went on much as usual, and what a lot my parents managed to pack into each day.

In early February they went on a visit together, up country. On the first day at Thaton, they visited two Tamil families, one Chinese, one Anglo-Indian, one English and one Burmese, also fitting in a marriage service, a baptism and an evening service with sermon. On the second day, Father celebrated Holy Communion at 7.30 a.m. before both went off by motor-bus, with the cook, to Duyingcik, where they paid a short and very pleasant visit to a rubber-planter and his wife, who had arranged much of their journey. At 9.20 they were on the move again, this time by motor-launch to Kyettuywe-thaung where they put their things in the Public Works Department bungalow, before finding the two Telugu Christians whom they had come to visit. After tea, there was a baptism in the village street of three other Telugu men, followed by some preaching to Burmese neighbours. Day three saw another celebration of Holy Communion, followed by a four-hour trip back by sampan to the River Salween, where they got into one of the regular launches and reached home about 5 p.m. His description of the visit ended with the words, "All well – the children quite boisterous."

As if this wasn't enough, on 19th February Father was to write, "I have an uncommonly busy month ahead of me. I suppose I shall get through, but I don't know how. Dilworth (my assistant priest) is off to Tavoy and Mergui for three weeks.

Mr. Tresham (headmaster) is off immediately, to try if he can get a Calcutta B.A. (he has been studying for a university degree.) Lent is just beginning with its special services and both the Anglo-vernacular schools must have their annual exams, which decide the promotions. The Governor of Burma is going to visit Moulmein, and he has intimated his intention of coming to evening service. I am very glad. It may help some others to find out that there is a church in this place! I shall have to preach myself that night, as the recognised chaplain."

Aunt Fan's diary records that on 2nd March the Governor, Sir Charles Innes, paid his very first visit to Moulmein, and that Charlie had to wear his frock coat for the reception. Father, meanwhile, describes it rather more prosaically: "With all the rest of the public, Marjory and I attended the Governor's arrival on Friday morning, and sat still while a lot of inaudible speeches were made – inaudible as far as I was concerned, and very uninteresting to those who heard them… then last night he came to church. We had a very nice service. Mr. West was with me, and read the lessons and the later prayers. I had to read the early part of the service, because Mr. West's rendering of the versicles is apparently even worse than mine! And I preached. What I was most nervous about was the hymns, because lately the organist and congregation have been taking two quite different lines, and the choir has not been strong enough to settle the matter. Last night, we sang together very nicely. Fifty schoolboys attended choir practice at the suggestion of the choirmaster, and I think that helped."

By Tuesday 13th March 1928 Sir Charles had moved to Mandalay, where Uncle Will's church was in process of construction. During this work, much to everyone's delight and surprise the original dedication stone had been dug up, having been lost for almost fifty years, all previous attempts to find it having failed. You may recall that it had been way back in October 1879 that James Colbeck had hurriedly buried it in an attempt to preserve it for posterity when he was forced to leave Mandalay at the start of King Thibaw's reign, and now, here it was again, safe and sound, and ready to be re-installed.

What follows is a copy of the introduction to the order of service, when the stone was replaced by Sir Charles: "The Form of Service used at the Placing of a Memorial Stone in the Church of the Lord Jesus Christ, Winchester Mission, S.P.G., Mandalay, by His Excellency SIR CHARLES INNES, K.C.S.I., C.I.E., I.C.S., Governor of Burma, Tuesday March 13th 1928.

The stone which His Excellency has kindly consented to place in the wall of the new church is the foundation stone of the church built by Mindon Min. The stone was originally laid on September 1st 1869 by Major E.B. Sladen, the British Political Agent, assisted by Capt. G. Strover, Asst. Political Agent in the presence of Princes Minetone, Thibaw and Thahgarah. It was accidentally found this year four feet below the ground, after all hope of its recovery had been abandoned.

The old church was of wood, which through the ravages of white ants and in the course of time had reached a condition beyond repair, and had to be dismantled. The new building is being erected on the same spot. The old church was built entirely at the expense of King Mindon, and its erection cost the mission nothing. The new church is being built by subscription at a cost of 54,000 rupees. The head of the mission will gratefully receive any donations towards this sum."

Uncle Will headed the Winchester Brotherhood then and must have taken the church service that followed, conducting it in English, Burmese and Tamil. So, it appears that the Governor had met both Garrad brothers within a fortnight, the elder taking the Moulmein service (where he had preached) and the younger taking the Mandalay service (but being spared a sermon). The stone still survives today; it was proudly shown to us, in situ, on our 2007 visit to Christ Church, and very fine it looked too.

But back in Moulmein, Father had just discovered that the *mali* (sweeper cum water-carrier) had smallpox. Fan writes, "We wanted to send him to the infectious diseases hospital, but he wouldn't go. We were all vaccinated." Charlie added, "Because he refused to go into hospital, we had to look the other way while some of his friends took him somewhere else. We have had the *mali's* place thoroughly cleaned out, and sulphur burned in it, and I hope it is free of infection, but we shall do it again presently." For a time, the family had to keep away from the neighbours, for fear of infection, and Aunt Fan wrote in her diary, "We felt rather dull, for all the other children were told it was best not to play with us."

By the end of March the heat was getting oppressive. Fan writes, "We arranged a mosquito net for Anne's bed, so that she could sleep on the verandah, and I had my bed pulled out at bedtime." On the following day: "Hot. Marjory felt the heat very much in the night. Charlie arranged the mosquito room for her and Baby on the verandah."

In April, visits to the leper colony are mentioned. Writing on Easter Monday, Father said, "I am now going out to give communion to a poor leper woman, a Eurasian, a young woman with a very old husband. But I don't see the husband on these occasions. I think he goes out; at least he does not appear."

By May, the weather was getting stormy, and on the 9th Aunt Fan wrote, "Tremendous storm in the night and we all had to hurry in from the verandah. Marjory and Baby got into Charlie's bed, and I pushed Anne's and my bed in, and then C. came and shut the doors for us." On the 21st, "Mr. Arthur Dilworth has come back from Thandaung, and he seems quite fit. Mr. West has also been here for the weekend, and took the English services yesterday, which was a great help. He has gone on to Kappali today. I don't envy him his residence in Kappali during the rains. Both children are unwell."

On 3rd June: "We are better here; the children well and happy again and Marjory very active." Then follows a remarkable few lines about Father's thoughts about the future of telegraphy, and the whole development of I.T. itself. He writes, "Wireless is very wonderful. I had to send a cable to Mr. Atwool the other day, and I found that I could send it at three annas a word, with a minimum of twenty words. They told me at the office that it would be sent by wireless direct from Bombay to England; I wonder whether that can be correct? So I suppose I pay one anna (which is a penny) per word for telegraphing from here to Bombay, one anna from Bombay to Daventry or wherever they deal with these matters, and one anna for the telegram in England! I don't think I shall stay here long enough to have a photograph of a letter like this delivered to you on the day that it is written for sixpence, but that will come. But there won't be any privacy, which will be objectionable."

In July 1928 the family were to say goodbye to Moulmein en route to Mandalay, but not before this triumphant letter, written a few days before the move. "Mr. Dilworth preached in Burmese this morning, for the first time. He seems to have got on very well indeed."

All sorts of farewell presentations were to follow. On 5th July Aunt Fan wrote, "Sent off a lot of things on a bullock cart to the boat. Charlie worked desperately hard. Ma Lucy and her children gave an entertainment in our honour at 3 p.m. We all went, and were all given posies of flowers and Charlie and Marjory had a lovely ivory figure, and I had a little brooch." On 7th July: "We went to tea at the boys' school by invitation of the teachers, and they presented C. and M. with a silver bowl. Then we went to St Agnes School at 5 pm, and the Tamils gave C. and M. a little clock."

On 9th July, "Had a very busy day packing, and Marjory and I, Sabetta and the children started for Rangoon in the evening. Charlie came with us to Martaban; we had a great send off, all Ma Lucy's children and all the Girls Friendly Society. Arrived at Rangoon at 6 a.m. the next day, and went to Bishopscourt. The Archdeacon and Mrs Cowper Johnson were there until the evening. Mr. and Mrs. Johnson (Burma Railways) came to breakfast, and others to tea. Mr. and Mrs. Atwool arrived from England in the morning and we saw them at Bishopscourt after tea."

Charlie arrived by the 6 a.m. train on the 12th and "We went shopping and then packed all our things and started for Maymyo at 1.15. The children were very good." The next day: "Will met us at Mandalay and we had *chota hazri* in the waiting room. We had our breakfast in the train. Mr. Thursfield (the local chaplain) met us with his motor at Maymyo and we came to Lansdowne again." Perhaps it was the sudden change to a much cooler climate, but both Douglas and I added to the complications of the move by having a bad attack of fever for some days, and Douglas also had nettle-rash. However, we recovered before too long and all was well.

By 5th August 1928, Father was back in Mandalay, and writes home, "Here I am, back in my old place. I don't take to it all kindly, I am afraid, but one has to go where one is wanted and that is the place that wants a man at present. Will is wearing himself out, but it won't be many weeks before he sets out for England, and those few weeks should not do him any particular harm."

In this letter, Father writes a great deal about the wonderful red brick building now standing proudly in the centre of their compound – the new Christ Church – pointing out that it was very nearly finished. This rebuild had been Will's project over many years, as head of the Winchester Brotherhood, and how heartening it was to find it reaching completion at last. Of course the Garrad brothers must have been sad to say farewell to the old historic church in which they had both served faithfully for so long, but it had become little more than a ruin. Gradually, over more than half a century King Mindon's wooden edifice had been rotting beyond repair, termites and torrential rain having taken their toll, and something had to be done about it. Recently, years of work in raising money had borne fruit in the construction of a fine brick building to replace the old.[14] Will made sure that much of the original carving was kept with Queen Victoria's font in pride of place as before, but I'm told that the compound didn't quite feel the same without the original old church, so dear to all of them. I was barely four years old at this juncture, and remember nothing about it at all.

The locally ordained clergy at Christ Church were delighted with their new place of worship, gaining much needed inspiration from it in their on-going attempt to preach Christianity in a Buddhist stronghold. The four who played the greatest part in the life of the tight-knit Christian community in Mandalay at this period were the Rev. George Kya Bin, ('*Saya* George' the translator), Rev. Asirvatham (the Tamil priest) *Saya* Ambrose and Rev. Chit Tway.[15]

Exciting news came on 19th August 1928. "You have seen no doubt that our new bishop has at last been appointed. Dr. Tubbs of Tinnevelly, India. Will has met him and is distinctly pleased at the appointment," Father wrote. "I rather think I met him myself once in Calcutta. I wish he were ten years younger." (He was, in fact, Charlie's junior by just four years).

In due course, Will and Charlie, accompanied by Mr. Caldicott, travelled down to Rangoon for the Bishop's enthronement. On September 19th came this comment: "I expect to get back on Saturday, but Will and Mr. Caldicott (who has had a bad attack of fever) will probably not come back at all, but start instead on the wanderings which are to take them at last to England, on furlough." Mr. Caldicott, always known as 'Caldie', was to give twenty-five years of his ministry to Burma, nearly all of it as Riverine Chaplain, an arduous job of frequent travel, visiting the scattered

The Three Bishops.
Left to right Bp. Tubbs 1928; Bp. Knight 1903-09; Bp. Fyffe 1910-28.

mission stations up and down the River Irrawaddy, remaining in post until the time of the Japanese invasion.

Later came this letter: "We had a great service in Rangoon on Thursday evening – the enthronement of the new Bishop. We all came away greatly pleased, feeling that we have got the man we want. We shall miss our old Bishop very much (I in particular have lost a great friend by his departure) but Dr. Tubbs is full of life, apparently very capable, and knows his own mind. He seems like the right man for Rangoon. He has appointed all three of Dr. Fyffe's Examining Chaplains, and so I took my place behind him at the enthronement. I must be getting awfully old (sometimes I feel like it) as I was the senior clergyman present on the occasion! There are two in the diocese senior to me, but both of them were away."[16]

Meanwhile, Father and Uncle Will were hard at work trying to turn the Winchester Brotherhood house at Christ Church into a suitable home for our family. For twenty-two years it had been occupied by a group of itinerant bachelors, with little time or thought for comfort, and a number of changes had to be made. First of all, a rotten post and beam had to be replaced and convenient doors made on the staircases so that dogs could be shut out from upstairs, and some discouragement given to thieves and trespassers generally, but, most of all, the electricity needed attention. Until now, it hadn't mattered much if the flick of a single switch were to cause lights to go on in two separate rooms (as had apparently been the somewhat strange pattern since it was first installed) but now, with children in the house, this simply wouldn't do. Just imagine the scene in Baby's bedroom, for example, if his light came on whenever the adults sat down to dinner! Something would have to be done about it, and done quickly.

Electricians were called in at once, achieving miracles under Will's guidance, so that Father was soon able to write, "Three of the five bedrooms are fairly straight now. Downstairs it is all a dreadful muddle… Will's study must become mine. My study must be made into a little drawing-room. The dining-room will need only a little rearrangement. The rooms of unutterable chaos must somehow become a nursery, and a sort of general study where Marjory and Fan or visitors can sit and write etc. The dirt is dreadful, the house never having had a mistress and having been just a warehouse for the last year, but the paint and whitewash are not bad."

With constant repairs going on, Father now decided to take on the job of Riverine Chaplain for ten days or so, in Caldie's absence. He wrote, "As his stations are likely to be badly neglected now he's gone, I didn't want the neglect to begin earlier than necessary and as I was doing no good at all in Mandalay I came away at once. It happens to be the really pleasant part of his beat. Three days up the river to Bhamo. Sunday at Bhamo. One day down to Katha. Services at Katha. One day down again to Thabeikkyin. Motor to Mogok, where I stay over Sunday, and then back to Mandalay. I had not the least realised what a peculiarly pleasant task I was taking when I very kindly offered my services!" Later he was to write from Mogok, "I have been having a very quiet peaceful time – five days of the river (three at a stretch and two separate ones) and most comfortable boats, with sixty miles yesterday of the most glorious motor-drive anyone can wish for. This place is much smaller than it used to be, because the great Ruby Mines Company has gone into liquidation. My great contribution to church life at Katha was repairing the harmonium. It had a dreadful cipher, and three or four silent notes, and was quite impossible to use. To get it right, I had to open it entirely, sound-box and all, and turned out half a dozen lizard's eggs and two baby lizards."

CHAPTER TWELVE

The Dedication of Christ Church and Adventures with a Motor Car (1928-1929)

On 23rd September 1928 came the stupendous news that Father, who hated all motor vehicles, had actually bought a car! "We have had tremendous discussions about a conveyance for getting the children out of the compound every day," he wrote, "and the upshot is that I have bought an old car. It is a Cowley-Oxford, pretty antiquated (1922) but apparently in good order. I am paying Rs 850 (£65) for it, and I hope it will carry me a long way before needing any serious repairs… my great fear is that it may prove to be like my first motor-cycle, that is excellent in the hands of its former owner who knew all its little ways, but hopeless in my inexperienced hands… the law of driving-licences in this country is a quite impossible one. I can't get a licence at present because they are granted only to people who can drive reasonably, and I am not allowed to drive without one! Of course I shall drive without one, and the responsible people will look the other way."

On 3rd October, Fan wrote, "Charlie's motor car came from the workshop and we all went for a ride." Father, writing home, put it this way: "My car has come, and I have had it out twice. Each time I have had a Burmese mechanic with me, to prevent me from doing anything dreadful. As a matter of fact I feel fairly confident now of doing nothing worse than holding up the traffic; that I am very likely to do. I haven't yet ventured to drive either in or out of my own compound, and I must tackle that now. It really is rather hard on a beginner, with two sharp turns, a steep little bit of rise, plenty of mud, and often several bullock carts or loose oxen as well as people walking. But I have to get through it."

A few days later, came this: "The car gives us some excitements. Just outside the compound the other day I was held up by some traffic and let the engine stop. It was on a slight hill but it stood quite firmly and so I didn't bother about the brake but got out and wound it up." [Earlier there had been trouble with the battery, and the self-starter had ceased to function.] "The vibration of the engine started it running backwards down the hill, and there was a bullock cart! I tugged at it for all I was worth, hopping along with one foot inside the guard. It only went very slowly, and there was a splendidly calm Burmese driver who quietly pulled the bullocks out of the way and the car came comfortably to a stand against the cart. Nobody minded in the least!"

Some days earlier on 28th September, the family had moved en bloc from Maymyo to Mandalay, at Mother's insistence. Fan wrote, "All the servants helped with the luggage and Mr. Gerald Thursfield (chaplain at Maymyo) took us to the station in his car. Ma Lane came with us to be *ayah* in Sabetta's place. Charlie and Marjory met us here and we came in a taxi, and the luggage in a bullock cart. It was the first night of the Light Festival, and the lights were very lovely."

On 26th October the new Bishop came up from Rangoon to stay with our family in Mandalay, with the consecration of Christ Church as the highlight of his visit. Afterwards, Father was to write, "Our great function is over, and very happily so. I think the service in church went well, though I had to do a good deal of running about to get people into their right place, to prevent the collection being taken at the wrong time, etc. As usual, the hymns were the great feature, and they really were very fine. The breakfast party was quiet and happy, the food well cooked, nicely served and available as soon as ever we were all ready. The Bishop is staying with us and is a very pleasant guest."

Hidden away, amongst my magpie collection of Burma papers, I found the service sheet of this great occasion, written in three languages, English, Burmese and Tamil, and the various scripts still stand out boldly from the printed page, just as they must have done all those years ago. Every hymn is fully written out, so that members of each race would be able to sing in their own native tongue, fully accompanied by the organ. Believe it or not, there were no less than eight hymns in total![17]

The only sadness on this auspicious day was that Uncle Will was not there to see it, having quietly slipped away on leave a few weeks earlier. Fan, writing home to her sisters in Bures, felt his absence keenly and wrote, "I wonder if Will is just about arriving home; at any rate, we think it is time we wrote to him, especially as we know how he must be longing to know all about today's festival. Everyone was regretting that he wasn't there, to see the climax of his work; there is only one opinion – that it is a really beautiful church, and shows in every detail what an amount of care and thought has been spent on it.

We had a very large congregation, but unfortunately nobody counted, so that 450 is only a guess. The Vardons think that they probably fed about 400 to breakfast, and we know that a good many people went away before it. Charlie took no end of trouble to ensure that everyone should know what to do in the service. There was a procession outside of the three choirs – Burmese boys, Tamil men and the choir from the English Church. The Bishop, attended by *Saya* George, had to knock on the door with his pastoral staff and they all filed in. The singing went well; we didn't attempt anything but hymns, but everyone sang and kept together remarkably well. The lady members of the English choir and Marjory sat up in the chancel, and the girls from the S.P.G. school were on the front mats, but I think the congregation sang just as much as the choirs. The Bishop gave a nice little address, standing up between *Saya* Ambrose and Joshua, and having each sentence translated into Burmese and Tamil as he went along. Most of the service was in English, for it was impossible to translate the consecration prayers, and the bishop liked to take the communion service himself. We had four to celebrate, *Saya* George, Joshua, the bishop and Charlie, so after all, the service was not so tremendously long – about two hours. It was all very inspiring and beautiful and everyone was happy. The breakfast too was a great success. Will knows exactly what it was like – great dishes of chicken pilau and rice, and I think all the tables and mats were arranged exactly as he does them… last evening we had the old diaries out of the safe to look at, and the Bishop was intensely interested in Dr. Marks. He stays here till tomorrow evening and then goes to Shwebo, and on to Maymyo where he will consecrate the new Tamil church. Charlie and Marjory are going up for a night so as to be at the consecration." Fortunately for all concerned, my parents decided that my brother Douglas and I were too young to take any part in the proceedings, apparently holding firm to this decision, despite our protests!

On 5th November 1928, Father wrote, "The Maymyo Church, too, has now been dedicated, with the name of St. Matthew. It isn't finished! Only half of the floor is down, and most of the walls are not yet pointed, but one has to get the Bishop when one can, and so we had the dedication service in spite of the place being unfinished."

Later that month, Father really got into his stride, going to Madaya, Myittha, and Kyaukse, following Will's pattern of pastoral visits round his 'parish', where he was much in demand as a translator, helping British missionaries to put their sermons into Burmese and training local catechists in English. By this time, Mother was also an expert in the local language, with the result that twice a year they were both asked to join a team examining British candidates in Burmese. This was a most rewarding but exhausting task, as they were expected to test people of all ages and abilities at a variety of different levels. Mastery of the Burmese script is, in itself, a complex undertaking, but to speak the language properly is even more difficult for it is tonal in essence, meaning that a word can have two totally different meanings, according to how it is pronounced. For example, an 'ee' sound can easily be muddled with an 'a' sound, so that attempting to say "quickly, quickly" on one occasion, one candidate had actually said "horse, horse" much to my parents' amusement! I believe I managed to jabber away in ungrammatical Burmese as a small child, but never learnt to read or write it, and haven't kept it up, unfortunately.

My father relates, in a letter home of mid November 1928, that after one of these strenuous language examinations, feeling tired out, they had to drive back along very bad roads, full of potholes, breaking two springs in the process. So, once again, they were without a much needed vehicle for several days, while the poor old car was being attended to in the local workshops.

There was good news at the end of the month, with the long awaited arrival of the first full time doctor at the children's hospital, Dr. Cicely Wilson. Father wrote, "The new doctor is here. She is first rate. I have high hopes of her when she has got hold of things, and she will get hold of them very quickly. We had been told very little as to who she was; she proves to be a daughter of Canon Wilson, sometime Headmaster of Clifton, and Canon of Worcester – a remarkable man whose daughter is sure to have good stuff in her."

Another arrival of note was that of the Viceroy, Lord Irwin. It was on the 26th November that Marjory, Charlie and Fan all went to his reception near the station, and two days later were invited, once more, to the garden party at Government House, when the car was, unfortunately, to get up to its old tricks once more. Father wrote, "There is nothing wrong with the car, but I got into such muddles with it in the squash at the Viceroy's garden party that I don't want ever to see it again. The dreadful thing was that in the process of parking, I touched the next car, and it happened to be a beautiful new brougham car. It was a very slight touch, but it did make a little mark in the paint just over the footboard, and the owners were very angry. Then, as we were all coming away, I was held up at the fort gate by some bullock carts and managed to stop my engine in the middle of the road, with half a

Outside the Queen Alexandra Children's Hospital, Mandalay (1928).

dozen or more cars in a string behind me. Fortunately the first turn of the handle started it off again. Despite all this, Marjory finds the car very useful and would not on any account part with it. I should enjoy it myself under other conditions; it is the traffic and the awful roads that make me greatly prefer my bicycle."

Our 1928 Christmas was a very worrying one, for my brother was none too well. Father wrote on the 23rd December, "Poor little Douglas is celebrating Christmas in his usual manner. His first Christmas he was very poorly and we had to get the doctor round on Christmas Day. His second Christmas was all right, as far as I remember, but he terrified his mother (while I was away) on New Year's Eve. Now just before his third Christmas he has got a nasty cough and a temperature of 103 degrees. Dr. Cicely Wilson came and examined him this afternoon; she says there is just a suspicion of bronchitis. She will come and see him again early tomorrow." A later diagnosis was pneumonia, but Douglas got better fairly quickly, and was soon up and about again. Despite all this, "We had our Christmas party as arranged. Marjory had to run upstairs several times, and sometimes stayed away rather a long time, but Mr. Park (chaplain at Mandalay) was in great form and the whole company were happy, I think. The feature of the dinner was, of course, the Bures pudding – very good, and recognised as such all round."

The New Year of 1929 started with the arrival of Mr. Clack as Riverine Chaplain. He was an old friend, having been chaplain in Moulmein when we were there not long ago; my parents were pleased to see him again, and I am told that my brother and I were delighted.

Douglas' third birthday on January 26th was celebrated in style. Father wrote home about it, saying, "Fan gave him a beautiful Bible, which (to my surprise) gave great pleasure. 'I can sing out of it' was his remark. Sometimes the two of them have short prayers in the household chapel, conducted by their mother (it is much too difficult for me) and then they both think it necessary to hold books for the hymn. Sometimes the books are the wrong way up! Douglas had a little toy railway signal with two arms amongst other things. 'I did want a signal' was his comment on receiving it. Half a dozen children came to tea in the afternoon. The great entertainment was a clean bullock cart with straw and a rug and flags, which carried them round and round the football field, first very sedately, then at a trot and finally at a canter, amidst shrieks of delight." I suppose I must have been four and a half years old by then, and I can, even now, certainly recall something of the excitement of that unforgettable, bouncy ride!

My greatest memory, at this time, however, was the daily ritual of seeing row after row of yellow robed monks, rice bowl in hand – many of them little boys of only nine or ten – queuing up in the street outside for their food offerings. This happened early each morning as well as just before dusk, and never ceased to intrigue me. Being female I was forbidden any sort of physical contact, but once, I remember being given a long handled wooden spoon, with which to dollop rice into some of their outstretched containers, and what fun it was. As a child, of course, I had no idea at all of the vital part played by these monks in the national life of the Burmese Buddhists; I just knew that in Mandalay they were there in their hundreds, for there were monasteries galore throughout the town.

In addition to his work at Christ Church, Father was much involved in the compilation of the Burmese prayer book, and though this was certainly one of his greatest interests, he found little time for it, telling us that there were never enough hours to go round. The Bishop came for a visit again in February, on his way up country to visit the Bible Churchmen's Mission, and the two of them went on a short trip together, a few miles south along the Irrawaddy. Father wrote, "I was only going as far as Sagaing to show him round a little and talk about other subjects for which there had not yet been time. We went and looked at Sagaing Church, which

Chota Hazri (or early morning breakfast) for the monks.

I had never seen before; it is quite a nice little church, but very different from the stone building which we planned in pre-war days."

In March, Father wrote to his sisters about the family, "Anne and Douglas do things together now much more than has been the case hitherto. They both say delightfully fresh things sometimes; I think one day I may take one of Douglas' latest remarks as the starting part of a sermon, and it ought to be a good sermon. The remark was 'Come into the chapel, Mummy; I want to help God to make me good'... I failed to get a letter off home last week; I was in too much of a rush getting started for Bootalet. I have thoroughly enjoyed my week out, except that the two days in the train were rather wearisome. There has been a breach in the railway for months, and it is likely to go on for months more. The unusual rainfall made a lake of many square miles; there are armies of coolies now digging a drain to clear it, but it is a big business and won't be finished for ever so long. I don't know how many villages are involved: I saw one flooded out - quite abandoned. The water has gone down now a little, and the railway metals just appear above it; goods trains creep through, and the line has not collapsed under them yet, but they dare not run the passenger trains through. Instead, they put us all into motor boats, and ferry us across to another train on the other side. The actual passage over the lake takes about a quarter of an hour. As I came back yesterday there were so many people in the train that the ferry boats could not take them all; so we had to wait a further period of one and a half hours while they went back and picked up the other people. But it is quite interesting to see once, and a great number of water birds have found their way there.

Saya Pyau [of Bootalet] had got my letter, and had made excellent plans, but I spoilt them all by a silly mistake; I wrote that I was going to arrive on the 3rd day of the waning moon, when actually it was the 4th. It gave a great deal of trouble, which was a pity. My boy Mg Hla Maung was with me, and we came to the end of our railway journey at Meza station early on Tuesday morning. We got a cart for our luggage, and walked off to Bootalet. About halfway we met a man who introduced himself as Maung Kyu, whom Will baptised not very long ago; he told me that he had been expecting us to breakfast the previous day! We could have done with that breakfast then, but we got some instead from another Christian (Maung Mya) two miles further on. All Wednesday we stayed in Bootalet, starting the day with Holy Communion. On Thursday as soon as it was light we walked over to Thapangine, and had Holy Communion there, and stayed there till it began to get cool again in the afternoon, and then returned to Bootalet. On Friday, *Saya* Pyau and I had a very pleasant walk by moonlight, back along part of the road to Meza, and had Holy Communion at Mas-u-kon – the place where we had breakfasted on Tuesday. Then I picked up my cart with Mg Hla Maung, (they did not start till daylight) and we went through to Meza again. Being early there, I took a local train northwards, and called on the Bible Christian Missionaries at Indaw, who gave me dinner, and after dinner I only just managed to catch the train for Mandalay. The nights were still thoroughly cold, though the middle part of the day has become quite hot enough, and I thoroughly enjoyed the walks. There are beautiful trees in blossom just now, the Cotton Tree and the Flame of the Forest, and I found some wild roses too. Some people have died, and others have moved away, since I was there nine years ago, but I found some very delightful old friends, and new people too. I have promised to go again after Easter, to visit villages for which I could not find time immediately."

Perhaps this trip had been rather too much for Father, because on his return to Mandalay on 10th March, he had a bad attack of malaria, and spent a whole week in bed with high fever. We were all very worried. At the end of this he wrote, "My doctor is a cruel man. He insists on fifteen grains of quinine daily for the next month, and ten grains daily for two months more, and I don't know how to get through with it. It will certainly mean that I shan't do any work worth doing for ages! Shall I rebel? I am very much inclined to, only if I do, I can't go to him when next I have an attack of fever. In the meantime I can eat and sleep and am really entirely well, only the floor keeps swinging and the table keeps jumping, and I found it pretty well a whole day's work yesterday to make answers on the prayer book from three divinity students!"

Meanwhile the weather was beginning to get unbearable, and plans were made for a family holiday at Anisakan, up in the hills, not far from Maymyo. Easter Sunday was celebrated in the usual way, and we left on the next day, Monday 1st April. "Very hot night and nobody slept well." Aunt Fan wrote, "All got up at 5. There were two bullock carts in the compound all night, and Charlie got them loaded up and to the station for 7 a.m. The children and I travelled first class to Anisakan, and Ma Lon, Po Yin and his family were close to us in a third class. We had masses of luggage. Charlie, Marjory and Hla Maung came up in the car, and to my great joy arrived first, and met us at the station. The house seemed rather desolate at first, but we all worked away and we got breakfast about 12 midday. It felt so lovely and cool when we arrived." On the 3rd: "C had an early tea and went back to Mandalay by the afternoon train. Thunderstorm in the evening, and a lot of rain and wind and it was rather dreary."

On 11th April, Father paid his promised visit to Bootalet again, still suffering from the after effects of malaria. Here he spent time with *Saya* Pyau at Tigyaing and other outlying villages, where he celebrated Holy Communion to the confirmed, and much enjoyed "the jungle walks and the simple lives of peasants." For the first time in his letters home, he muses a little about his health, saying "In a way it is a relief to get back to the railway, as one can't help wondering sometimes what would happen if one got a nasty bout of fever twenty miles from anywhere, though I never have been caught like that, and twenty miles from anywhere is the very extreme limit to which I go. I doubt whether my five days' walk has been more than thirty-five miles, though it seems very much more over the rough tracks, and so I suppose I have always been less than twenty miles from one end or the other. Only Tigyaing isn't 'anywhere' when you get to it; it only becomes 'anywhere' when a steamer arrives. Anyway, it has all been extremely pleasant, only I am horribly conscious of not having risen to the social side of it, because I am still on quinine and pretty considerably deaf."

In early May Father was at last able to get a few days in Anisakan, but writing home on the 12th he says, "I am back again at headquarters; I can hardly call it 'home' just now – all that makes 'home' is at present at Anisakan. They all seem very happy there, and splendidly well."

He was soon off again, however, this time travelling with Mr. Asirvatham to Namtu. They looked up all the native Christians there (about a hundred of them) and "had some curiously mixed services". Father explains that "The Burma Corporation, mining silver and lead and some other metals too, is a big company. It is said to employ 28,000 men. One of them told me (though I doubt very much whether he really knows) that they have a daily income of £50,000, and a daily expenditure of £40,000. I expect that there are outgoings (depreciation of plant etc.) that do not appear in that statement. I stayed first at the Public Works Department bungalow, and found it very comfortable, perched on the top of a big hill, which was splendid when you got there, but rather a severe climb three or four times a day. I had to leave that because the Sawbwa (Shan Prince) came, and then I went to the Corporation's rest-house, which is also very nice.

The whole place is much better laid out than it was when I was there before, and it is fascinating to watch their little trains running about everywhere, and in particular, to see the slag being poured out. Sulphur smoke is the bane of the place, but they have got it so arranged now that it seldom comes into the town. From the smelting furnaces they have a flue running half a mile or more up a steep hill, and a big chimney at the top of the hill, and it is only a very perverse wind that brings the smoke down now. All the same, there are hardly any animals. Two or three ponies, two goats and one dog were all that I saw while I was there. No milk is to be had, except out of tins."

Writing from Christ Church, Mandalay on 19th May, Father says in his usual forthright way, "Mr Neal (the headmaster of The Royal School) is a great man now, made a member of the Mandalay Municipal Council on the nomination of the government. I am really very sorry about it, as it is an exacting business, and an honest man can do very little good amongst a company of clever knaves. But he thinks it is his duty to try what he can do, and it certainly is an honour to be picked out for the post." He adds, as a postscript, that, "The new Riverine Chaplain has come – Mr. Stevens from St Philip's Church, Rangoon."

In early June, Father had fever once again, and managed to get a whole week away with us all at Anisakan, where he swiftly got better in the cooler weather, particularly enjoying playing with Douglas and me. In one of his letters he describes a bonfire we made together, which I vaguely remember as being most exciting. "Anne got as far as poking the fire lustily once when I wasn't looking; she didn't burn herself, happily, and did no harm beyond nearly putting the fire out."

Although we had already been away from the heat of Mandalay for two months, Mother now accepted an invitation to stay for a further couple of weeks at our old home, Lansdowne, in Maymyo, where the Snow family was currently on holiday. Mrs. Una Snow was our hostess, the wife of Mr. Dick Snow, the much respected head of the country's education service. She was a wonderfully warm, hospitable person – a former missionary herself – who befriended us on many occasions, and was a great friend throughout our time in Burma. She had four children, Elizabeth, Audrey, Nicholas and little Ursula, and we all got on really well together. Audrey and I were much the same age, as were Nicko and Douglas, and this was one of several shared holidays, which I remember as being great fun. Of course we went for long walks and played interminable games of hide and seek, but best of all were the wonderful dressing-up sessions, when we pretended to be Burmese people, puffing away at homemade 'cigars' and spitting out bright red 'betel juice', which was really permanganate of potash as used in the kitchen to sterilise our food! The stained red lips and teeth of many Burmese villagers today, as we discovered on our recent visit, show how strongly this rather revolting habit is still ingrained, betel nuts being chewed into a pulp and then forcefully and accurately ejected in a well-directed stream of saliva.

Meanwhile, Father was still hard at work in Mandalay, and how he put up with the dreadful heat day after day I simply can't imagine, for although rudimentary electricity existed, air conditioning hadn't even been thought of. In our main sitting room, however, was a large swinging fan, made of some sort of cloth, stretched on a rectangular frame, suspended from the ceiling on rafters, and worked by a cord. Our 'punkah-wallah' (fan operator) would sit on the floor, with the cord attached to his foot, moving it endlessly, up and down, up and down, in an effort to provide some respite from the overpowering heat. Despite this attempt to cool us down, my abiding memory of the hot season is of prickly heat, when I was covered from head to toe in itchy pink spots, desperately trying not to scratch.

At the end of the month Father (who also found the temperature unbearable) received a letter from his sister Edith in England, telling him that the family at Bures had been entertaining the Thursfields – missionaries in Maymyo when I was a baby. Father replied, "I hope we have told you that Mr. Gerald Thursfield was kindness itself to us when he was at Maymyo, and when his family had gone, wanted us to share the parsonage with him. He is a thoroughly good fellow, but his sermons are apt to be peculiar, and it is commonly reported that when he was leaving Rangoon [for England] he offered his bicycle for sale in the middle of one of them!"

This titbit was by way of being no more than a light-hearted preamble, for Father continued "I have had a letter from the Bishop saying that Maymyo badly needs an assistant chaplain, and asking whether I should like to have the post, combining it with some Burmese writing. The weak point of the suggestion is that he thinks we might live in the Anisakan house. The last feature is entirely impossible. I like the house as a holiday house, but as a permanent residence it simply won't do. It is too small, too distant, and too flimsy. Whether the assistant chaplaincy can run to the rent of a house in Maymyo, I don't know; if it can't, the idea must be dropped so far as I am concerned. The chaplaincy at Kalaw [which had obviously been discussed earlier] as a light post with time for writing, seems to me more possible, and the Kalaw country is delightful… either would suit us very well."

CHAPTER THIRTEEN

The Beautiful Hill Station of Kalaw and a New Arrival (1929)

In July 1929 Father wrote to his sisters to say, "We have been thinking a lot about 'number three.' Marjory is now writing to Katie and George and Frances Wood to ask them to be god-parents, and we may presently ask the archdeacon as well." Thinking back, I must have known for some time that I was going to have a new brother or sister, but as the event grew nearer and nearer, the excitement grew even greater.

More good news was to follow, for on 5th August 1929 Father returned from the Diocesan Council in Rangoon with a huge smile on his face. "My next move is to be Kalaw, and that is delightful. Beautiful hilly country, with rolling downs and pine trees, splendid for the children, and for their parents too. It is higher than Maymyo, and colder, also wetter but I think not so wet as seriously to matter. The idea is that I should have a thoroughly light post and get to work on Burmese writing. It has several outstations – Taunggyi (still higher up the hills) and Thazi, Meiktila, and Myingyan in the plains. The Bishop would take these last three off me if he could see any means to do it, as he is really keen to give me time for writing, but I expect I shall have to serve them. Apparently it means being out twelve days each month.

At Rangoon I stayed with the Snows. Mrs. Snow was also a member of the Council and went to almost all the meetings, but even when she didn't go she managed to let me have their car and in that sort of way it was delightful. She is a simply splendid person. I didn't see much of the children. They all seemed very happy."

On 12th August he wrote, "We had our annual Transfiguration Festival yesterday at Christ Church, and it was all very nice. I was rather frightened beforehand, when

I found that I had got to translate the Bishop's sermon for him, but he was able to give me the outline of it in advance, and it was not too difficult. Fan played the organ." The 30th September was to see the birthday of Queen Alexandra's Children's Hospital, Mandalay, and Father wrote, "Mr. Arthur Lee (the chaplain at St. Mary's) came and preached in the chapel in the afternoon."

On 8th September, "We are all waiting rather anxiously, ready for a journey to hospital at any moment." On the 15th he wrote, "The baby [born the day before] kept us waiting a week, and seemed as if she would never come, but she seems a beautiful baby now that she has come. Fan, of course, has told you all about her and everything connected with her, and if I set out to do it again I shall only be repeating what she has said. Anne is simply delighted with her, and has already been allowed to nurse her; Douglas too is greatly interested. Marjory is wonderfully bright." Aunt Fan's letter has not survived, but her diary entry says: "14th September Dr. Wilson came at 1 a.m. to tell us a splendid baby girl had been born at 12.05 a.m." Charlie went to see Marjory at 5.30 a.m. and he and I went at 9 a.m. and the children and I went for 10 minutes after tea. M. was wonderfully well and happy."

It was also at this period that Father was beginning to make plans for his new posting. "I have been making enquiries about the journey to Kalaw, and a friendly railway official will help us a lot. He will reserve a second class compartment for us, on production of four tickets, although according to the rules that is only done for night journeys; and he will reserve two rooms for us at Thazi station for the night, although generally only first class passengers are allowed to use them. The Kalaw train leaves Thazi at 8.30 a.m., so we have to travel as far as Thazi (three or four hours away) the previous day. But we aren't starting for Kalaw tomorrow! We are likely to be a tremendous party, as in addition to the family, there will be the butler with his wife and two babies, two sisters of the butler's wife, and an Indian *ayah*. I did wonder about engaging what they call a family-coach, in which we should all be able to travel right through without changing, and cook meals for ourselves on the way; but it proves too expensive, as one would expect."

Thinking of the hill terrain he would have to traverse on his future 'parish rounds', Father had also realised the need to get hold of a suitable vehicle for the purpose. "I have made an offer for a two-year old Chevrolet car recommended to me in Rangoon – £100. I don't know yet whether I shall get it, and if I do it remains to be seen whether we find it a good bargain or not. It is a good type for the Kalaw hills. I believe nearly every car on the road is either a Chev or a Ford. Apparently the

English cars do not do well on very long hills. We have not yet made any effort to sell our old Morris, we can't spare it yet. I fear it has deteriorated in our time, and we are not likely to get what we gave for it, nor anything near it. But it has a first-rate engine. The actual engine has never given us any trouble at all, except that it heats very much."

Aunt Fan, meanwhile, more concerned with babies than with motor vehicles, noted in her diary that it was not until eleven days after the birth, the 23rd September, that Mother was allowed to get out of bed for the first time, arriving home three days later. While she was still in hospital, Father had written, "Anne and Douglas go to see their mother and their new sister every day. Today they were both on Marjory's bed, lying one on each side of her – an ordinary single bed and something of a tight fit. We are very glad to know that Katie and George [his sister and youngest brother] are both willing to be god-parents. There is no reply yet from Frances Wood; it looks as if she must be away. I have registered the baby's birth with the names Frances Elizabeth; I am not quite sure that the registrar has accepted it, as he prefers that babies should have no names!"

Mother's return was badly timed, for Father had to go off to Myittha straight away, and then, at the request of the archdeacon (who was unwell) to Maymyo for three days. On his return, Father wrote, "Baby has got a tremendous lot of prickly heat, so bad as even to make big blisters, but Marjory quite hopes that the worst of that will clear up very quickly; she thinks that there were so many nurses and *ayahs* taking turns at the hospital that often the child was wrapped up too warm, and that the same attention was not paid to details as would have been done if some one person had been responsible."

Fortunately, as he was always a huge support to our family, Uncle Will came back from furlough in England at this juncture, "ever so well and full of energy," as Father remarked, adding, "I hope he will keep it a good long time".

Baby's christening took place on 13th October 1929 at Christ Church, in Queen Victoria's magnificent font, and that very same day, Father wrote to his sister Katie, the new godmother, "Your god-child was christened this afternoon, and by proxy (through Fan) you not only made the promises but you held the babe and gave the name, Frances Elizabeth. There was a considerable congregation for the christening – most of the Burmese girls' school, those of the boys' school who have not gone away for the holidays, *Saya* George and his wife, Mrs. Joshua (wife of the Tamil priest), two of the Mission ladies and Miss Seeley (head of St. Mary's Girls' School),

Mr. Lee (the chaplain) the matron and one of the sisters of the General Hospital, two ladies from the Wesleyan Mission and one from the Baptist Mission, and a few more. We had to divide the party after service. The English part had tea and cakes in the verandah of the house, and the Burmese part had fizzy drinks and cakes under the trees, and a keg of ice-cream went round the whole lot. Will officiated at the christening; I represented George, and Marjory represented Frances Wood. Elizabeth has not told us yet what she thinks of her new Bible, but her parents think it is a very nice one and thank you very much. Anne and Douglas both came to the service and behaved very nicely indeed."

"With the new baby has come the new car", he wrote a few days later, "so I am making a splash! I don't mean that the new car is here; I mean that I have heard from the Snows today that they have made the bargain and bought it for me. A Chevrolet, two years old, tested by their chauffeur and found in very good condition. I am hoping that the travelling allowance attached to the chaplaincy will pay for its running expenses."

In the same letter he recounted that, "All the last week has been spent in packing. After about three days it seemed perfectly hopeless, but I think that we shall get through now. I have bespoken a fifteen-ton truck, and also a motor-lorry and six coolies to take everything and put it in the truck. The loading is to be done on Tuesday. The house now is chaos, the piano in a packing-case, packing-cases in the drawing-room and verandah, about twenty-five of them full, and others being filled, book-cases boarded up to protect the glass etc. House-moving is no joke, even when you are going – as in this case – into a furnished house. We are supposed to be going to Kalaw for two years; I hope we shan't be moved again at the end of six months!"

On 20th October, Father wrote to Edith, grandly heading his paper with the new address, "St. Katherine's Cottage, Kalaw, Southern Shan States, Burma." He had gone ahead of the family to make preparations for our arrival and wrote, "I have just finished my first Sunday in my new beat. The regular cycle of Sundays is (1) Kalaw, (2) Taunggyi, (3) Kalaw, (4) Meiktila, and if there is a fifth in any month, it goes to either Myingyan or Thazi, which otherwise have only weekdays. Myingyan will probably not get a visit more than once in two months. There were just under twenty people in church morning and evening, and ten children at the children's service; I'm afraid that I can't hope to keep even up to that, as there are many visitors here, all government business having stopped for the ten days of the Buddhist Annual Festival.

"It is simply glorious country, all amongst the mountains, with fresh air and pine-trees and beautiful flowers. In my garden there is a fuchsia in blossom, and just outside it are willow herb and other things like that. It will suit us splendidly."

"The house too is quite nice, a single-storeyed building of five rooms, not including kitchen, two pantries and four bath-rooms. We shall need them all, and shall still feel squashed after the roomy houses we have had at Moulmein and Mandalay. I have arranged them all in my mind, making (1) a dining-room; (2) a drawing-room; (both of which the children will use, but there is also a verandah for them); (3) a bedroom for Marjory and me and Baby Elizabeth; (4) a bedroom for Fan and Anne and Douglas; (5) a study and a dressing-room divided by a big book case. But I haven't half told you our resources. There are servants' quarters, a garage and (a great asset) an annexe of three rooms much too draughty (through walls and floors) to be of any use in the cold weather, but invaluable for visitors in the hot weather. We have a lot of ground, with roses, and I don't quite know what other flowers, and lots of pine trees, and a drive of rather an uncertain nature, and jolly little paths with steps in them."

When, at last, my sons and I managed to locate St. Katherine's Cottage on our 2007 pilgrimage to Burma, the drive was of an even greater 'uncertain nature' than ever, being nothing but a steep slope of bare earth and tangled vegetation, but the wonderful welcome we received more than made up for this. The house is still the property of the S.P.G. and still serves the little church next door, as well as its surrounding 'parish', its occupant at the time of our visit being a Burmese Canon of Christ Church Cathedral, Mandalay, Rev. Stephen Pah Ei. He was born in Taunggyi to a Christian family, was ordained in 1969, and has three daughters and one son, his wife sadly having died recently. He seemed overjoyed to show us round, and with the help of the local innkeeper as interpreter, told us something of his present day duties, echoing much of Father's work of eighty years ago! He said the congregation at St. Katherine's was currently around thirty.

The delightful wooden bungalow was much as I remembered it, and looked exactly the same as the old black and white photograph we carried with us, but how tiny it seemed to me in retrospect. However did all six of us fit in I wonder, let alone our furniture, and where on earth did the family find space for the piano and all those glass-fronted bookcases?

Father certainly found it a squeeze, for only a short while after we moved in, he wrote home, "We are getting a little more used to our quarters now, but are still

St. Katherine's Cottage, Kalaw in 1930.

rather conscious of creeping round chairs and things to get anywhere. I expect we have plenty of room really, but we have been used to such big places that this seems small. The children are outdoors a large part of every day". Later, when the warm weather came and visitors were about to arrive, he added "I can't think how three extra people are going to fit in; they have reasonable bedrooms in the annexe, but they will have to get into the dining-room somehow. As regards the drawing-room, they must just take it in turns; there simply isn't room for the whole party there."

My own scribbles jotted down quickly after our visit in 2007 note that "there is just one big room and another of reasonable size, but the remaining three are quite small, and the veranda (which I recall was our playroom) is no greater than seven or eight feet in length. I don't think the annexe still exists – at any rate we didn't see it – and what is left of the grand-sounding 'four bathrooms' now appears to be just one rickety little outdoor structure, made mainly of bamboo. The living room is comfortably furnished and contains a stone chimneybreast and mantelpiece, while another fireplace is set into the wall of an adjoining room where sleeping mats are laid out on the floor. The main bedroom holds a mosquito-netted double bed,

St. Katherine's Cottage, Kalaw in 2007.
Our interpretor (left), Anne and Canon Pa Ei.

wardrobe and chairs, but otherwise there is little furniture, illumination being provided by a few electric bulbs hanging haphazardly from the ceilings. A lean-to provides a cooking shed without refrigeration, the 'cooker' being a single electric ring, supported by a charcoal burner."

The church is also a simple building, without a tower, and we were told that it had been effectively abandoned for ten years before Canon Pah Ei arrived, when the roof was full of holes. But now the church is well used, the old wooden roof having been replaced by a corrugated iron one, and only the previous week the forty-seventh anniversary of Anglican Youth had been held here, and had included the Baptists. "There are four Christian churches in Kalaw now; Anglican, Roman Catholic, Baptist and Evangelist", Canon Pah Ei told us.

Writing about St. Katherine's, Kalaw, for the publication *Burma News* in late 1970, Rev. Aung Hla said "We are here since October 1969. I started cleaning the church. It was covered with dirts of sparrows, it took me a good many days to scrape

Outside St. Katherine's Church, Kalaw in 2007.

the floor and polish it to bring it back to presentable condition. The compound is fairly big and it was covered with Lantana bushes and thick jungle, it took me two months to clear all the jungle."

So both church and cottage have had their ups and downs over the years, and that both still survive to serve the community seems to me something of a miracle. We certainly loved living there, and Father's letters sing the praises of the surrounding countryside. Writing from Taunggyi on 10th November, he wrote happily, "This is simply wonderfully beautiful country. I have been here before on visits, twice, but I never thought that the time would come when it would be my own beat. From the point of view of a raw motorist, it is distinctly alarming, but not nearly so bad on this side of Kalaw as the first twenty miles on the other side. For one thing the road is much wider, and there is room for cars to pass almost anywhere. But there are hills, even on this side. In the first thirty miles the road drops, sometimes very steeply, from 4300 ft to 3000 ft, and in the last twelve miles it rises again to 4600 ft. One gets glorious views of mountains and valleys on the way, only of course I dare not look at them; I have to keep my eyes glued to the road, which is well-made, an immense improvement on the Mandalay roads."

On the home front, writing about the family, Father said, "Anne and Douglas are both full of life. Fan keeps taking them out for walks etc. and already knows our immediate neighbourhood far better than I do. Elizabeth is growing fast, but doesn't know much yet beyond her pram."

I remember these walks as happy, exciting times, as the three of us explored new territory together, with Aunt Fan – who loved the countryside – pointing out the different flowers, trees and birds as we went along, doing her best to teach us their unfamiliar names. We kept nature diaries, recording the amazingly rapid growth of bamboo – sometimes as much as an inch a day I seem to remember – and counting the number of 'bul-buls' we saw. These dark little birds with tufted heads were about the size of sparrows and flitted about from bush to bush in considerable numbers, their repetitive song being one of the jungle sounds that I can still recall with relish. One day, a visitor came to stay, joining us on our walk before bravely setting out next morning on her own, and proudly announcing at lunch time that she had found a 'cow-cow's nest'. How we children managed to stifle our giggles, I shall never know, but I do remember Aunt Fan's conspiratorial wink of approval.

Meanwhile, Father was beginning to explore much further afield, and wrote, "Taunggyi is the headquarters of all the Shan States, and there are about fifteen real Englishmen here, many of them with wives. I don't suppose they are often all in, as they have to administer a huge tract of country, and I have made acquaintance so far with only half at the most. But there are Eurasians too, and a few Indian Christians and I have found my time fully occupied in looking people up. I expected to stay at the Circuit-House, with my jungle boy providing meals for me, but I found a note waiting for me from the big man of the place, the Commissioner of the Federated Shan States, inviting me to stay with him, so here I am at the Residency, in great comfort. The Commissioner is a Mr. McCallum, who was Deputy-Commissioner at Patokku (not far from Mandalay) in the long-ago days when I used to go there every month. When I come next I shall probably find twenty or more Shan Sawbwas gathered in council, and the whole place very festive. Accommodation will be short, but the principal of the Shan Chiefs' School (a very nice Englishman with a very nice wife) is willing to take me into his house, so I shall be all right. A delightful feature this time has been the keenness of the colonel of the Military Police (soldiers really) who rushed at me with "Padre, when can I have a little talk with you? I want to bring my buglers (not Christians) stationed outside the church tomorrow morning, to play the Last Post and Reveille at 11a.m."

Christmas at Kalaw was celebrated in style with church services, a Christmas tree, a roaring fire of pine cones, plenty of games like charades and 'I packed my trunk and in it I put my…' and of course a splendid meal finishing with the Bures plum pudding.

Just four days later on 29th December, Fan wrote in her diary, "The Kalaw Hotel caught fire at 6 pm. It was a tremendous blaze. Charlie and all of our men servants tried to help. The hotel was full of visitors. C. brought one here to dinner and sleep, and he turned out to be the ex-Prime Minister of Hungary, Dr. Sheemoney." Father adds, "We gave him a camp cot in the drawing-room," and described the catastrophe thus "The hotel chimney got on fire, and then the wooden tiles of the roof, and to climb up the roof with pails of water proved so difficult that enough water did not arrive to put the flames out, and in less than a couple of hours the whole building had gone."

The recollection of this fire is burnt deeply and indelibly into my memory. I vividly remember standing on our little veranda at St. Katharine's Cottage looking across to the hotel a short distance away down the valley, holding tightly onto Aunt Fan's hand, as huge flames shot into the air and explosive noises reverberated around us. Later on, when the hotel was re-built some months later, we were all invited to its re-opening and I was greatly taken with the new wooden wainscoting in the dining-room. How extraordinary, then, on our 2007 pilgrimage, to be able to stay in the very same hotel, and to be able to eat our dinner in the very same room whose panelling had intrigued me as a child all those years ago. Of course I recounted the whole story to the hotel manager, who was fascinated to hear it, having had no knowledge at all of the building's exciting past.

CHAPTER FOURTEEN

Burmese Fashions, Earthquakes, Bluebirds, Snakes and Troop Movements (1930-1931)

January 1930 started with Father's departure for the Burmese capital, as Aunt Fan explained in her diary: "Charles, Marjory, Baby and Antonia (the *ayah*) started after breakfast in the car for Thazi en route to Rangoon. C. was going to an ordination retreat, and M. to stay at Mrs. Snow's, to go to the dentist. The packing up was very hectic; Anne and Douglas both wept over the departure, but were very good afterwards. Old *Ayah* (Antonia's mother) slept in the drawing-room bathroom."

Things did not work out quite as planned, for a few days later Father wrote, "I have come down to Rangoon at the Bishop's summons, to conduct a retreat for four English ordinands (ordained yesterday) and to preach at the ordination service. Marjory has come with me, needing the help of the dentist. Baby has come with Marjory, because she could not stay without her. And the *ayah*'s daughter has come with Baby. I am staying at various places; the rest are with Mrs. Snow. And now Marjory has dysentery, and is laid up in bed, and has to have injections every day, and must not attempt to feed Baby! The Snows are kind beyond all words, and either Miss Hogg (their nurse) or Mrs Snow herself see to all Baby's bottles. They seem to be acceptable today; yesterday was rather stormy. We ought to be going back today (Monday) but the Doctor says M. can't possibly go before Thursday."

They all arrived home in due course – and what a welcome back I remember giving them – while Fan wrote "Marjory had to go straight to bed but was none the worse for the journey. The Indian doctor came and gave her an injection. I had to learn how to make Baby's bottle." Mother recovered fairly quickly, but was stiff from the injections for a long time to come.

Meanwhile, Father continued to have adventures with the Chevrolet (which my brother tells me had a powerful engine – 23 horsepower). Writing home soon after

The old Chevrolet with the Garrad family on board.

the Rangoon visit, he said, "I don't think I have told you how I put my car into the ditch one day. It was *not* with Marjory, Baby, Antonia and three or four cwt. of luggage; if it had been, it might have been serious. Neither was it on one of our precipitous roads. It was in Kalaw itself, when I was driving the car empty. I met another car, and to give it plenty of room I deliberately ran onto the grass edging of the road. But it wasn't grass; it was a ditch and two feet deep obscured by long grass! Fortunately it was a soft muddy ditch, and when a dozen men had collected and by tremendous exertions had lifted the thing out, it proved that no damage was done. I left four gallons of petrol in that ditch, as it simply ran out through the hole for putting it in, and that was all the harm done. I shall be more wary of grass in future."

On 26th January, writing from Meiktila, he said "This is Douglas' birthday. I believe there is a birthday tea tomorrow, for which I must be back. His great present this time is a second-hand motor-car, one in which he can sit while he propels it by pedals. It comes from the Snows, who are beginning to get ready for their departure for England. In a Myingyan shop I found one of those tin monkeys which climb up a string when you pull it tight, so that is on its way, and my boy has added (entirely on his own) a beautiful wooden rabbit which wags its ears as it is pulled along the floor.

It so happens that I am visiting all my five stations one after another now, and the car is pretty busy. By the time I get back to Kalaw tomorrow (I *hope* it will take me back alright, but I always have the uncomfortable feeling that if it stops I shan't know the least what to do), the gauge is likely to show five hundred and fifty miles in eleven days. A nice little round of pastoral visits!" The following week he wrote home, "I have actually had a Sunday at home – the first for three weeks."

On the 2nd February, Fan's diary tells us that we now had a new *ayah*, a Burmese girl called Heliman, to whom we all became very attached. She was young and pretty, I remember, and I loved hugging her because she was so kind and always smelt delicious! Most days she wore a beautiful scented flower in her long, shiny black hair, which was coiled tightly on the back of her head, and she had a wide selection of brightly patterned *longyis*, which came down to her feet and were tied with a special knot round the waist, always topped by an immaculate blouse or *aingyi*.

On her cheeks and forehead she often wore a light-coloured creamy substance, which looked like some kind of powder. "It's called thanaka", she said, when I asked about it, "we grind it ourselves from the bark of a tree and mix it with water to form a paste. It's very cooling in hot weather, keeps the flies away, and looks nice too."

Most Burmese people we met in the bazaar or at the market had strange dark red teeth, I remember, but Heliman's were beautifully white. "Why?" I couldn't help asking her. "Because it's usual in this country to chew betel-nuts, and then spit out the juice," she explained, "but I don't like the taste much, or the spitting, and anyway it spoils your looks, because it stains your teeth red."

Another fashion at this time, particularly among women, was cigar smoking, though luckily for us, Heliman didn't enjoy this either. Tobacco was a prolific local crop, and stalls on the side of the road were always piled with cheap and chunky, hand-made cigars for sale. As children, we even used to play a game of counting the number of smokers we saw on our forays into town, gaining special points each time we saw a woman dropping ash over her baby, as she fed him by the wayside. In particular, I've never forgotten the odd occasions when we saw a stressed mother remove a soggy, half-smoked cigar from her own lips and stuff it into her fractious baby's mouth in an effort to shut him up! It seemed to work.

It wasn't until much later that I learnt that Heliman belonged to the Muslim faith, for the diaries recount the occasional days off she had in order to attend her special religious ceremonies and she didn't come to church with us. Looking back, I think that my parents must have recognised her caring qualities when they appointed her, accepting that 'to love one's neighbour' is central to every faith, and not just the sole property of the Christian.

At this period Father's main task was supposed to be the compilation of the Burmese prayer book, but with all his other duties he had pitifully little time to give to it. However on 23rd March he wrote, "This month has five Sundays, so I am giving one to Thazi. I came down yesterday morning, and tomorrow morning I move on to Myingyan. After that I go to Meiktila, and stay over there next Sunday. This arrangement gives me a couple of days or so more than I really need, but *Saya Yo* (from Myittha) is here, and I hope to have some useful time with him correcting and polishing a little material which I have prepared." Later, after the visit, he wrote, "The Bishop wants the baptism, confirmation, marriage and burial services of 1928 in Burmese – at least he thinks he does, subject to the opinion of the missionaries – and we have now got out some drafts which I think are quite good. Of course they will have to be considered by other people and no doubt they will have improvements to suggest, but I hope they won't cut them to pieces, as I believe they are good. But 'nice Burmese' is so much a matter of opinion that one never knows what people will say."

Some weeks after this, having apparently been given the grand title of 'Chairman of the Prayer Book Committee', Father wrote, "I have been having meetings lately of people interested in the Burmese prayer book. There are two things to be done. (1) to put our book into order ready for a new edition, (2) to see whether we can get other missions (Wesleyan, Baptist. etc) to agree on one rendering of the Lord's Prayer, creeds etc. Both seem to come largely onto me. I could cope with the first one nicely if I might just go my own way, but of course that cannot be; the second one is difficult, but in three meetings in my house of some of the Wesleyans and some of ourselves, we have tentatively reached a good deal of agreement. But it is the Baptists and Roman Catholics that really matter, and I am afraid that neither will combine with us at all." Poor Father! He'd met these very same problems years ago when he was working on the translation of the Bible, and now here they were once more, in all their worrying complexity. It must have seemed something of a repeat performance.

On 6th April, Father wrote, "Visitors are coming up to Kalaw now. I got my two Pegu jars before I left Meiktila – nice earthenware jars for holding bathwater. They were rather bigger than I meant, the other size being out of stock, but they sat in two corner-seats behind with a roll of bedding between them, and they travelled beautifully like that. I suppose they weigh nearly one cwt each. Now I think we have enough. Marjory has one, I have one, the kitchen has one, each of our visitors has one, and Fan (who wants endless water for the children) has a big metal drum which once contained Mobiloil. But the third room in the annexe still needs other things, which must be supplied quickly. I have instructed a carpenter to put down about twelve square feet of new floor-boards, as the white ants had a good feed some time ago. If I add some clothes-pegs and mosquito-net hangers, and Marjory adds curtains, that will about do. There is a comfy bed, and a make-shift cupboard, and a make-shift wash-stand, with a little table and a chair, and what more does a holiday-maker want?

Are you interested in motor-car doings? On the way up the hill on Friday, my car stopped, and the engine refused to start again. I was just thinking of unscrewing the carburettor and seeing whether the petrol was coming through all right, when I noticed the suction pipe broken right across the middle. (The suction pipe makes a vacuum and so draws in the petrol. It is a little brass tube and only air passes through it.) I held the two broken ends together, and bandaged the place with a rag, turned the handle, and came through into Taunggyi without a falter!"

As though he hadn't enough to do already, Father was to write on April 27th , "I broke some new ground early in the week. There is a silver and lead mine at Bawsaing, and I thought it was up to me to see if they had any use for a chaplain. I got an invitation from the manager, and on Monday I went off – twenty-three miles along the main road to Taunggyi, nineteen miles more of metalled road, one and a half miles of unmetalled road, and then I seemed to be at the end of everything – but no, the track proved to go on, very steep up and very steep down, and after an exciting half mile more I found myself in the camp. The manager is a very nice Englishman, with a very nice English wife. There are two other young Englishmen, and two Eurasians. There are two other mines, two miles away and eight miles away, each with an English manager. We arranged to have Evensong with a service at 3 pm, in working kit, and all eight people were there. Now I am invited to go every month; I doubt whether that will succeed so well, but so good a response at the first visit means that I must have a try. The mine has no great output at present, but it is getting ready for one. Machinery to the value of £13,000 is to go in during the next twelve months. I went right down the mine, something over 300 feet. The manager himself took me down, and as he wanted to inspect the sides of the shaft we were lowered very slowly, so slowly that my arm ached horribly from hanging on to the rope, and I was exceedingly glad to get to the bottom. We stood side by side on a solid piece of timber, rather like the seat of a swing, only it doesn't swing because it runs in guides. Down below there were a lot of galleries, some rather stuffy but mostly well ventilated, with bits of ore visible for those who had eyes to see it. My eyes were too good; I found no end of ore that wasn't ore at all! I stayed two nights, and came back on Wednesday. On future visits one night will be enough, and the manager (whose name is Garrett) won't hear of my putting up anywhere but in his house."

In early May 1930 there was dreadful news. "You will have heard of the earthquake in Pegu and Rangoon. It seems to have been terrible. They say that there were a thousand deaths in Pegu and that would mean something like one person in every thirty killed. The accounts that we get represent the place as wiped out. First the earthquake brought down most of the bigger buildings and then a fire swept up all the little buildings, and as the water-main was severed by the shock they could not fight the fire. Rangoon has suffered a great deal, but not like Pegu. Just one quarter of the town seems to have been badly damaged, while other quarters were so little shaken that people were not sure that it was an earthquake."

Burmese accounts say that not only was the ancient capital of Pegu completely destroyed, as well as parts of Rangoon, but that there was also an after-shock, followed by a tsunami in the coastal areas. "Was this an omen that British rule would end?" the papers asked.

Rain was falling in torrents in mid-May, and Father wrote from Meiktila, "I am afraid that last week again you did not get our letters. The train was held up on the way down the hill, by a landslide. I heard all about it the next day, at Thazi, from the driver. He was rounding a big curve, on a downward slope of one in twenty-five, when he saw some earth on the metals. He jammed on his brakes, and brought his train to a standstill as quickly as he could, and saw a considerable bit of the hillside moving down. It wasn't a big slide, but enough to be nasty, and movement continued for something like an hour while the train stood there. His engine was just eight feet away from the place. I asked why he didn't go back a little, to get into a safer place, but he said that it was quite impossible; he had a load of 300 tons, whereas the maximum load for going up hill is 145 tons, and his engine was not strong enough to move the train upwards. However he knew that he and his passengers were safe, as there was good solid rock beside them at that point."

Worse was to come, for on 1st June Father wrote that "Burma is not a very happy land just now, at least at Rangoon – first a horrible earthquake, and now an appalling riot. We hope the riot is over, but we don't know. Burmese and Indian coolies have been out for each other's blood and seem to have been getting it too, in spite of civil police, military police and British troops. Our latest news says that the hospitals have received 100 dead and 800 injured (mostly badly hurt); but how many other cases there may have been, unknown to the hospitals, can only be guessed." A week later he was staying in Taungyyi where by chance he was to meet the chief police officer of Pegu, and wrote as follows: "Apparently Pegu would have had murderous riots of the same sort as the Rangoon riots, only our friend managed to nip them in the bud. As far as I can make out, two thousand Burmans were making their way to the railway quarters, in order to attack the Indians, only happily he was able to stop them with his police and arrest the ring leaders, and nothing came of it. Things seem to be quiet again in Rangoon, but how far the passion has died down we don't know."

Thankfully, up in the hill station of Kalaw, Father was to write, "Here we go on quietly, undisturbed by the troubles elsewhere. The only thing is that there has been a nasty epidemic of enteric in the Methodist School, but all the cases are improving."

At the same time, Aunt Fan's diaries talk of our wonderful family walks, picnics, shopping, swimming, playing in the garden, the sand heap or on the swings at the Club (our happiest occupation) as well as of less enjoyable things like bouts of slight fever, grazed knees, headaches, tummy troubles and, naturally, a great many coughs and colds.

Since our arrival in Kalaw Mother had started giving me daily lessons, partly based on her own teaching experience, and partly on the curriculum of the Parents' National Education Union, and Douglas joined in when he was old enough. It was no sinecure, because we were expected to do homework each day, and our end of term exam papers had to be sent to headquarters in London, but I enjoyed our schooling together, trying my hardest to learn to read, so that I could share in her love of books. I shall certainly never forget the day that I was summoned to read aloud for the first time to Mrs. Snow (Mother's delightful but erudite friend) who was staying with us. I was scared stiff, I remember, but felt terribly proud when she praised me at the end.

I don't know how Mother found time for all the things she did, for she was involved in nearly everything that went on. She ran the Mothers' Union and the Girls' Friendly Society; she trained the local choir and taught at Sunday School and even started Girl Guides at Kingswood School, and much of this, of course, was in Burmese.

Happily, in due course, the typhoid epidemic at the school began to come to an end, and Father wrote home, "The enteric cases are getting on excellently, all except one little fellow (a Baptist) who is still very ill. The little school hospital has a very different appearance now, instead of all lying limp with ice-caps, they are reading picture papers etc." and it wasn't long before we were once again allowed to play with our friends there. I'd missed the companionship of girls of my age, and now longed to join in some of their more formal activities, setting my heart on becoming a 'Bluebird' – or 'Brownie'. After much cajoling, I was allowed to join when I was six, and it was one of the highlights of my young life. We were called 'Bluebirds' rather than 'Brownies' because most people had light brown skin anyway. Very wisely, Guide Headquarters had given some thought to this, deciding to give junior members in India and Burma this different name, which made us feel quite special.

We had a great time, following the Brownie programme to the letter, with all its important rituals, meeting outdoors when it was fine, and in the school hall when

Anne as a Bluebird in Kalaw (1930).

the rain poured down in bucket-loads. Even Douglas, my little brother, was keen to join in our activities, often attending meetings and becoming a sort of honorary member! 'Tawny Owl' was our much loved leader, an Anglo-Indian girl of about twenty, I suppose, with the most beautiful, velvety brown eyes. She gave me a paper bluebird, with "Love from the 1st Kalaw flock" written on the back. I have it still. It is one of my most treasured possessions.

Those early days, playing with children of so many different races and religions – Buddhists, Muslims, Hindus and Christians from Burma, India, China and Europe – had a great effect on me, paving the way for a firm belief that all children are equal, whatever the background they come from. This tenet is basic to all that the world-wide Scout and Guide movements stand for, and is the reason why, more than eighty years later, I'm still a member of Girlguiding! Now, far too ancient, of course, to take children to camp or to run Guide meetings, I'm a member of the Trefoil Guild, a group of older (mainly retired) leaders who try to give back-up help to our younger colleagues in their vital role of training the next generation.

Recently, some of our Guild members in my home county of Norfolk have been supporting the Burma Children's Fund, the small go-ahead, hands-on charity which grew from the dedication of the 'Feed My Lambs' window in All Saints' Church, Maymyo, and is now giving hope and education to many deprived youngsters throughout the country. Through their auspices, we are sponsoring two orphans whose parents died from malaria within a week of each other, and both children are doing splendidly though unable to join in the fun of Scouting and Guiding – currently banned by the Burmese government. Things may change, however, as Aung San Suu Kyi, leader of their National League for Democracy, was once a keen Guide herself, her mother having been the founder of the Burmese Guides.[18]

But to return to the Kalaw of long ago, it was always something of an adventure to travel any distance on those precipitous roads, and sometimes Bluebird gatherings were in another town. For example, in June 1930, when I'd just joined, Father wrote home, "My journey down by road on Tuesday was quite straightforward. The only unusual features, beyond a certain amount of mud, were a big boulder which had been washed down a high bank (fortunately there was room to pass) and a little further on a milestone right in the middle of the road, evidently washed there by water flowing across. I rather wondered what I should find on the way to Myingyan. You know that Burma abounds in water courses that are generally dry but become torrents after rain, like 'The Rivers of the South' in the Psalms. Two such have to be crossed between Meiktila and Myingyan. I believe that for three days cars were held up, but by the time I reached the streams, they were not more than three or four inches deep. Two Englishmen in Meiktila were less fortunate. One poor fellow, half full of dysentery, was trying to cross a similar stream in the dark and failed; he had to get towed out backwards and return home. Another got unexpectedly into a hole two and a half feet deep and when his car had been pulled out the petrol tank was full of water and the gear box was full of water and altogether there was a lot to do before the poor old car would move on."

A month later, on his usual visit to the mine at Bausaing, Father wrote, "Today I did a silly thing. I wanted to get my car under the bungalow, to shelter it, and I could not determine whether it would go or not. I manoeuvred it into position, took the hood down, and began to back. Of course my head would be cut off if I sat up, so that I had to crouch right down, and when the critical moment arrived and I saw that the windscreen would not go under I missed the brake (being in a strained position) and now I have no screen! It was a job to get home on Tuesday, as I was nearly blinded by the rain. I have sent to Rangoon for a new one." It arrived a week later and Father wrote, "I have a wind-shield again. It arrived at Kalaw at 3 p.m. last Monday and I left Kalaw at 7 a.m. on Tuesday, so there wasn't much time to spare. I was glad to see it. It is the wrong shape, and I don't know what to do for a permanent arrangement; I have got it on, but being the wrong shape it won't open or shut. I have written to Rangoon to see how they propose to get it right. I can't send it back to them, as I can't go without it until I get another."

It seems that he did get it put right eventually, writing only a few days later that, "I went down to Meiktila again last week. A Tamil Christian died there, and they telegraphed to me to come for the funeral. I thought about replying that they had better call in the Baptist missionary, as seventy-five miles each way is a long distance to go for a funeral, but he was a man I knew quite well and liked, and it seemed better to go. I was silly enough to make the journey ten miles longer than I needed. I stopped at Thazi, and left my boy at the bungalow to cook me a dinner; then I changed out of my thick Kalaw clothes and went on. After going five miles, I remembered that I had left my cassock and surplice etc. with my bedding, and I had to go back to Thazi and get them!"

In his letters home, so as not to worry his sisters, Father usually made light of the frightening state of the country around him, where constant riots and banditry were still going on, but in mid June he wrote "We have had an odd story of Mr.

Appleton and his wife (Kemmendine missionaries) and Mr. Procter (chaplain of St. Philip's) being in a nasty scrape, and finding at last that their assailants – Burmans – were special constables who mistook them for *dacoits*! Mr. Procter has an odd face, and often dresses in an exceedingly slovenly way; also he is so sunburnt as to have quite a dark complexion. So perhaps people in a jumpy state of mind may be pardoned for being suspicious of him, but the Appletons are quite obviously the most peaceful people in the world and I can't think how the situation can have arisen. Happily no one was hurt, only the car (a new one of Mr. Procter's) has lost some of its beauty." He added as a domestic postscript, "Tomorrow the chimney sweep is to come. The local method seems to be to tie a big of straw onto a rope, and then let the rope down from the top, and pull it alternately from both ends. I expect it will make an awful mess." (It did!)

Once the house was straight again, a Mr. and Mrs. Littlewood were invited to tea, with their small boy. Father wrote home, "Mr. L. is on eight months' medical leave, and thinks of spending it all here. He spends his time catching butterflies, but I rather think it is a new game. At any rate he informed us that already he had secured five hundred, and when we expressed our surprise at their being so many species in Kalaw, it came out that he meant five hundred butterflies altogether, including about thirty-five different species. So we think now that he enjoys catching every butterfly he sees. But we shall know more about it on Thursday, when we are going to tea there, and shall be shown the collection. Even thirty-five different species will be interesting as we know nothing about our local butterflies. One day as I came up from Thazi there were so many of them for seven or eight miles that they quite dazzled me, almost like snowflakes in their numbers, all of them orange-tips or something of that sort."

I remember those butterflies from our daily walks through the beautiful Kalaw countryside, when we were always accompanied by one of the grown-ups, who taught us a great deal about the natural history around us, constantly keeping us on the alert as both snakes and poisonous spiders lay in wait for the unwary. Father, in particular, was especially vigilant, carrying a heavy cane with him at all times.

One day, we were passing under a tree when he suddenly shouted "FREEZE!" and we stopped in our tracks. Looking upwards, all I could see was a small brown twig hanging from a branch, but Father had noticed it move and knew it was a snake, about to drop onto us. Lifting his stick, he gave a hefty swipe and down tumbled a dead krait, an innocuous looking little brown creature, only about seven or eight inches long, but very deadly. We stared at it in disbelief, for Aunt Fan had only just finished reading us the story of Rikki-tikk-tavi from Rudyard Kipling's *Jungle Book*, all about the brave little mongoose who saved a boy from almost certain death by snake-bite. One short passage in the story reads "Something flinched a little in the dust, and a tiny voice said 'Be careful, I am death!' It was Karait, the dusty brown snakeling that lies for choice on the dusty earth; and his bite is as dangerous as the cobra's. But he is so small that nobody thinks of him, and so he does the more harm to people." Kipling relates that Rikki-tikki rushed to the rescue and killed Karait, so becoming the hero of the hour, just like Father.

A short time later, a letter arrived from Uncle Will which recalled this frightening incident. He wrote, "I had to hurry this week for the funeral of a child of two and a half who died of snake bite. Most evenings it played with its little friends in the Commissioner's garden (the Commissioner being away) but a snake had been seen there and the child was kept at home in its own garden. The father went out to play tennis and the child with two others was playing on a log when it suddenly started to cry and said something had bitten it. His mother was out too, and auntie thought it was an ant or something and did not take much notice until she happened to see a snake under the ivy. Being a sensible woman she rushed indoors and collected a piece of rag and put a tourniquet on Baby's leg. There were no *gharries* about, so she picked up the child and went straight to hospital. The doctor was in and got to work at once, but could not find any signs of a bite on the ankle, until the auntie realised that in her excitement she had tied up the wrong leg! The result was that the baby died, a very very precious baby, and the parents are heart broken." From then on, the *mali* (or sweeper) was instructed to keep a special eye on us, as we played in the compound.

Snakes aside, it was the prayer book that was always at the forefront of Father's mind, for he wrote on 19th October, "I am very busy over the Burmese prayer book. Just now I think it is getting more time than the parish is. The Bishop is back, and tomorrow I must try to get our report to him into order, and then we shall hear what he has to say about it all. But there is a lot that I want to do before I meet *Saya Yo* (Will's catechist at Myittha) next Friday. He is the only Burman with whom I can compare notes at fairly frequent intervals. I think he is quite the most useful of the Mandalay staff for this purpose, and it is fortunate that I can get hold of him from time to time. It is the Collects that are occupying me at the moment. I suppose I have been revising them for fifteen years, and now I have to get the results into order for the consideration of other people.

"Last week I wrote from Taunggyi. From there I went as usual to Bawsaing, and found them in rather a sad frame of mind. The price of lead has gone down to such an extent that it no longer pays to produce it, and the whole staff has been given provisional leave to go. They are confident that the price will recover before very long, and they are continuing with the erection of their machinery and generally getting the camp into order, but in the meantime they have stopped production, and it is likely that some of the people really will have to go. The Garretts were as kind as ever, and I stayed the night with them."

On 4th December Aunt Fan wrote in her diary, "There was an earthquake shock at 1.40 a.m. Marjory and I felt it, but the others slept through it." Its epicentre was miles away in Toungoo, and Father explained, "The earthquake was nasty enough, but nothing like the previous one; thirty people killed; fifty people injured and a dozen or so of brick buildings down with several bridges (both road and railway) rendered unsafe."

There's some light relief from this tragedy in Father's letter from Meiktila, written shortly afterwards: "The evening service is always very small, and so it was this time, but there was an excitement. All that I knew at the time was that Mrs. Blaker suddenly stopped playing one of the hymns, and we had to finish it without the organ, and that she pushed somebody else onto the stool to play the last hymn. It seems that while she was playing, a mouse came out of the organ, ran up to the top of the hymn book, and there sat and looked at her!"

Writing from Taunggyi on 9th November, Father described the journey in style, saying, "Marjory and Baby have come up here with me this time. We were such a load yesterday! In front were just Marjory and I; in the back were Baby and her *Ayah* and the boy, with a stack of things more or less from floor to ceiling in the middle of the seat, and an oil-stove under the boy's feet. On the carrier were Marjory's great trunk, then a good sized pack of mine, then a folding pram, then the boy's roll of bedding, then (tied on as an afterthought) my little *pah* [or canvas box] full of books etc. and then (tied on a mile along the road, when we reached her mother's house) the *Ayah's* big roll of bedding. It all travelled quite safely, but a good deal of the road up the hill required second gear where top gear generally suffices."

A little later, he wrote, "I had an interesting walk a few days ago. After tea I started off to see Mr. Browne at Loian, and I tried a short-cut, by which I expected to get to him in about two and a half miles. But I didn't get anywhere – just kept on a jungle path for about four miles, and then found myself in a village right beyond

Baby Liz having her bath (1930).

Loian. It was sunset time, and I consulted a villager as to how to get back; "If I go back the way I came, I shan't get through before dark, and then I shan't be able to find the way."

"No, you can't go back that way. I have twice been caught by the dark on the path, and I heard the bears all round and was terrified." However, it was all right. He took me about a mile in another direction, and there was the high-road from Taunggyi."

Once safely home again, Father noted, "The children give us great fun. The other day at breakfast, I asked Anne a question, and she replied with great deliberation: "Bless my heart, I don't know". Douglas, he added, went into the vestry to 'help' arrange chairs, when he "looked out a cane chair with more holes than cane in the seat, and was heard to remark to himself, 'I think Mrs. Harris must have sat in that chair'. It was a splendid idea, as Mrs. Harris (wife of one of the old Baptist missionaries) weighs about 15 stone."

Back in Taunggyi on 14th December, Father wrote, "Taunggyi is very full just now. All (or nearly all) the Sawbwas are here, engaged in their annual council on affairs of state. Yesterday I went to the sports at the Shan Chiefs' School and in the evening to a big dinner party at the chief engineer's house. And it was quite interesting. Three of the bigger Sawbwas were there. When the ladies left the table,

I found myself seated for a few minutes next the Sawbwa of Kingtung, and I had a little conversation with him in Burmese; he is an old man, and I am told that he is the only one left who does not speak English."

Soon, Christmas was upon us, with all its excitements. Even Father thought it went well, being encouraged by the arrival in Kalaw church of two couples who had never appeared before. "Such a happy Christmas we had!" he wrote home afterwards. "Presents for the children, and even for their parents, had been coming in for days, and they were supremely happy in unwrapping them. They are well set up for toys now for many a day; the question is whether we can get on without moving into a larger house! Wherever we go, we seem to stumble over toys, or else over Baby, who is now here, there and everywhere."

At this time, the political situation in the Shan States was reasonably stable, but there was worrying unrest elsewhere. At the end of his Christmas letter, Father wrote, "Thayarwaddy is north-west of Rangoon, far south from us, and has for many years been a district full of crime; apparently taking occasion from the hardness of the times, they have got up a very nasty little rebellion now. We hear that not only Military Police but English soldiers also have had to be called out to deal with the situation. Up till now we have not suffered greatly from the general depression of trade, as paddy has fairly maintained its price, but the bottom has now fallen out of the paddy-basket, and things are going to be difficult for the Burman. P.S. I haven't told you that the plum pudding was just as good as ever. Thank you very much."

On 4th January 1931, Father wrote, "On Monday I moved back as far as Thazi, and found the place very full of Christmas. Nearly every house wanted me to have cake and wine; I daresay I had cake at ten different places, then went to dinner and was fed with peacock at a railway guard's house. Thirty-three people came to church. On Wednesday I was off again, to Loilen this time, a place which I have never visited before, sixty miles beyond Taunggyi. We had a congregation of five, with two communicants in the P.W.D. Bungalow, and I was glad that I had gone. Taunggyi is about 4500 feet high, and successive points on the road are 3600, 4300, 3500, 4800, 4200 (Loilen). I should have liked to look about me all the time, as parts of the road ran through most interesting country, but the driving needed too much attention for that."

A week later our family had a wonderful day's expedition to Inle Lake, a huge stretch of water set high up among the hills, where there were floating markets, houses on stilts, and fishermen who rowed with their legs. It is a truly magical place,

Fisherman on Inle Lake (2007).

and I have never forgotten the sheer wonder of that golden day, when I was only six years old. Our boatman knew just where to take us, first through channels of reeds stretching high above our heads and then through open stretches of glittering water, before finally inviting us to land at a temple set deep into the hillside. Today, long-tailed motor boats are on hand to whisk the occasional tourist from place to place, where one may visit skilled craftsmen of all kinds – among them silver smiths and silk weavers, umbrella makers and cigar manufacturers – but (as we discovered on our visit recently) though Inle Lake may have changed somewhat over the years, it has lost none of its intrinsic character and charm, its fishermen still row with their legs, and its stunning beauty is undiminished.

But much of Burma, way back in the third decade of the twentieth century, was far from being a country of peace and stability. Writing on 18th January 1931, Father said, "There have been no end of excitements this week, rumours floating about everywhere about the movements of rebels in the neighbourhood. It is believed now that there never was anything in any of them, but that they originated with a telegraph man, who – following a wire through the jungle, as is his duty when it doesn't work satisfactorily – came across a gang of men searching for a stray elephant and took them for rebels. But it was so far believed at the time that a lot of Military Police were sent out to scour the jungle for three days. I am glad that I happened to be at home, as it really was rather alarming. Of course I couldn't have done anything at all if a party had taken it into their heads to try their luck at our house, but Marjory and Fan find comfort in having a man in the house and would have felt rather nervous by themselves. I am afraid that round Thayarwaddy (Lower Burma) trouble still continues. As a rebellion, the movement is entirely at an end; but there are a lot of roughs still prowling about in those parts, occasionally burning a village or shooting a man. They have a pathetic belief in charms as rendering them immune from injury; in spite of seeing their comrades shot down by the rifles of the soldiers they still retain their belief, only supposing that the men who lose their lives had been careless and not carried out the charm correctly. It may be months before the district can feel quite secure again."

Despite the dangers, Father was determined to continue on his rounds, as usual. Writing from Meiktila on January 25th, he said, "*Saya* Yo has come again to correct and improve my Burmese drafts of the Burmese prayer book," adding that Mother – wanting to make the most of his travels – was keen to get him to carry out some domestic tasks on his way home. The letter reads, "On Wednesday I shall have plenty to do. First there will be church at Myingyan, with or without a congregation. Then there will be the drive here – sixty miles. Here I have a little business at the Deputy Commissioner's office, and the church accounts. I must also pick up two old ragged carpets which I have bought from the church for Rs 2, in order to have something on our annexe floor. The next stage will be only to Thazi, fifteen miles, and there I must put *Saya* Yo into the train. Then comes the sixty mile drive to Kalaw, broken in the middle by a pause to dig sand out of the bed of a stream to furnish the children's sand-tray. Marjory is very keen that I should manage somehow to carry up enough to make a real heap in the garden for them to play on, but I can't do that. The poor old car will have already two people and a lot of luggage, and it can't take a cart load of sand in addition. And so the day goes, and is bound to go. It is a curious kind of chaplaincy!" Later, with the help of two others, he did manage to bring a whole sack load home, but, as he ruefully remarked, "Baby has got rid of nearly all of it already. Baby is very active."

In early May 1931, Father commented, "Now there is another excitement. 120

of the British troops at Maymyo are to be stationed in Meiktila, which used to be a garrison town but has been abandoned for several years. Whether the idea is that they are too far off at Maymyo in case of the rebels giving sudden trouble, or what the purpose is, I don't know, but the order has been given and the troops are expected next week. It is announced only as a temporary measure and so I don't think I need expect to be told to move my headquarters from Kalaw to Meiktila, but I shall have to come down more than I have done, if it can be arranged."

Starting his letter "From Meiktila", Father wrote home on 17th May, "It seems likely that this address may appear pretty often at the head of my letters. The soldiers are here; one company (about 120 men) of the Oxfordshire and Buckinghamshire Light Infantry. They have three officers with them – a captain and two lieutenants – and a major of the R.A.M.C. to keep them all well. The officers all seem delightful fellows and the men (as far as I have seen them) strike me as nice straightforward English lads. I took three of them for a drive yesterday, and was foolish enough to let them persuade me into racing the car. They were very keen to see fifty miles an hour on the indicator, so at last I had a try, and we touched the fifty miles all right, but we also shook the silencer to pieces. However, I have been able to get the silencer put together again. We had parade service this morning. The Te Deum was rather a fiasco and threatened to break down all together, but it did just keep going and otherwise things went very well, at least, well enough. I am wondering what we shall find this evening. A parade service is in Orders, and men have to come. Unfortunately – according to Army Orders – they have to come in specially clean kit, with rifles and ball ammunition. Other services are voluntary, and soldiers come or not as they like, just like everybody else. We may find a nice little crowd tonight, or we may find nobody."

Eight days late, Father wrote from Kalaw, "It is Monday morning, and I have not yet written home, which is very bad of me. When I got back last Monday, I found the household in some anxiety because both Anne and Douglas were not well, and their temperatures were so funny that Dr Reardon (Taunggyi) was afraid that it might be enteric. Happily it has proved nothing serious. We think now that it was influenza. At any rate they are up and about again, though a little thin and weak. Douglas came to me yesterday with 'Daddy, my red motor wants oiling so badly. It won't start unless somebody pushes it.' It isn't oil that it lacks; it is strength in his little legs. But that is coming back all right. All our five long-term visitors have gone, but we have another now – Rose Davidson, from the blind school at

Douglas' motor car (about 1930).

Moulmein. She has brought us the latest news of Father Jackson, which is very bad news; he has cancer, as was suspected before, and the Rangoon doctors can do nothing for him, but under their advice he is going to England in the hope of getting there an operation which will enable him to go on with his blind school work for a time."

A fortnight later, back in Meiktila, he was to write, "The movement of troops here is all uncertain. We have been told (amongst other things) that Meiktila is to be a Brigade Headquarters, with a general and his staff, and that it is to have a cavalry regiment, but now it is thought that neither of these thing is coming off, but that we are likely to go on much as we are, only with some of the Manchester men instead of the Oxfordshire and Bucks. I hope it all means that the rebellion is really to be crushed. I believe I wrote a long time ago that it was crushed in the first two days, but it wasn't, and it is spreading. The difficulty is to crush it without killing a good many innocent people. A generation ago they would have taken severe measures, but today we are much more careful about individuals. Some of us are beginning to think that the former was really the kinder method, that the innocents who might suffer under severe repression would be fewer than those who suffer from gangs of rebels. Whether our policy is directed from Maymyo, from Simla, or from London, nobody seems to know; probably all have a finger in the pie, and the result is a pie that is no good to anyone."

Much of Burma was in a state of turmoil, and just a week later Father wrote, "In consequence of a deliberate act of train-wrecking, whether due to the rebels or more ordinary bad-hats, trains have now ceased running in the dark over one section of the railway. Consequently we are all hurrying up to get our letters into the post tonight, as tomorrow's post won't catch the mail in Rangoon."

On 21st June he reported, "Our former company of British soldiers here has gone back to Maymyo, and a company of the Manchesters has come instead. At present we do not know very much about them. They had a terrible journey, crossing Northern India in the very worst heat of the whole year and then on the boat from Calcutta being at very close quarters with their own mules, with a day of storms thrown in. Consequently at the moment there are twenty-five in hospital, and the rest are feeling very seedy. A church parade was ordered this morning but it consisted of only fifteen men! We have also a Field Ambulance newly come, consisting of R.A.M.C. doctors (three British and one Indian) and something like 150 Indian men. Whether there will be anything for all these new soldiers to do up and down the country we don't know, but there is no denying that it is a great comfort to have them here. What one hopes, of course, is that the mere sight of them will show the rebels that that they have no chance whatever of winning in the end, and so bring peace without much in the way of skirmishing first."

The following week there was a further report on the railways: "Our trains are running much as usual now. For a time they stopped running any train at night over a section where tampering with the lines was feared, but they have re-started it now, only a little more slowly than usual. They send another train (not open to the public) just ahead as a pilot, so that if any train has to be derailed it may not be the full passenger train. But in spite of that precaution, I hear that the ordinary passenger train is anything but full. Everyone now prefers to travel over that section by daylight, and the night train has only about a sixth of its usual complement. Even up here, where all is perfectly quiet, we are all heartily weary of this rebellion; in the worst areas life must be ghastly for the villagers. If it were a matter of open fighting, the troops would soon put an end to it, but is a very difficult matter to deal with these *dacoits* who swoop down and are off again in an hour to their hiding places in the jungle."

His next letter says, "Trouble seems to succeed trouble, and the lack of rain is very serious. Just round here they will probably get a little of their cotton and sesame crops in, and their paddy may be all right, but in the Myingyan district where cotton is the universal crop, they have not been able even to plant it, and famine relief works are being started. Rice is extremely cheap, but even so they have nothing to buy it with. In parts the cattle are said to be dying for lack of anything to eat." As a postscript he added, "Fortunately, the children are all splendid."

In July 1931 the two Garrad brothers, Charlie and Will, were both at the Diocesan Council in Rangoon. Before he went, Father wrote, "I am rather dreading the Council. The Bishop is excellent, but at times he needs keeping in order, and I don't like the job! Generally the Archdeacon does it splendidly, but he is away in England, and so others of us will have to be on the alert. Also I have to preach at the Festival service, and Rangoon Cathedral is a very difficult place to preach in, it just takes one's words and puts them away in a sponge somewhere. Well, I suppose we shall get through." On his return, he commented, "Rangoon was rather strenuous, of course, but the arrangements left us more freedom than often is the case. Will spoke at length once, and did it exceedingly well. Only he suffered from being one of a string of nine missionaries, charged each to speak of his own circumstances and plans, and there were too many of them. My sermon seemed to fit the occasion well."

Mother was getting increasingly tired now and her health was causing some slight concern, and Father wrote, "The doctor gave her quite a good report. He found that nothing whatever was wrong organically. But he thinks she has been too busy, and says that she must go slow until she is stronger. So the Bluebirds have been handed over to the teachers in the school, and I don't know what is happening about the Burmese Wesleyan women; I rather expect that the weekly class will cease." (Luckily, with Mother's support in the background, the Bluebirds went on just as before, and I continued to enjoy our meetings.)

The climate in Burma never does anything by halves, and in early September the rains returned with a vengeance. Writing from Meiktila, Father said, "The whole countryside was full of water when I came down on Friday and at one place the road had only just escaped being carried away. The railway line was breached for a few hours. Then yesterday there was another heavy storm in the evening, and there has been one this afternoon, so we are doing well at last."

A week later he was in Taunggyi. "Up here," he wrote, "I am staying with the burra-sahib, the Commissioner of the Shan States, Mr. Clague by name. He became Commissioner only a few months ago. He has a wife, a daughter aged six, and a smaller son. They are very simple, homely people, and one can go to bed at 9.30 p.m., whereas it used sometimes to be a matter of 1 a.m. as dinner parties were very frequent when the McCullums were here."

Among the visitors at breakfast the following morning was the redoubtable Miss Cam, the nursing sister who followed Miss Patch as matron of the Mandalay Children's Hospital and later, for umpteen years, was to teach nursing skills to many Burmese ladies in the Rangoon Delta. 'The Camel', as she was known, was a great friend of our family throughout our time there, and a significant personality during my childhood, whom I admired greatly.

CHAPTER FIFTEEN

Charlie says "Goodbye" to Burma and a New Bishop is Welcomed (1931-1935)

On 27th September 1931 comes an unhappy letter, giving a foretaste of some of the problems that were to force Father into retirement later on. "I have been a bit out of sorts for some time, so I went to the doctor at Meiktila; he thinks it may be a mild attack of sprue, and has put me onto the peculiar diet which belongs to that. It consists of milk, and liver soup, and milk, and spinach, and milk, and a little fresh fruit, and milk, and a few almonds, and milk... and it has made me feel pretty empty." (Father hated milk at the best of times, so this must have been purgatory.)

Writing again from Meiktila on 4th October, Father said, "I am writing by lamp light and insects of many kinds are busy. Obviously the best thing to do will be to get into bed pretty soon, and put the lamp out. I am not overflowing with energy, but I am able to do what has to be done and I think the doctor expects me to pick up soon. I came down by train this time; it takes all day, nearly, but it is much less tiring than driving the car. I go back tomorrow. There are once again plans for making Meiktila (plop goes a bat off the doorway curtain!) into a larger military station. (The bat is now walking up the mosquito net of my bed.) It is expected that within a few weeks all the Manchesters will be here, the whole battalion, instead of only one company as at present."

On 11th October he wrote from Kalaw, "Such a funny household! Anne has whooping-cough, Baby has not, and Douglas has a wee bit of cough which may or may not prove to be it. So the aim is to keep all three apart from each other. The orders for tonight are: Anne (as usual) with Fan; Douglas (as has been the case lately) with Marjory; Baby in the drawing room with Heliman. I am for the present sleeping in the annexe. I have myself distinctly made progress during the week, though the weighing machine does not recognise it yet, but I have to go very quietly and shall probably have to wait some weeks before getting energetic again. That is why I am at home today. The bishop is going to Taunggyi a fortnight hence, and so he bade me leave out Taunggyi this month. I shall go down to Meiktila and Thazi as usual at the end of the week, but I shall probably go by train.

I had a visitor on my way up from Meiktila last Monday. As the train was going slowly round a sharp bend after leaving Singaing station, a Chinaman crawled through the window and grovelled at my feet on the floor saying something in unintelligible Burmese. I had an idea of pulling the communication cord, but it was pretty evident that he meant no harm, and I let him be, only relieving him of a clasp knife which he took out of his pocket with some keys. But I didn't greatly enjoy his company, and I thought that the tunnel which lies on that stretch was never coming to an end; I expect it is really about 200 yards long (I must try and estimate it next time I go) but it seemed to be two miles and more! When we got to the next station of course I insisted on his getting out, though it was necessary to call up both Guard and Stationmaster before he would leave my carriage. (He had a third class ticket Toungoo to Kalaw; I was travelling first) and then to all appearances, he went entirely mad. I should think that he *was* mad, but another passenger on the train told me that he was feigning madness in order to defeat an excise officer who suspected him of smuggling opium. I don't know what the truth was, but I don't want him again."

The following week both Douglas and I had whooping cough (allegedly a gift from the Bluebirds) and spent most of our time in the garden, I remember, where we chose a special out of the way patch, behind a fallen pine tree, in which to be sick from time to time. Father's letters, meanwhile, showed that he weighed only eight stone ten pounds and for a six foot man that certainly was not enough. Ever the optimist, however, he wrote, "The doctor is pleased with me, and is giving me a little more to eat. The last prescription is tripe."

On 1st November he wrote from Meiktila, "The regiment has come, and we did not know ourselves at Parade Service this morning – the body of the church nearly full with 120 men, fourteen officers (as well as the usual little group of civilians) in the chancel, and in the space by the side, thirty bandsmen giving us music. It comes almost as a new experience to me, accustomed to regard thirty as a big congregation."

By 8th November he was down in Taunggyi. "His Excellency the Governor and Lady Innes are here just now. They were both in church at 8 o'clock this morning, and nearly everybody else was late, which made things very awkward. However they quite realised that in these jungle parts our clocks are all different and nobody knows the time. During the morning, a note came down inviting me to lunch. It was embarrassing, as governor's invitations are commands, so the only thing to do was to accept the invitation and ask to be excused the food. I have just come back from the lunch. There were no other guests, only the two big people, two aides de camp and a private secretary. They were quite simple and homely, and it was all quite easy."

On 22nd November, Father wrote, "We are all doing splendidly. The whooping cough is nothing now, nothing – that is – except a bar to mixing with other children. And when I last weighed, I found that I had put on well over a pound in eight days.

The church (here at Kalaw) has got to be repaired this week. Its walls, between the wooden posts and beams, are made of matting, covered with mud-plaster and white-washed. Some of the matting has to be renewed; much of the mud-plaster has also to be renewed, inside and out, all the plaster (old and new) has to be white-washed; and the woodwork has to be earth-oiled! Happily it does not cost as much as it sounds; £5 should very nearly suffice, but I expect it will make a mess. After church tonight I made a start at dismantling the place and I hope the *durwan* [caretaker] will finish before the men come in the morning."

By 13th December he was staying with Mr. Clague, the Commissioner, at Taunggyi, and wrote, "The car has been a little troublesome lately, especially in respect of the battery, which would not store power enough to work the self starter in the morning. But I found my regular mechanic when I arrived on Friday and left the car with him for a day, and I think that it is all right now. Only the battery still needs working up, and as I must get off early tomorrow, the mornings are cold and I am not yet up to hard work with the handle, I have planned to leave the car tonight on a nice slope in Mr. Clague's compound, and so get a running start in the morning."

The last of Father's letters to survive was written on 27th December 1931 from Kalaw, to his sister Katie. "Such a Christmas! The children most thoroughly enjoyed it, and so did their elders. There is no doubt that you must have a family to keep Christmas properly, and if it is rather tiring, it only comes once a year. The whole Blaker family from Meiktila came here for it, six of them; we gave them the annexe and such beds as we had, and those who could not get beds slept on straw on the floor and professed to like it much better. It happened not to be very cold, and I

St. Katherine's Church, Kalaw, 2007.

think they were all right. For dinner there was the Bures plum pudding, which smelt excellent and I'm sure tasted so, and our own home grown turkey, of which I had a mouthful without any obvious bad results.

The cherry blossom has come out early this year, and the trees are a wonderful sight. Marjory and Fan decorated the whole church with it, and it looked beautiful. Congregations were much as other years, nothing much, but enough to give hearty services. Baby came to church for the first time."

Aunt Fan's diaries continue to record the happenings of the next few months, but she gives us few details. It seems that life jogged on much as usual, with Father doggedly sticking to his demanding routine (despite his declining health) until mid April, when Kingswood, the local Methodist School, was to give a concert. I well remember the last minute preparations for the show (in which I played Pooh and my brother played Christopher Robin) and our disappointment when Father in Fan's words "was not at all well and couldn't go to see it."

On 17th April 1932, "Charlie had slight fever but managed to take the morning service" and the next day was no better. "C. lay on the sofa or in bed all day". On 20th April, with Father's temperature rising alarmingly "We got Colonel Jones who was staying at the hotel to come to see him. The doctor settled that we must go to

England." Father's fever gradually subsided, his condition being confirmed as tropical sprue, a very nasty disorder of the intestines that causes failure to absorb nutrients from food.

Uncle Will was summoned and joined us from Mandalay on 9th May, when the diary relates that "He started to help pack directly after tea". He could only stay for four days and after his departure neighbours rallied round to assist. The weather was far from kind and on 20th May: "Tremendous storm of rain at midday and Marjory's bedroom, where her clothes were spread out to be packed, got flooded." On 23rd May the heavy luggage went off by goods train, and the next day "We all went to tea at Kingswood School, partly to celebrate Empire Day, and also as a farewell."

On 25th the Commissioner and his wife, Mr. and Mrs. Clague came to the rescue, sending their car down from Taunggyi so that Aunt Fan, my brother and I could go to stay with them and get out of everyone's way. We had a lovely time, I remember, playing with their children and even being allowed to ride their ponies. Annette Clague was about the same age as me and we used to hold dolls' tea-parties together. Back at Kalaw on Sunday 29th May, Fan wrote "Our last Sunday at Kalaw. I went to church three times." Uncle Will came to stay our last two nights, and on 30th. "There was a farewell tea at the Club, and presentations to Charles and Marjory."

On 1st June 1932, "We left Kalaw for England." Mother, Aunt Fan, we three children and our *ayah* went by train to Rangoon, with Father and Uncle Will travelling in the faithful old Chevrolet. Aunt Fan relates (in her understated way), "We put a camp bed in the middle of our carriage for Heliman; it was rather a squash. Mrs. Tubbs met us at the station and Will had all his meals at Bishopscourt too."

The diary entry on June 4th is in capital letters: "SAILED FOR ENGLAND ON THE KEMMENDINE AT 11.30 A.M. A GREAT MANY PEOPLE CAME TO SEE US OFF. THE BISHOP AND MRS. TUBBS AND CHRISTOPHER (THEIR SON) DROVE TO THE WHARF WITH US. HELIMAN WAS DREADFULLY DISTRESSED. WILL WAS ALLOWED TO COME ON THE LAUNCH WITH US TO THE SHIP; HE NEARLY GOT CARRIED AWAY WITH US."

There was a nursery on board, and a small swimming pool, and Douglas and I enjoyed the run of the ship, despite being greatly worried over Father. The grown-ups had a much worse time, as the seas were very rough, the fiddles were on the tables, Father was badly ill and Mother and Aunt Fan suffered constantly from seasickness. In addition, I suppose, it didn't exactly help when I fell out of the top bunk into my aunt's wastepaper basket, but at least I bounced back quickly!

We arrived at Tilbury on 9th July and the previous day Douglas gave everyone a fright by running a high temperature, which was to last for several days. Nevertheless, somehow or other, we all managed to travel to Reigate in Surrey, to stay with Mother's sister Mrs. Agatha Macfarlane in her comfortable house, while Father went straight to the Hospital for Tropical Diseases in London as an in-patient. Ten days later, Aunt Fan and I travelled to the family home at Bures, calling in to see Father in hospital on the way, finding him much better, to our great relief. By the end of the month, he was considered fit enough to be discharged, and there was great rejoicing when he and all the rest of the family were able to join us.

Meanwhile, the powers that be at S.P.G. had managed to find us a flat in West Malvern, Worcestershire, where we could live while Father regained his strength, and in early August we all moved in. For ages, Douglas and I had set our hearts on at last being able to live in a proper English house with a staircase, so imagine our disappointment when we discovered that 'Rose Court' was a ground floor flat, spacious, but without stairs! To make up for this, there were wonderful walks up the Malvern Hills from our back garden, and we soon settled down, with Mother being our teacher as before. She kept us at it from 9.00 a.m. to 1 p.m. daily, and must have taught us well, for when we started 'proper school' later on, we found ourselves equal to our peers and even a little ahead in some subjects. I, naturally, clamoured to join the local Brownie pack and soon had plenty of new friends to play with, though Douglas was not so lucky. He was too young for the local Cubs, but now too old to be an honorary Brownie.

All in all, 1932 had been a difficult but triumphant time for us, and Aunt Fan's final diary entry for 31st December puts everything into perspective with this pithy comment: "Charlie had his first mutton chop for one and a half years."

The following extract from the minutes of the S.P.G. Burma Advisory Committee for June 1932 is something of which I am very proud. It reads:

"RETIREMENT OF THE REV. C.E. GARRAD."

"The retirement of the Rev. C.E. Garrad, M.A., on account of serious ill health was brought to the notice of the committee, and it was unanimously agreed that the following message of appreciation of his services to the Society and sympathy in his illness should be forwarded to him.

The committee deeply regrets to hear of the enforced retirement of the Rev. C.E. Garrad, M.A., from the Burma Mission Field on account of ill health. It desires to place on record its appreciation not only of the invaluable services rendered by him to the Society in the translation of the Burmese Bible but of the selfless devotion to duty and the integrity of character which were such outstanding features of his life and work in Burma.

It requests the agent to forward to Mr. Garrad a copy of this minute and to express on its behalf its deep sympathy with him in his illness and its most sincere desire and prayer that he may steadily recover full health and strength in the home land."

Uncle Will was now our only family link with Burma, and though letters went backwards and forwards between us, none of these survive today. We know, however, from old tattered copies of the periodicals *Burma News*, *Burma Calling* and the *Rangoon Diocesan Magazine* that though Father was no longer living in the country, his work there was to survive and grow, with the publication of his prayer book in the latter part of 1932, the very year he had had to leave the country in such a hurry. Indeed, in front of me, at this moment, is a beautiful black leather edition, inscribed on the front page "To the Rev. Charles Edward Garrad in grateful recognition of his services on the Diocesan Liturgical Committee." Signed "Norman Rangoon (and the Bishop's cross) Whitsunday 1934."

Once he had regained his health, Father was appointed to the small rural parish of Barrow Gurney, Somerset, six miles from Bristol, and in the diocese of Bath and Wells. The vicarage was large and welcoming, but was very exposed to the elements. It sat in a commanding position on top of a steep hill, overlooking the distant city, and we all suffered from the cold; the windows were ill-fitting and rattled when the wind blew from the north so draughts were extensive, and we soon discovered that itchy chilblains in winter were almost as bad as prickly heat in summer.

School was a new and exhilarating experience, and a bit alarming at first, but we children settled down quickly, enjoyed it, and did well – at least some of the time! Of course I joined the local Brownies, and Guides when I was old enough, and later ran the Barrow Gurney Guide Company, all these activities continuing to be very important to me.

At last we had a stable, permanent home which was to be our stronghold for the next eighteen years, the springboard from which we three children were launched into adulthood. The first six years were wonderfully peaceful, but before long the war descended on us, shattering everything, with Bristol being particularly badly bombed. Father immediately volunteered to man our first aid station, while Mother joined the Auxiliary Territorial Service (the women's army) on a local basis, before signing up with the Red Cross. Aunt Fan ran the household, welcoming the refugees who thronged our spare rooms and attics and managing, somehow, to prepare meals for all and sundry, despite food rationing. Douglas and I were just old enough to join up before hostilities ceased, he in the Royal Naval Volunteer Reserve, and I (following Mother's footsteps) in the A.T.S., both seeing service overseas – but that is another story.

My most consistent memory of vicarage life, both before and during the war, is of Father at his desk in his north facing study, muffled up in his scarf, great-coat and woolly mittens, the room barely warmed by a small and smoky peat fire, as he worked on endless corrections to the Burmese Bible. He would fill page after page of foolscap paper with meticulously written corrections to the published text, painstakingly inscribing his revisions of the Burmese script, line by line, and verse by verse, making his way through every chapter of every book of both the Old and New Testaments. He just couldn't bear imperfections in meaning, let alone in grammar, spelling or punctuation, and was relentless in their eradication. Later, long after the war ended, he collated his papers and sent them to the Burmese Bible Society in Rangoon, where, much to our astonishment, we were to re-discover them on our recent pilgrimage to that city, some sixty years later.

I shall never forget our first visit to their headquarters at 262 Sule Pagoda Road, Rangoon on the 15th of November 2007. The Burmese Bible Society has a shop on the ground floor, where one can buy interesting cards and books, but our destination was a first floor room, up a steep and mysterious unlit stairway. Here we were met by the Rev. Khoi Lam Thong, the Bible Society's Translation Officer, a young man who impressed us greatly with his knowledge and enthusiasm. He told us he was a Chin from Manipur, and that the Society was working on projects involving the translation of the Bible into eighteen separate languages, spoken by ethnic minorities in Burma.

Khoi (pronounced choy) had evidently done his homework before our visit, for he spread out before us a number of different Bibles, including the very first 1926 'Geratt' edition (presumably a corruption of Garrad and Sherratt), riddled with woodworm and termite holes, placing beside them a tall, faded heap of files containing Father's corrections. I found it extremely moving to be confronted with all these pages, each in his well remembered handwriting, being overjoyed to find that they were still in existence. Khoi explained that although the language of what he now called 'the Garrad version' is considered somewhat academic (echoing that of the old Royal Court of Mandalay) it is still used for daily worship in the cathedral as well as in many churches, being constantly referred to, when the meaning of a passage is in doubt. The trouble is, he said, that there are now very few copies left in circulation, even the 1991 reprint being almost unobtainable.

During the course of this meeting, the Archbishop of Burma telephoned in person to ask us to visit him, so we hopped immediately into a battered old taxi and drove to Bishopscourt, where the great man himself was waiting to receive us, standing on his steps barefoot, dressed in a plain white surplice. Despite our dishevelled appearance – for it was hot and we had toured the Sule pagoda before visiting the Bible Society earlier – he ushered us into his reception room as though we were royalty, seating us on beautifully upholstered teak settees, and serving us tea. During our half hour's conversation together, we were much struck by the bishop's wisdom, humility and scholarship, learning that though no attempt has as yet been made to put a stop to church worship (except perhaps among the Karen people, though this is a political rather than a religious issue) job promotion is heavily dependent on membership of the Buddhist faith. Despite this, it appears that a number of young men are still coming forward for ordination, a major problem of the Christian training colleges being that Bibles are in increasingly short supply. "The scholarship of 'the Garrad version' remains unchallenged," we were told, "and we desperately need more copies."

When it was time to say farewell, our host insisted that we should be driven back to the hotel in his private conveyance. What sort of car would it be, I wondered, naively anticipating something of a reasonably modern vintage for a figure of his importance, in contrast to the many pre-war wrecks we had encountered on Burma's roads during the past few days. Disillusionment quickly set in, however, for it was only minutes later, as I climbed, somewhat gingerly, into his very elderly, rusting pick-up that I began to realise the extreme poverty of the Anglican church in Burma. No wonder Bibles were in short supply.

After this momentous meeting we put our heads together and eventually, with

The Archbishop of Burma with Anne and Thomas in 2007.

much deliberation, having further consulted the Bible Society and the Dean of the Cathedral we came to an agreement that our family – the Garrad clan – would be prepared to sponsor a new edition of Father's Bible, provided that this would incorporate his corrections. The work would take time, of course, but we were assured that this could be carried out at a reasonable cost, and the Burmese Bible Society declared itself to be delighted. For our part, we felt overjoyed that all those years of dedication would now bear fruit, but were aware of the huge task ahead. We would all have to be patient.

Over eighty years have now passed since the Garrad bible was first published in 1926 and it's necessary to go back to those times in order to realise how much the new translation was valued, for "we just couldn't have done without it" seems to have been the general feeling among all those working for the S.P.G. and the B.C.M.S. (Bible Churchmen's Missionary Society) at this period.

So let's put the clock back to 1934, to the second year after Father had left

Burma, when Bishop Norman Henry Tubbs was to startle everyone by announcing his forthcoming retirement. Who would be the next Bishop of Rangoon people wondered? A local priest, perhaps, or, more probably, someone brought out from Britain for the purpose? I can recall my parents animatedly discussing the issue at meal times, as we sat round our circular oak dining table in far away Barrow Gurney, and remember their considerable surprise at the final outcome.

In his letters, Father mentions Mr. West from time to time, but these brief entries tell us next to nothing about the man, other than that his principal – and successful – sphere of work was in Kappali, among the Karen people. You may remember, for instance, that my mother and Miss Fairclough sailed up the River Salween to visit him on 20th November 1927, while on 2nd March 1928 on a visit to Moulmein at a church service attended by the Governor, Sir Charles Innes, Father wrote (somewhat tongue in cheek) that, "Mr West's rendering of the versicles is apparently even worse than mine."

So, in late 1934, it's a somewhat unexpected discovery to find that this very same Mr. George Algernon West had just been chosen by the newly autonomous Church of England in India as their next bishop, being consecrated on 27th January 1935. Tucked away among Uncle Will's private notes, I came across this entry: "West is a big man physically as well as spiritually. In the 1914-18 war, he was in the Royal Garrison Artillery and knew all about handling fifteen inch shells. Incidentally, he collected a Military Medal, which shows he is a big man in other ways too. He came out to Burma as a deacon, being appointed to the Karen mission at Toungoo and was ordained priest in Rangoon. That particular mission always had a lot of touring attached to it, and it was West's ambition to pioneer. Sitting still in headquarters did not appeal to his temperament and he went further and further afield. The area round headquarters was thoroughly worked, so he visualised a campaign on the other side of the Karen hills and went to the Salween valley to investigate. The death of a dearly beloved wife settled him in his decision to leave the beaten track and make his home in this altogether new district.

It was while he was working and living there, that the diocese had to choose its new bishop and attention was focussed on him. A remark of one of the indigenous clergy at the council caused some merriment: 'We want a man who will live among us and Thra (his nickname) is fond of the jungle, just look at him', and we all looked at West, who had not seen a tailor or been near a barber for many months and had almost forgotten what English food tasted like. He was the man who was elected, the big man with the big spirit, who lived up to what he preached. Since then, he has been giving us the lead, and if we have not always followed him, this has not been his fault. Sitting in Rangoon and presiding at committee meetings does not appeal to him, such things and all money affairs are better left to an archdeacon. His mind is constantly visualising new schemes and key people to direct them."

It was during George West's time at St. Peter's Mission, Toungoo (between Mandalay and Rangoon) that he was to meet his future wife, Helen Margaret Scott-Moncrieff. You may perhaps recall her as a friend of Aunt Fan's, who features in the diaries as the first nursing sister to join Miss Patch at the Children's Hospital, Mandalay, tragically dying in childbirth not long after her marriage. After this devastating blow, which Uncle Will described so succinctly, Mr. West was to find a particular niche in working with the Karens, later featuring them in his books, *Jungle Folk* (1933), *Jungle Friends* (1937) and *Jungle Witnesses* (1948).

At this period, Uncle Will was still resident in Mandalay, soldiering on as head of the Winchester Brotherhood. In October 1935, at the S.P.G. monthly meeting, he reported that they were languishing for lack of recruits and that the recent tendency had been to give greater responsibility to native workers. He is reported to have said, "The schools form a large and important part of the work done by the Mandalay mission. St. Mary's School has 200 girls on the roll, and has a boarding house for twenty-five. The children attend St. Mary's Church and the chaplain takes his share in their religious instruction. At St. Andrew's School, all the teaching is in Burmese. This is also nominally a girls' school, and has about 180 children in its seven standards. The teachers are all Christians and religious instruction is given daily, but only a small proportion of the children are Christians, and most of these are members of the St. Andrew's boarding house under the charge of one of the ladies of the mission.

"The Royal School has now fallen on rather bad times and its position is precarious. The reason for this turn is very tragic. Until the last few years, all middle-school pupils were required to sit for a seventh standard examination conducted by the government education authorities, and the better schools gained the higher proportion of passes. Nowadays, financial stringency has compelled the government to give up the expense of this examination and each school examines its own seventh standard and issues its own seventh standard pass certificates. This withdrawal of control is pressing very hardly on the better-class schools. In practice the schools which have the lowest standard of efficiency, and therefore allow the highest percentage of pupils to pass, are decoying the children from the better schools which are still trying to maintain a reasonable standard of learning. The Royal School has lost a large number of pupils, who now go to The National School, where they receive rapid, and to our minds, quite unjustifiable promotion."

On a more up-beat note, however, he praises the women's work, particularly at the Queen Alexandra Hospital, saying, "A fully qualified English lady doctor is in charge, and there are with her three English nursing sisters, and ten Burmese nurses trained or in training. There are thirty cots in the large upstairs ward and when they are full, the overflow has to sleep on the floor. Burmese children are very charming and you can tell certain times of the day by the noise going on. They are not old enough to look at the clock, but like the animals in the zoo, they know when it is feeding time and take good care that others know also!

Another point about the hospital is that it is sending out year by year more trained nurses to work in the villages and help the jungle people. It is becoming much more of a diocesan institution, and a definite 'jungle nursing service' scheme is under consideration, whereby villages will contribute towards the cost of the training of their own girl or girls during their time in Mandalay. The going out of Miss Cam from Mandalay to start medical work in the Delta has proved a great success, and she has started several of our nurses in useful centres there."

The work of these nurses was to prove especially valuable in a few years time, for in 1941 the Japanese armed forces were to invade Burma, and medical services were much in demand as casualties grew. Bishop George West was still, nominally, head of the Rangoon Diocese on the outbreak of war, though he was far away from the country at the time, "recuperating in the United States of America from a serious motor car accident," Uncle Will reported, "which had left him unconscious for three weeks and dangerously ill."

Fortunately, the bishop was to make a full recovery, spending his time abroad learning about the Oxford Group, later named the Moral Re-Armament Movement, of which he was to become a leading member. Indeed, it was in North Carolina in May 1943 that he married for the second time, his new wife being the redoubtable Grace Hay, with whom he later travelled to India. Determined to get back into harness as soon as possible, it was in mid 1945, even before hostilities in the Far East had come to an end, that they were both able to make their way back to Burma, to learn at first hand about all that had been going on during these difficult years.

CHAPTER SIXTEEN

The Japanese Invasion and the Trek into Burma (1940-1945)

The war in England started in earnest a whole year earlier than the war in Burma. It was on the night of 24th November 1940 that the Luftwaffe bombed Bristol for the first time, dropping huge numbers of high explosive and incendiary bombs on the city. It is said that the blaze could be seen from forty miles away, and we certainly had a terrifying, grandstand view from our hilltop in Barrow Gurney vicarage. By this time, we had a Czech refugee and two evacuee children from East London as well as a couple of their teachers living with us, and there wasn't much room to spare when we all crowded under the sturdy oak dining-table that served as our air-raid shelter. Fortunately, Barrow Gurney escaped relatively unharmed, and, as a teenager, I would watch, fascinated, as our search-lights swept the winter sky for marauding German planes. There were gun-sites all round us, and though I didn't know it at the time, one of them was under the command of a nineteen year old lieutenant, who was later to become my husband. I didn't meet him till after the war, when I was astonished to discover that he had not only helped to keep us safe during the blitz, but had also spent the greater part of the war in Burma, fighting the Japanese. His name was Claude Carter, and this is part of his story.

After serving with the Royal Artillery in Bristol and Plymouth, he volunteered to join the Indian Army, in response to an urgent plea from the War Office, and, in due course, found himself aboard a converted French liner, which had seen better days. The journey east was cramped but largely uneventful, he told me, except for the plumbing, as nothing but cold, rusty liquid ever emerged from the hot taps, while the toilets were constantly being flushed with boiling water! Once in Burma, he was posted to the Royal Indian Army Service Corps, being the only European officer in his unit, and quickly having to learn the native language of Urdu in order to survive. For three long but exciting years he had been in charge of some fifty three-ton lorries, carrying men and supplies up and down the precipitous Burma road (never knowing when and where the Japanese would strike next) and being mentioned in despatches for his efforts. Enemy ambushes were frequent, but an almost equal hazard was the unexpected behaviour of some of his troops. The drivers, being Muslims in the main, (supposedly prohibited from drinking) soon discovered that there was alcohol in the brake fluid, which they drained when no one was looking. After several terrible accidents, when vehicles went over the edge, brake inspection before setting out became the order of the day.

The Battle of Kohima (sometimes called 'the Stalingrad of the East') was one of the final turning points in the war, Claude's convoy of vehicles apparently being almost the last to carry troops (the Royal West Kents) across the frontier from Burma into India, and up the Imphal/Kohima road, before the Japanese managed to commandeer it. The final showdown took place in the early summer of 1944, the battle at last being won on June 22nd, when our British and Indian soldiery managed to overcome the retreating Japanese, before eventually being able to re-open the road once more. Claude was not in that first convoy out, having been holed up in a ditch for some days, without food or water, and covered with lice. He was reported

Captain Claude Carter, Royal Indian Army Service Corps (1945).

as 'missing', he found out later, but fortunately there was a delay in getting the news home, so his parents were spared that particular agony. He was an only child, and this would certainly have caused them great and unnecessary distress.

On the outbreak of war in Burma in 1941, the European priests and workers had been instructed to evacuate to India by orders of the government, as it was thought that the their presence would be an unfair responsibility to the indigenous church, and would add to their difficulties. The first mission to come under Japanese occupation was Moulmein,[19] followed by Kappali, and Rangoon came next. How were these missionaries to get away?

Following the Japanese occupation of Lower Burma, everyone tried to escape as best they could, and filed away amongst Uncle Will's collection of papers are several accounts of people's horrific experiences as they made their way to India by whatever means possible – train, plane or on foot – and here are some of their stories.

It was on December 23rd 1941 when the first bombs fell in Rangoon, that Miss Jean Forrester from the mission (a volunteer ambulance driver) wrote, "I happened to be on the morning shift and had drawn ambulance no 1. We always drew lots for ambulances, as some were easier to drive than others. Suddenly the siren went.

'Number one ambulance driver,' said someone.

'Here.'

'Here is your nurse. You will sit by the door. When the first message comes, your doctor will call you. You are not to go till your doctor calls you. Got your tin hat?'

In ran a messenger. I was near enough to the control table to hear what he said.

'Merchant Street, corner of 42nd Street – casualties.'

I leapt to my feet, and then remembered that I wasn't supposed to move without orders. The doctor and stretcher bearers went out. Some one wrote, 'Merchant Street, 42nd Street' on a piece of paper and thrust it into my hand. The nurse joined me. We slipped on our tin hats and went out. The doctor and stretcher bearers piled into their bus. The nurse and I got into the ambulance.

In about two minutes we reached 39th Street. An A.R.P. warden stopped us. As we stopped we heard an enemy plane swoop down on us from above. We yelled to the stretcher boys to stay in the bus, and to the Indians who were running wildly round in the centre of the road to get under a strong porch.

'If I'm going to be killed, I hope it's quick', I thought and closed my eyes as the shriek of the plane got louder. There was a crash and I opened my eyes. About 100 yards ahead there was the grey dust cloud of chipped masonry and broken road surface. A bomb? Machine gunfire? But if the warden hadn't stopped us we should have been at that exact spot. I looked at my foot jittering on the clutch, and realised that I couldn't stop it. I prayed, 'Please don't let me be afraid.'

Once the ambulance was loaded, my foot steadied when it had work to do, and off we went to the General Hospital, as quickly as we could without shaking the casualties up. Then out again to pick up more casualties and back again for two hours." Rangoon was in chaos, and people had to make their way north as quickly as possible. On January 1st 1942, Miss Forrester was sent to Shwebo to take over the All Saints' Boys' High School from David Patterson, who was about to become an Army Chaplain. The Rev. and Mrs. Dyer came up at the same time to look after the mission itself. Little did she know it then, but Shwebo (and later Myitkyina further north) were to become evacuation camps, almost entirely under her control. An extract from Miss Forrester's article reveals that "From March 5th we took on the welfare side of the Air Evacuation Scheme, which was initiated by the Director of Civil Aviation, one of the most efficient people I have ever met.

An average of three planes went each day from Shwebo, taking away about 135 people, including children. Convoys came in every few days varying in numbers from 100 to 200, so our numbers in camp fluctuated considerably and the catering for each meal was difficult, as was also the allotting of beds or floor space. As we had only eighty-seven beds and at times nearly 500 in camp, this demanded tact! 'Either a bed or a mattress' we said 'not both, please' – and people co-operated willingly. They were not able to take their bedding on the plane, so we gradually accumulated a store from which we were able to supply those who had come without any. We were able to get milk, butter and bread locally, also vegetables and enough meat for one meal, but any other stores, including dal and salt were flown over from India in the planes taking the evacuees away. Burma itself was far too disorganised to send us anything, although there was a good deal in the country, as looters later disclosed. So long as we were getting on with the job the government officials were willing to give us anything we asked for."

By the beginning of April they had to move north to Myitkyina, where the evacuation camp was to be in the American Baptist Mission. "I found two of the mission there and four others arrived after a few days, so we had our organising staff. By this time Mandalay had been bombed out. Evacuees began to pour in by their hundreds. Planes were very erratic. We were supposed to have two Chinese

National Airways planes doing two flights each and every day, but they didn't always turn up. Hygiene was the biggest problem. What I saw of people's habits and lack of responsibility in the direction of hygiene made me feel that this should come before even the three 'R's in our educational programme."

"One gala day we evacuated 450 people but the next day our hearts sank, because no planes came at all, and we learnt later that the reception camp in Assam had forbidden them to come because they had not been able to deal with all we sent them the day before. This was sheer nonsense, for by that time we had 2,000 in camp and news of 5,000 more to come. I was sent for, to help with the reception at Assam. I think this was really an excuse to get me out, while there were still planes, for we were very near to the end. About ten days later the Japanese bombed Myitkyina aerodrome, and air evacuation had to cease while there were still thousands left behind. For these people there was now nothing but the long trek out."

And what of Mandalay and Uncle Will? He was out of town on Good Friday morning, 3rd April 1942 when the first bombs fell, but Miss Chapman (originally of Kemmendine, Rangoon) wrote as follows: "I was sitting in the Mission House with Nellie Linstead. In a few minutes we should be going to St. Mary's Church, where Padre Wilson was to conduct the Three Hours' Service. She was telling me about the final arrangements she had made for the blind women who had been evacuated to Shwebo after the fall of Moulmein, and she was planning now to go to Shwebo or to Myitkyina to help in an evacuee camp. As we talked we heard aeroplanes overhead, either very low or a good number… and a sudden fear. Were they our own? But there had been no alert… bombs, and very near too, for the mission compound was between the post office and the telegraph office, and not far from the railway station. We lay on the floor on our faces, for there was no time to get to a trench. It seemed to be over, and we went across to the Children's Hospital which was a first aid post, to help Rosina Simmonds and her Karen nurses as much as amateurs could. But Mandalay had begun to burn, and the compound was surrounded by fire. In the afternoon we had orders to evacuate. First the patients, stretchers, lorries, ambulances took them off to other hospitals. We bundled hospital equipment, medicines and bedding into our own cars and took them down to the Winchester Mission, and drank tea in Padre Garrad's house. Returning to the hospital compound for the eighth or ninth time that afternoon, I found the clergy busy extinguishing a fire which had broken out in the chapel roof. There was no hose pipe, no pump and no ladder, but just three petrol tins, one of which leaked, and the well. They saved the chapel somehow.

"Padre Garrad returned to the Winchester Mission to find not only his house full but the school buildings in the compound full too, with Indian, Chinese and Anglo-Burmese people from bombed quarters of the town. Some wanted rice, some had no salt, and some had nothing to cook in. And was there going to be enough water in the compound well for everybody? Some had not found a place where they could sleep. I thought of the 'feeding of the 5000'.

"April 4th. Mandalay was still burning, but in a different part. The clergy cleaned up St. Mary's Church for Easter Day. It had been partially damaged by the bombing. An evacuee camp was organised ten miles out of Mandalay on the Maymyo road for the people in the bombed quarters. Air evacuation from Shwebo was discontinued and people were waiting for trains to take them farther north to Myitkyina aerodrome. On Easter Day I went with Padre Garrad to Sagaing where he took the Easter Eucharist with a congregation of a dozen. Coming out of Mandalay with its confusion and noise to the peace of Sagaing and its altar made him feel, he said, like the disciples who found their Lord at Emmaeus. I was glad that he had come away from it for an hour or two, and I hoped he was taking courage from the great failure of Good Friday when he saw the place where he had worked for thirty years past, being destroyed. As we re-crossed the Irrawaddy by the fine Ava Bridge on our way back to Mandalay, we wondered how long that would be left standing."

Uncle Will left Mandalay on April 14th 1942, with Messrs. Wilson and Matthew staying behind for another week. The front page of his notes is missing, only starting on 2nd May, without a location, but by this time he was probably up country at Katha. He writes "A prayer meeting to be conducted by Appleton was announced for 8 a.m. in church. Present, the B.C.M.S. men, Miss Simmonds, Hardy, Websper, Tidey and self. Spent most of the day preparing things to start on trek on Monday or Tuesday. The blind school and the deaf school are being evacuated to Bilumyo and our Q.A.C.H. nurses are going too. There is an excellent spirit among them.

"In the evening I was having a bath, a knock came at the bath-room door, and I was asked to wrap myself in a towel and open the door. On doing so, I found Major Parry (Royal Army Medical Corps) of Maymyo, who said that he had heard that I was proposing to walk with the party, and had come up from a hospital train at the station to invite me to travel on it and then fly. He asked my age (sixty-one) and then spoke so kindly that it seemed ungrateful not to do as he said, and I agreed to dress hastily and go and get on the train. On arriving there, I found the longest train I have ever seen, drawn by a Garrett hill-climbing engine. When I had been there for sometime, who should come along but Appleton. Major Parry had heard that he had sore feet (which was quite true) and had been up again to the Mission House and had sent him down.

"Sunday May 3rd. The train reached Myitkyina about 7 p.m. and we detrained by the side of the line and were at last taken in trucks to the hospital. I felt an utter sham but got into the bed next to Appleton. As there seemed no sign of a meal, we went to sleep but were woken up again at 11.30 for supper, two cold sausages on a plate. Having eaten them and gone to sleep again, we were again woken about 2 a.m. and made to stand on a pair of scales and have our weight taken!

Monday May 4th. We had breakfast in hospital, porridge and eggs, and then names were read out for those to go to the aerodrome in an ambulance. My name was read, so we started off all together about 9.30 a.m. There were a number of people waiting at the drome, so we waited too, and eventually a plane came and took about thirty. Then there was another wait until another plane came. At midday, a message was received that enemy planes were about, and we had to disperse into the jungle. Then about 3 p.m. came another message that no more planes would be coming that day, so we prepared to return to Myitkyina, but before we had gone very far, another plane came, so Appleton and I decided to stay all night at the drome in case a plane should come by moonlight (it was full moon). We managed to find a well of reasonable drinking water and fill up our bottles. A good many men of the King's Own Yorkshire Light Infantry were there too, and the soldiers gave us some of their biscuits and sausages and shared their mugs of tea, after which we spread out our rugs and lay down. There were one or two light alarms of rain during the night, but nothing serious and we had quite a good night. Almost at the first streak of daylight, three planes appeared, all alike, Douglas DC2, but with different markings, one American, one Chinese and one British. I was allowed on the American plane, but at the last moment, was told to leave my suitcase and take only a Shan bag. I hastily put a few things into this bag, and then was told that I might take the suitcase after all. The result was that my prayer book got left behind, also my rug and my Burberry. Appleton managed to get on to the second plane. After an hour or perhaps a little more, we saw an aerodrome beneath us and made an excellent landing. Appleton got out of one, to my joy, and Cardew of the Burma Railways was in the third, so we three formed a little party and stuck together."

"After waiting about for an hour or so, we got into a lorry and were driven off to D....h, about 25 miles away, where we were put down at a Roman Catholic Church. There we found all the people who had flown from Myitkyina yesterday, Miss Simmonds, Websper, Hardy etc. and there was tea to be had, followed by a large plate of rice and vegetable curry. The ladies slept in the chancel, the men in the nave. After tea, Appleton and I (Cardew had a tied up leg) took a walk round and found the Anglican church, but it was locked up. If it had been open, my intention was to steal a prayer book in place of the one I lost at Myitkyina. When we got back to the camp, we found people boarding lorries to take them to a steamer en route for Calcutta, so we joined them, and found places on a good sized ferry boat. Mattresses and blankets were to be had for the asking and we got bread and stew from a bazaar shop, and spent quite a comfortable night. Various people had to move when it rained but we were all right where we were.

"Wednesday May 6th. All day we went down the River Brahmaputra on the *S.S. Duffla*. It seemed to be very similar to the Irrawaddy except that we saw no pagodas on the banks. At night we again had bread and stew for dinner, and the decks were rather hard."

"Thursday May 7th. We arrived at Tezpur at dawn, and went on the narrow gauge railway en route for Calcutta. It was very crowded. At Rangapura we changed to a metre gauge train, getting off at Rangiya where, after a meal in the refreshment room, we got into an empty luggage van on yet another train (smelling badly of fish, so that we had to have the door open) and stayed there till we reached Parbatipur where we changed again. We had missed our connection and had several hours to wait. During breakfast, a man in a white cassock walked in and we wondered who he might be. I made friends with him, and he told us he was a Brother of the Oxford Mission at Calcutta, to whose headquarters we were trying to find our way, and from there on, he took charge of us, and we felt much happier.

"The Calcutta train came in at last and an intermediate compartment was reserved for us evacuees. It was rather a mixture, men and women on top of each other, with lots of children, but after all we had come through, nobody seemed to mind. We arrived at the fish market part of the goods station, where we got gharries, arriving at Cornwallis Street, filthy and hungry, but safe and sound.

What has happened to the Christian people of Mandalay, I do not know. We can only commit them into God's hands and pray for them. Their distress may be the great opportunity to build themselves into a really national church, and we must hope that it is so. The ark of the church which the missionaries have been trying to build for many years has been, at the last, plunged into the maelstrom, rather than launched, but we trust God that she is afloat and to use Kipling's phrase, 'finding herself'."

One major casualty of the exodus was that of Rev. Higginbotham, who had recently taken over from Rev. Lee as Archdeacon of Rangoon. In bravely attempting to drive his car through Japanese occupied territory, carrying all the diocesan papers with him, it seems that he disappeared, and there is little or no evidence as to how he died.

Fortunately for Uncle Will he knew nothing of this, nor, at this stage, of the other big tragedy in the getaway, that of the Bishop's Home children from Rangoon, who, together with a few of St. Matthew's children from Moulmein, had unsuccessfully tried to walk to India. They had been travelling north, under the care of young Miss Tilly, the newly appointed principal of St. Matthew's, Moulmein, when their train was bombed, Miss Tilly dying on the platform from her injuries. Undefeated, Miss Bald, the second in command, took over, bringing her charges safely to Mandalay where she asked for a communion service in Miss Tilly's memory. Uncle Will took this, and wrote, "It was a beautiful service, the children singing hymns which they had learnt by heart, with about twenty communicants." The next day he took Miss Bald to the Commissioner and got free passage for the party on the Thabeikkyin ferry. They left the following evening for Mogok, and all arrived safely.

From there, they eventually had to make their way to Myitkyina airfield, becoming stranded there on 6th May 1942, just two days after Will himself had got away. An army staff sergeant spent the next days ferrying some 200 people (including the children) up to milestone 102, the starting point of the westward trail into Assam via the dreaded Hykaung Valley. The little ones were then taken to Sumprabum to a convent, while Miss Bald and the older children started the trek on foot, under British Army guidance. S/Sgt H.J. Shaw, Royal Engineers, wrote later, "We were faced with hardships on the very first day; five of our six bullocks were lost with almost all our rations. It had continued to rain hard, none of the girls had waterproofs, only their thin summer frocks. (Capt. Young managed to buy about ten umbrellas from Kachin villagers). The mountain tracks were very difficult. Usually we started each day with only plain tea to drink, having one meal of rice at the end of the day's march. After about two weeks of this, several of the girls were ailing and Sgt. Major Norcliffe was suffering from sunstroke.

"Capt. Young decided to go on ahead alone to Maingkwan and arrange with the political person there – Mr. North – for the housing and rationing of the whole party. Mr. North informed Capt. Young of a suitable bungalow to accommodate the party, but that he could only supply rice, but we managed to get hold of some bully beef and chickens. The following day (Saturday 6th June), we set out for the Govt. camp at Shingbwiyang, having added to our party fourteen women and children who had been detained at Maingkwan for several days. We were forced by sickness throughout the party to remain at Kiapha Ga for three days. The physical condition of the whole party by this time was becoming desperate. There was a good supply of rice at Gawbang, enough for one month or so at least, and so it was decided that Capt. Young and myself – being the most fit in the party – should continue the journey to Assam and try to get assistance."

Both these soldiers were to fall ill with malaria while they were away, and then the monsoon intervened, so they were unable to return. Capt Young died in August, and despite heroic efforts, there was no way S/Sgt Shaw could get food or clothing back to the party. We are told that only one child eventually reached Calcutta, though, happily, most of the younger ones who had been taken to the convent, did manage to survive.

The Hykaung Valley, through which the ill-fated party had journeyed, was a fearsome place, my husband Claude told me later. He had ventured into this terrain with his men on one occasion and had found it harsh and inhospitable. After the 1942 exodus (when relays of people had tried to trek through it in their escape to India) the harrowing sight of human and animal skeletons, strewn along the valley, as well as many burnt out wrecks of vehicles, was something Claude could never forget. It was so dreadful that he'd tried to make a record of it, feeling that such horrors should never be forgotten, but the photographs he'd taken with his battered pocket camera were unsuccessful, being grainy and badly focused. The strange thing, he noticed, was that the bogged-down, abandoned trucks he'd come across were always full of bodies, presumably not the original occupants who'd been forced to get out and make their way by foot through the glutinous mud, but others who came afterwards, seeking some sort of shelter from the elements, being too exhausted to go a single step further.

Despite all this, the Rev. George Tidey's party did eventually get through and I am just so thankful that Uncle Will wasn't with them as he had planned to be, because it's very doubtful, being elderly, that he would have survived. The group started off by train from the B.C.M.S. hospital at Mohnyin, travelling forty miles north to Samaw and spending the first night in the club there, with a supper of rice and two sardines per man. What follows are extracts from Tidey's moving account, in Uncle Will's possession:[20] "After supper," he wrote, "some of us who had been some time in Burma discussed our chances of reaching India. We knew it wouldn't be an easy journey and that there would be much more to it than the actual walking. The Samaw people were most kind and lent us a truck to take our kit to the end of the day's journey, and so we were able to travel light. Some of our optimists decided that since it was only twenty five miles, and that since any one could do three miles an hour, they would finish the day's march in eight and a half hours. They started off in great style and by their own account did four miles in the first hour. They were soon far ahead of us. Those few of us who went 'softlee' caught them up after twenty miles where they were strewn along the bank side, begging anything with wheels to give them a lift. We heard no more about mathematical calculations and fancy schedules after that day.

Already one man was down with dysentery, which didn't promise very well for the remainder of the journey, but here at Kamaing we got two ponies which we used for carrying sick men's kit. This was a very hot day and we did only ten miles before we came to a clearing with some coolie huts and here we decided to halt. There was a stream here and we all felt better for a good soak in it. When we came back to our huts, a convalescent officer told us he had arranged for a lorry to be at our disposal next morning and sure enough, next morning it was there. We found that the truck had been bequeathed to us for as long as the road lasted. It was a poor enough road which a good shower would have finished, but still we made progress, and however uncomfortable, we all felt it was better than walking. At Maingkwan we had to wait a day for two of the party who had been delayed, and some of the men began to get a bit jumpy at the delay. There were reports that the Japs were infiltrating and coming down a nearby river. That evening, two R.A.F planes flew low over the bungalow where we were resting. We saw them drop small parachutes and four men went back a couple of miles to find out what they were. There was a certain amount of food and a cheering message.

Next day we set off for the river. We were determined to get the lorry as far as possible. This was our introduction to the mud we got to know so intimately. The track went through the jungle and one man had his hand crushed as we scraped against a tree. The Jeep which we had acquired got through to the river, but the truck stuck in the mud and we had to unload our precious food and heave and haul with scarcely a foothold. Eventually, we drove on through the night without any headlights and reached the river bank about ten. We had a piece of goat which some one had found, with rice and tea. There was no shelter and so we lay on our groundsheets and slept until about midnight when the first monsoon storm of the season burst on us. By daylight we were uniformly wet and cold.

There were lots of bullock carts waiting to cross on the small rafts, crowds of people and several lorries like our own which had to be left on this side. In the late morning when most of the people were over, some of our men with amazing ingenuity managed to get the Jeep onto a raft and ferry it over. We all carried a certain amount of kit to give the Jeep a reasonable chance and off she went in a cloud of mud, skidding and slithering, but making a fair speed. After three miles, we found the Jeep stuck in a mud hole up to her nose. We must have spent a couple of hours before we would admit that we were beaten, but we were. We had now more food than we could carry without the Jeep, and so we distributed the spare among the people who were passing at the time. As events showed, we gave away the wrong stuff and we soon regretted that we had been lavish with the sugar. But some bullock carts appeared and we were able to persuade their drivers to help us to the next village, otherwise our sick people could not have managed.

That evening, after we had arranged ourselves in a broken down hut, we went to look at the river. It was running very fast and the raft had been destroyed. We swam in the shallows and after supper had a short service around the fire. The following afternoon the raft was ready and so we went down to the waterside to take our turn with the other people, some of whom had been waiting quite a time to cross. Just when everything seemed set, a number of Frontier Force men rode up. They were all armed and seized the raft, and were quite ready to shoot people who objected. We had some very anxious and unpleasant minutes. With the delay they caused it took us all day to cross the river, but there was quite a good place to camp on the other side. The main difficulty we had found so far was the complete lack of information about the route and the distances between stages. We had seen little sign of what the government had done to help refugees to reach India, but some who passed us told us that a few days previously, an official had put up a notice, 'Entrance to the Hykaung Valley; certain death for women and children', (as indeed it had turned out to be.)

The next night we spent at a very dirty camp. We slept on our groundsheets in the mud. As we set off next morning, we were told that the day's march was fifteen miles, but it must have been nearer twenty. The mud was very deep and sticky and we found it hard going. One of our airmen who had lost half a buttock in a raid, walked twenty minutes and rested twenty minutes all the time in great pain. We reached a small stream after nine miles and washed off the mud, drank plain cocoa, and after a sleep, pushed on. The heat was very trying. There had been storms on this part of the road and every mile or so we came across trees which had been blown down and blocked our way. We reached Shinbwiyang in the dark, but found there both huts to sleep in and food which had been dropped by plane. The next day some of our people were too tired to go on, in any case we felt we ought to do something to help the man in charge. Planes came over twice that day and dropped food in sacks or by parachute. Our work was to try to rescue the food as it fell, for proper distribution. In this camp we saw the first cases of cholera."

Here we found the Maingkwan mission elephant had been left for us. Maggie was small and had a low trick of picking up mud and water with her trunk and slinging it at whoever was walking immediately behind her. She had no great beauty, but she made all the difference. About half the day's march was over when it began to rain. We had just begun a climb of 3000 feet which would have been difficult enough in any case, but with the path turning to deep and sticky mud, to make any progress at all was a labour. After the first 1000 feet, we began to see pack bullocks exhausted and left by the side of the path to die. And then we saw elderly men and women standing weeping at difficult corners which they had not the strength to round. Then, as we climbed further, we came across dead animals and dying people. The camp was near the top of this hill, but when we reached it after ten hours' hard going, we were very disappointed to find what a poor thing it was, a small clearing on a steep hillside with a few leaf huts, already falling down and befouled. There was no one in charge, no food and very little water. Next day, we made a fairly short march of five or six hours and reached a similar camp, tumbled-down and filthy.

The following day, which was the Sunday after Ascension, was the worst of the whole journey. We had chosen a small gravel island scarcely above water level as a better camping place than the camp. It was raining when we got there, but soon we had a fire and a shelter thatched with plantain leaves, but the weight of water brought the roof down. Our second attempt was more successful and the hut lasted till morning, as of course, did the rain. Next morning, we had to wade down the river about waist deep for perhaps 600 yards, climb up through the stinking camp and then on to the mud path up the mountain side. Soon it was the same thing again, people weeping from weariness and despair, and then the dead. The camp we were making for, we were told, was the highest of the journey, and we came to something like despair at times when the height we had so laboriously gained on the path, was lost on some precipitous descent.

It was raining heavily when we reached the camp. We had a bad night. We tried to make a floor of sorts to keep ourselves off the mud by laying bamboos together, but it wasn't successful. With a little fat on our bones, the bare mud could have been more comfortable. We slept a little until the cold became too much for us, and then we lay and waited for daylight. One man had fever. Others had such bad feet by this time that it was torment to struggle into sodden boots. All this time we were hemmed in by thick, monotonous jungle, but some miles further on, we had a great relief, and came to where the trees were thinner and where the grass began, and through the clouds we could see range after range stretching to the north with occasional clearings and Naga villages. As we began the descent to the river, some ten miles away, we caught up with a European of sixty or so who had been greatly cheered by the unaccustomed openness. 'Ah, this is God's own country' he exclaimed. He was drowned next day, trying to cross the river.

We didn't reach the river that day. About six miles short, we heard a shot and saw an English soldier with a rifle. He had been trying to distribute food dropped by plane for people on the road, and was moving on that day. We said we would take over, and stayed in this deserted Naga village for two days. Food was getting short, and people on the river bank were dying in scores from exhaustion and cholera as they waited to cross. At this stage, Maggie's driver refused to go any further. Just when we thought she must be abandoned, a Siamese was discovered in the camp. He had formerly owned elephants and offered to drive her. The river was running very fast and one look decided that it was useless to try to cross. We slept in a leaf shelter. Next morning we got the rope over with Maggie's help, and people began to cross a little further upstream, knowing that if they were swept away, they could always catch hold of the rope. Maggie spent most of the day ferrying women and children, so we could go no further, because she was worn out. It was something to know that many people who would never have made the crossing without her help, had got another stage on their journey.

We had a dry night and set off in great style on a path which we thought would be les muddy, but which wasn't. This was the first day the party straggled. Previously, two of us had always acted as 'whippers-in'. We were fit and could put up with the very real strain of having to go at the pace of the slowest and wait until the weaker had recovered enough strength to make a further effort. Twice we came to the usual sort of camp, full of dead men's bodies and all uncleanliness. The next day the party from the sugar factory in Burma who had earlier showed us such kindness lent us a riding pony, which was a great help. We used to walk for hours without speaking at all. The next camp was like the others, quite unusable, and we made a clearing in the jungle and camped there.

On the outskirts of the camps as we passed through next morning, the doctor and I who were the last of our party, came upon an English officer lying in a hut alone, and looking very poorly. He showed us his legs which were badly swollen and covered with huge and painful sores. His party had gone on without him, leaving him a tin of bully. The doctor did what he could, but we had very little with us in the way of medicines. The trouble was sandflies. After the third river, these dreadful flies often made our nights sheer torment. We all agreed that the fiercest mosquitoes and the worst leeches with which the road abounded, were trifles compared with these flies. Since most of the bites were on the legs, as we sloshed through the mud, the bites became infected and that was the start of serious trouble.

The next camp we came to was run by a soldier and some planters, but it wasn't properly organised yet. They were making a clearing so that food could be dropped by planes and in the meantime, some was being brought by coolies, but not in very large quantities. Still, there was a little for everyone and, what was far more important, we got the longed for feeling that something was being done, and that eventually it had dawned on someone that many people were having a long walk in considerable discomfort. We stayed here for some hours and helped as far as we could. In the evening, we were given tea at a similar camp, and told that as they had no food, the best thing was that we should push on another seven miles where there was a camp with abundant supplies. There was a river to cross on the way, but here we found a proper raft with men to work it. When we reached the camp the Scots planter in charge made us most welcome, and gave us food and a bench in a hut to sleep on.

Our troubles, we felt were now as good as over. We were made very welcome at the camp in the evening, and given as much rice dahl and onion as we could eat, and then a meal out of tins before we went to bed. Coming down the hillside to this camp was the worst place for falls on the whole road, and some of us averaged about seven good shaking falls to the mile. One of our men had such bad fever that he could not even cling on to the pony which had been provided for him, and so we had to make arrangements for coolies to carry him on a litter. But for our doctor, he must surely have died. As it was, when he reached camp, it was obvious that he couldn't go on without a day's rest. And so to save overcrowding in this camp, all of us but four pushed on to the next. Next day we made a start but the road was so steep and so deep in mud, that sometimes we made only four or five hundred yards in the hour, and two or three times, in spite of every effort these magnificent coolies made, the litter tilted and shot the sick man into the mud. We only did six miles that day, and there was no accommodation. But the English planter in charge said we could spend the night there, and he also gave us food. Next evening we reached camp without difficulty, but the following morning it was soon apparent that something must have been wrong with the food we'd had, and there were frequent and sudden stops.

But everything was comparatively easy now. The rivers were bridged, there was tea to be had on the march, and we knew that only a day or two more would bring us to the railway. Our next camp was a village on top of a heavy hill. Here again we got good food and a dry place to sleep, and were told that there was only one more camp between us and the railway. There was a small hospital here, where I had my hand lanced. Some days back I had fallen on a razor sharp bamboo which had sliced through my hand which was badly swollen and poisoned by this time. One of my ankles was in a similar condition, but since it had held out for several days, there didn't seem much point in stopping here with so few more miles to go. We were on a Jeep road now, no longer a track, and after a steep mile or two, down-hill all the way, we rounded a corner and could see, far below us, railway lines. We all began to laugh and talk together, until someone began to sing 'Now Thank We All Our God' and then we all sang according to our ability.

It was really a small mineral line but it led to the line we wanted, and soon we were rushing along in a railcar to the junction where we piled into a coal truck. As we passed through the stations, we could see motor cars and officers in nicely starched uniforms, and all the things which had lately become so unreal to us. But amazingly, above everything, we were moving without walking, without a ha'porth of effort on our part. And so we got to India."

CHAPTER SEVENTEEN

After the Japanese had Left (1946-1948)

One of the first groups of British soldiers to enter Rangoon when the war with Japan was coming to an end, was to include Capt. Claude Carter of the Fourteenth Army, (later to become my husband), the erstwhile young gunner who had done his bit to defend Bristol in 1940, later leading endless convoys up and down the Burma road, before finally ending up in India, at the battle of Kohima, just across the Burmese border.

War in the Far East ended officially on 14th August 1945, following the bombing of Hiroshima and Nagasaki, but it appears that a huge problem arose as to how to alert the scattered Japanese troops on the ground to the fact that the conflict was finally over, for they were under orders to fight to the death. As a result, Claude told me that he was to witness a strange manoeuvre over Mingaladon airport, Rangoon, which was to lead to the surrender of the 33rd Japanese Army, apparently only founded in Rangoon in April of the previous year. Watching closely, he saw twenty-four British Spitfires led by a group captain of the R.A.F. flying in ever lower circles over the city, forcing down a large transport aircraft emblazoned with huge, unmistakable red Japanese insignia, alleged to be carrying Field Marshal Count Terauchi – commander of the Southern Expeditionary Army Group of the Japanese Imperial Army – and other very senior officers. The chief of staff of the British Twelfth Army took the surrender, and the encircling British aircraft finally persuaded the Japanese soldiers that all was over.

Once Mingaladon was safely in British hands, Bishop and Mrs. West were able to return, and this they did with all speed. Mrs. West was serving with the W.V.S. (Womens' Voluntary Service) and got down to work immediately, while the Bishop attempted to contact what remained of his scattered flock. They found the Cathedral and Bishopscourt still standing, but in a despicable condition.

Capt. Peter Tubbs (whose father was Bishop of Rangoon from 1928 to 1934, and whom I'd played with as a child) entered the city at much the same time as Claude, and gives us this description: "We went along Commissioner Road to the cathedral. The main hospital on the right and the two schools on the left of the road were undamaged though closed. We turned into the cathedral whose outer appearance, except for a few windows, seemed unchanged. As we went in by the porch a foul smell greeted us, and as we stopped at the font and looked around it was difficult to recognize the inside as having been a church. It had been transformed into a toddy distillery and the foul smell came from fermenting yeast and huge dead rats lying about. The whole of the north aisle was taken up by two large presses made of heavy timber, and broken bits of large earthenware jars lay near. The whole nave was bricked in to form a large room fifteen feet high, and as we had no torches we struck matches and peered around. Part of it seemed to have been a cattle stall and part a store for materials used in distilling, and rats ran around everywhere.

We emerged by a small doorway in the bricking opposite the altar and by the communion rails. All furniture, ornaments, tablets, lectern, pulpit, in fact everything had gone. There was another bricked-in room in place of the altar where we peered out and found the same sort of contents. Outside on the south side were huge ovens of some sort. We were glad to get away from the smell and into the fresh air again." His experiences at Bishopscourt were no better. "Three cows stood on the verandah chewing the cud, and looking at us as if we were intruders! We went in and over the whole house, which was just a shambles, and of course every bit of furniture and decoration had gone, except for the two safes in the study which lay battered open on the floor."

But what of the indigenous clergy themselves who had remained in Burma? Had they survived? The bishop was able to meet ten of them from the Delta, only a week after his arrival and said, "They had come through a flooded and *dacoit*-infested country. Their frayed and tattered garments spoke of the impoverishment of the past three years. Deprived of their buildings, their European advisers and colleagues, their organizations, their salaries and church funds; threatened and bullied by the Japanese authorities, their people killed and massacred sometimes before their eyes, themselves or fellow priests strung up and mercilessly beaten – even their thoughts and motives probed and extracted by cross-examination, and sometimes even by torture – all these they had survived, and they told their story in simple and matter-of-fact terms. All they asked was to begin again and to get their churches back." Of course, during the Japanese occupation, services had continued to be held up and down the country, but always in secret, in private houses or jungle clearings.

One of Bishop West's first measures was to appoint three priests as archdeacons, all of whom had proved their mettle in time of war. John Aung Hla was placed in charge of the Mandalay area; Hla Gyaw was given the Toungoo beat; and Luke Po Kun, the Delta region. Shortly afterwards, the venerable George Appleton returned from England to take up his post as director of public relations. It was he who had escaped to India with Uncle Will, and who had acted as archdeacon (after Rev. Higginbotham had died) carrying out his post as best he could from the U.K. Now he was to be made head of a government department, with control over the chief English newspaper as well as the radio and the vernacular press, and was just the right man to give spiritual leadership to a country in disarray.

Some of the old Christian schools – closed for the duration – had already sprung up again, almost of their own accord, and were ready for development. In Moulmein, a few children armed with a slate or two were found squatting under a house learning their lessons, while in Mandalay they were being taught in the church, and Hla Gyaw had meanwhile started a whole host of village schools.

All this resurgence of life came together on October 16th 1945, when His Excellency, the Governor of Burma, spoke at the dedication service of the Cathedral, now cleansed of its awful smell, but still without illumination. On this great occasion, the place was lit by the headlights of Jeeps and other military vehicles, which completely surrounded the building, while this prayer was said: "Nothing can withstand a mighty onslaught of the spirit. We have shown our greatness as a people in the darkest hour of adversity. Humbly we ask God to make us great in simplicity and obedience, as we seek to bring to birth a human society in which it is normal for men to love one another."

Meanwhile, throughout the whole country, the political situation was tense. Aung San and his deputy Ne Win headed what was then known as the Anti-Fascist League, becoming the People's Volunteer Organisation in 1946, their main aim being to see Burma returned to full independence once again. Throughout the first year after the armistice, there seems to have been a battle of wills between the newly returned Governor of Burma, Sir Reginald Dorman-Smith, and Aung San, with the charismatic Burmese leader growing in popularity and stature. Nevertheless the whole country was in a mess, with constant strike action and very little law and order. By now, Lord Louis Mountbatten of Burma had become Viceroy of India,

Rangoon Cathedral in 2007.

following his years as Supreme Allied Commander of the Southeast Asia Theatre of War. It was he who had received the final surrender of the Japanese, and it was he who was now beginning to see the start of Burmese nationalism in a somewhat more positive light than some of his less adventurous colleagues, being prepared to give his backing to the new Anti-Fascist League.

In September 1946, Sir Hubert Rance arrived to take over from Dorman-Smith as the new (and last) Governor of Burma, and quickly set up an executive council, heading it himself as chairman with Aung San as his deputy. Full scale strikes were averted by this move, but in exchange, Aung San demanded elections for the following year and full independence by January 1948, when Burma would also cease its membership of the British Commonwealth. At this time, and under pressure, Prime Minister Attlee declared, "It is for the people of Burma to decide their own future… for the sake of the Burmese people, it is of the utmost importance that this should be an orderly – though rapid – progress."

Uncle Will came back to Burma in the middle of all this, arriving on 19th May 1946, having served as an army padre in Shillong, India, before enjoying two years' furlough in England where he had acted as priest-in-charge of Acton, a Suffolk village neighbouring Bures. He must certainly have wondered whether this was to be his last visit home, and setting out for Burma on 12th April 1946, on the S.S. *Durham Castle,* wrote from Southampton: "It was difficult saying 'goodbye' this morning, but you were all very helpful. John and Fan sent me off at Bures station, and when the train started, I found myself sitting next to one of my Acton parochial church councillors We did not travel together long as he got out at Chappel, but he helped me over the first ten minutes which is the difficult period. My love to you all, Edith, John, Katie, Bess and Fan – your loving brother Will."

It was to be a crowded journey, for on 21st April he said, "We landed our Italian prisoners at Naples, 1,500 of them, and since then there has been a reshuffle of the decks and we have a good deal more space to walk in." Later, he told them that it only took eighteen days to get from Southampton to Calcutta, compared with the six weeks and four days of the wartime journey in reverse, two years previously.

On 19th May he wrote, "This is my first letter with a Burma stamp on it for four years, but it is not a familiar Burma, everything at present is very strange. Rangoon is a very sad place, the destruction on the banks of the river and the wharfs is terrible; there are large holes in the roads, bomb craters not yet filled in, and it will take a long time to get back to its pre-war condition. I am told there is a train to Mandalay twice a week, covered trucks, you sit and sleep on the floor and the journey takes two days. In the meantime I am here, and the service at the cathedral this morning seemed very familiar."

On 2nd June he had managed to cadge a lift to Mandalay with George Tidey (now back in Burma and in good heart after his desperate trek to India) and reported: "St. Mary's church has been very badly knocked about, but Matthew has got a new roof on it and a reasonable floor, though the windows are still just gaping holes. The whole town is a mass of ruins and little bamboo huts, but the Christ Church compound has remained practically untouched since I came away, and Queen Victoria's font is undamaged. I understand the whole place was used as a hay store and has not suffered badly at all. The Royal School was also a hay store and is similarly undamaged. The Brotherhood House is in good order too, and is now serving as wards for paying patients, both upstairs and downstairs."

For the next few months Uncle Will was to be stationed at Holy Cross College, Rangoon, (where he was sharing a room with Mr. Tidey), his task being to train the Divinity students and to take his turn at preaching and leading services at the cathedral. A great deal of looting was going on, and the college was often a target.

On 1st September 1946 he writes from Rangoon, "I have one great piece of history to report. The consecration stone from the altar which we buried in Mandalay in 1942 has been found. When I was in Mandalay a month ago I left some money behind to pay for digging (to a depth of seven feet) and this week I have heard from *Saya* Chit Tway that he has now got the stone in his house safely. So now that stone has survived two evacuations; it was originally let into the wooden altar in 1872, buried from1879-1884, replaced in the same wooden altar, buried from 1942-46 and now awaits inserting in a new altar in the same position as formerly. I feel so pleased about it all."

In September Rangoon was strike-bound, with the police demanding more money, the post offices closed and the trains only running intermittently. By mid October, when everyday life had returned more or less to normal (under the joint leadership of Governor Rance and Aung San), an Anglican Diocesan Council was held in Rangoon, using Burmese as the principal language for the first time, with interpretation into English when required. Uncle Will approved of this change of procedure now that the indigenous clergy far outnumbered the British, but found the whole rigmarole somewhat slow.

By January 1947 the political situation had worsened. Strikes were now occurring everywhere with most of the banks and markets closed, school children being told to stay at home, and the university also shutting its doors. Uncle Will rarely made political comments in his letters, but now there were constant references to the tense situation, as he wondered – in some trepidation – what was going to happen next.

On 16th March he wrote to his sisters, "I have some news for you. You must get used to a new address, Christ Church, Mandalay. It won't be my home because the buildings are not yet released by government, but the bishop sent for me three days ago and said that my special work at Holy Cross would end with today's ordination service and that the military were relinquishing charge of St. Mary's Church at Mandalay, and he wished me to go back there."

Back in his beloved Mandalay, Uncle Will soon settled down to the old routine, taking services at St. Mary's with *Saya* Chit Tway, helping Archdeacon Aung Hla at Christ Church, and visiting the outlying stations of his 'parish'. He was lodging with Mr. Thursfield from the Bombay Trading Corporation (cousin to Padre Thursfield of the old days, the priest who advertised his bike for sale in the middle of a sermon). On 30th March he wrote, "I have had a busy week and a happy one, trying to find out where people live and get in contact with them. The destruction in Mandalay is just awful and people live in funny places which one would have formerly considered quite impossible as a house."

On 13th April comes this entry: "Polling has been taking place for the last three days for U. Aung San's government, but there was fortunately no contest in Mandalay. I believe the opposition to U. Aung San has been negligible, and I hope he will be given a reasonable opportunity of showing what he can do. No doubt, some things will be wrong, but so they were under British administration."

May was unbearable and he wrote, "Very hot, and I am a mass of prickly heat which I don't usually get at this time of year, only in September. I am glad that my little tract on Buddhism is at last being printed, but it seems a very inopportune moment for it. It was written three years ago for the benefit of soldiers in Burma, and to print it now when soldiers are leaving as quickly as ever they can seems rather stupid."

On 20th July 1947 comes this brief but ominous entry "Both congregations were very thin today. Yesterday, U. Aung San and several more ministers were shot in Rangoon, and people think it wiser to stay indoors today." A week later he wrote "After the assassinations of 19th July, the bazaar and all businesses were closed for three days. It is all rather sad, as Aung San in his last address had finished up saying something like this: 'If this country is to be really free, people must learn to work, work, work', and within eight days of his death, there have been four days of doing nothing at all, and when the state funeral takes place a month hence, there will be more holidays I expect."

It seems that during a meeting of the Burmese Executive Council a group of men in army fatigues had burst into the council chamber, killing the guard outside, before firing at Aung San and his team. Only three of the men in the room survived, and with the death of their leader, the peaceful future of Burma lay in tatters, with the dangers of a communist uprising hugely increased. Shortly afterwards, agreement seems to have been reached that Thakin Nu should succeed Aung San with Ne Win as his deputy, and much useless speculation followed as to who the assailants might have been, for there were inevitably widely differing factions among the compatriots. No mention seems to have been made of the fact that Aung San left behind a grieving widow and a beautiful two year old daughter, who would one day, in due course of time, become a winner of the Nobel Peace Prize, known to the whole world as the leader of Burma's National League for Democracy, Aung San Suu Kyi.

On 17th August, just a month after the assassination, Uncle Will wrote, "All English officials seem to be leaving this country now, the Commissioner of Mandalay left a fortnight ago and the Sessions Judge had a farewell dinner last evening." Three weeks later, "A party of thirteen English people left this week for England, not to return." But the church did its best to remain constant, continuing as always with its ongoing life of prayer and worship.

In September, Uncle Will was saddened by a visit to Madaya, not far from Mandalay. The mission here had been started many years ago in memory of the Rev. James Colbeck, the valiant priest who had rescued so many members of the Burmese royal family from imprisonment and death at the start of Thibaw's reign – a great hero of my uncle's. In his letter home, Will reported that, "Madaya is a sad sight, worse even than Mandalay. The whole place was burned down in a village fire about 1940 and it was burned again in the fighting in 1942 and again in the return fighting of 1945."

In October he wrote, "I am now gazetted as an officiating chaplain to the forces" and was more than a little surprised about this, saying, "We no longer have any British or Indian soldiers in Mandalay, and the NAAFI shops were closed down a fortnight ago, so I do not see any point in my appointment."

Will was now in process of moving house again, the newly arrived Commissioner in Mandalay, Mr. Foster, having invited him to share his home. On 19th October came this description of the move: "I managed to borrow a handcart with pneumatic tyres (one of them very flat) and moved my books and bookcases and my big box in four trips – the whole distance is only 200 yards."

A Diocesan Council at Maymyo, in which Will played a major part, was to take place later that month, followed by many adventures with a Jeep that a friend had lent him. Like his brother Charlie, Will much preferred his bicycle to a car, and wrote, "I took the Jeep to Myitnge for evensong on Monday, and had trouble with the lights on the way back. I expect the wires from the battery had got mixed up; when I drove fast, the lamps were bright; when I drove slower they became less bright, and when I met some bullock carts and had practically to stop, the lights went out."

Will celebrated Christmas 1947 with all the usual joyful services, and on 28th December wrote home about these, adding that, "Quite a procession has just gone past the house. Thakin Nu has arrived in Mandalay. The procession was something like this. Jeep… Jeep… car… two 15 cwts full of soldiers… car… very big car… two Jeeps… station wagon… Jeep… Jeep. The circuit house where he is putting up is at the end of this road, and Thursfield has facetiously commented 'And we are all within hand-grenade range.'" He adds "What a business it is to be an official in a country like this! Next Sunday we shall not be allowed to pray for George our king in church, or I may be run in for treason!"

The 4th January 1948 was Independence Day, with U Nu appointed as Prime Minister, taking over the government from Sir Hubert Rance, who immediately left the country together with the last British Regiment on Burmese soil, the King's Own Yorkshire Light Infantry. Uncle Will wrote home, "I don't know what is happening in the town but today is Independence Day and there are great goings on. They began at four a.m. with everything that could make a noise doing its utmost: factory sirens, steamer hooters, railway engines and some big bombs which made the house shake. I was in bed and remained there, but the Commissioner had to be on duty to pull down the British flag and pull up a Burmese flag: red, with one big star for Burma and five little stars for Karens, Shans, Kachins, Indians and… (I wonder whether number five is for Chinese or English people). Everyone is out in the fort where there was a big parade and march past at eight o'clock. I could not go as it coincided with church."

On 11th January: "We are now feeling quieter after four very noisy days of independence festivities and it is good to be quiet again. Mandalay has been full of sports and races of all kinds, children, adults, ponies, bullocks, boats… I believe the girls' cycle race was one of the most exciting events. Girls on cycles is quite a new idea, and they require a wide berth in the road as they have not realised as yet any rules. I believe the race was equally devoid of rules and there were several collisions.

I spent two days this week at Maymyo, and invited myself for the night to the Lewis house". (He was the chaplain there.) "They have given up the old parsonage near the Garrison Church – the Garrison Church is closed and the parsonage has reverted to the Public Works Department and they now live in one of the 'quarters' which used to belong to the Club. The Club is entirely gone and only one building of the quarters is still standing, but it is close to All Saints' Church and is the right size for a newly married couple and they will be comfortable there.

Maymyo was just as noisy as Mandalay, but rather a different kind of noise. Mandalay people were very pleased about independence and were genuine in their rejoicing. Maymyo people were not quite sure whether they were pleased or not, and so they rather over decorated their buildings and made a big noise to pretend they were very happy. It was strange driving into Maymyo from Mandalay (I went with the Commissioner) as an enormous flag staff had been erected right in the middle of the cross roads below All Saints' Church. The crossroads always need care to negotiate, and I thought as we approached that the authorities were making a roundabout there to simplify the traffic problem, but I was wrong; it was a big flag staff planted right in the middle of everything."

On 1st February 1948 he wrote "I don't like the news of Mr. Gandhi's death a little bit. He seemed to be the one person in India to keep people together. I hope it will not have repercussions in this country too."

Archdeacon Aung Hla, in the meantime, had decided to go to England for a period, to 'look and learn on the job' as he put it, and Uncle Will was deputising for him, which meant many journeys to Rangoon and back. At the end of May, he wrote, in some desperation, "One difficulty just now is communication with Rangoon. Last Sunday the railway was breached by the communists between here and Rangoon, and they also breached the road, so there has been no communication between Upper and Lower Burma except by wireless. The communists are being a real nuisance; they have been getting at the headworks of the Mandalay Canal and cutting off the water supply. The one thing that Burma can really do well is to grow rice and the world wants more food badly, and the communists are now trying to hinder the irrigation of the fields on which the rice crop depends. Of course they get chased off by the soldiers, but as soon as the soldiers are withdrawn, they come back again."

On 8th August 1948, Will wrote home about the big Festival Service at Christ Church. "It was a very nice service indeed. *Saya* Chit E took the service in a very loud voice, supported by his brother *Saya* Chit Tway, with another loud voice, and Bishop's Commissary Archdeacon Hla Gyaw preached a simple sermon in a very gentle voice. My business was to play the St. Mary's harmonium which was brought round for the occasion, and to eat mohinga (rice noodles in fish soup) after the service was over."

Meanwhile, the country was still in chaos, as described by Uncle Will at the end of August. "Much trouble from the communists everywhere. The rains are getting near their end, but the farmers are intimidated and dare not go near their fields." This letter was written from a little mat hut inside the Methodist Mission compound, to which Will had just moved, overjoyed to have his own quarters at last, however basic. "The hut is a great success. It has a thatched roof and mat walling and has three rooms, sixteen feet by twelve feet, with an electric light bulb in each room and a little verandah on the north. Last night we had a heavy rainstorm, but the roof only drips in one place, a very little drip." He was to share meals with the Head of Mission, and adds this heartfelt comment: "A bonus is that his cook makes homemade bread, really lovely English bread."

Later he wrote, "At last I have got some galvanized iron to mend St. Mary's church roof; it has taken many months to get it. Parts of Mandalay are having a plague of woolly caterpillars, millions of them; fortunately this compound is not yet in their direction, but St. Mary's church has been full of them, and squashed caterpillars make a nasty mess on the church floor. The Burmans, of course, are particular about killing things, and they just collect them in boxes out of their huts and put them by the roadside and they crawl into someone else's house. I should think last night's rain may have drowned quite a number."

In October, Will was to preside over talks about the possible re-opening of the Queen Alexandra Hospital, Mandalay, a prospect very dear to his heart. It was noted that "The government won't allow people to come in as clergy or evangelists, but they might allow people in as doctors and nurses."

My uncle was now hard at work preparing no less than seven addresses – in both Burmese and English – which he would shortly have to deliver in Rangoon at a big retreat. On 5th December he wrote from Mandalay, "We sleep at the station tonight ready for the 5 a.m. train tomorrow morning, seven clergy, and we hope to reach Rangoon in due course. The train has been running seven days consecutively, so I think the chances are that we shall reach Rangoon in two days, but in case we don't I have a tin of cheese and a tin of bully in reserve, and will buy a loaf of bread before I start. It was my early service at Myitnge today, so altogether I am rather muddle-headed. Retreat addresses are only more or less finished and packing more or less incomplete. I wonder what I shall leave behind. There is great excitement today because the newly printed Burmese hymn book has arrived; it is a joint Anglican/Methodist book and has a good selection of hymns."

The following letter from Rangoon is dated 13ᵗʰ December 1948: "I left my *basha* (hut) last Sunday evening and slept at Mandalay railway station on my camp bed, and we reached Rangoon on Tuesday evening without misadventure, except that I think I picked up a germ somewhere, because at Rangoon station I started a bilious attack and arrived at Bishopscourt to be sick and go straight to bed. It was rather a bad attack and I had to go and see a doctor, but he gave me some sulphaquinadine tablets and told me to take two every three hours day and night for three days, and I am now much better. We are well into our 'retreat' and as so often happens, are already rather in difficulties. We are all of us, thirty or more, at Holy Cross, and last evening we were told that something had gone wrong with the water pipe-line and since we arrived all the bathroom and sanitation appliances have ceased to function, which is very awkward when we are full up with people. The Bishop of Calcutta arrived on Friday, and gave us his charge on Saturday and preached a big sermon in the Cathedral yesterday. He was a fellow army chaplain in the 1914-18 war, and was Bishop of Assam when I was working at Shillong, so he was an old friend, and that was why I was invited to Bishopscourt to stay. Yesterday afternoon I moved up here."

On returning home, Will added a postcript, "Rev. Aung Hla has returned from England, full of zeal, so I happily am no longer acting archdeacon."

CHAPTER EIGHTEEN

Anarchy in the Streets and New Burmese Bishops (1949-1950)

January 1949 opens with Bishop West asking William Garrad to consider becoming his assistant bishop. My uncle was now sixty seven years old, far and away the most senior of the four English Anglican clergy remaining in Burma, the other three all being in their thirties. After much thought, he wrote home, "Ten years ago when the matter came up, I declined after having had plenty of time to consult with others. This time, he asked me to wire my answer, and I found it very difficult. The indigenous people are hardly ripe just yet, though in a few years time they will be. One great trouble is travelling. I am not as young as I used to be and things are taking a bad turn again. The Monwa train had to be cancelled for four days because it was being shot at. The Shwebo train got held up one day and did not reach Mandalay at all, and had to go back. Yesterday's paper reports the Bhamo mail post being fired at so heavily, only a few miles from Mandalay, that it had to turn round and return. To be bishop and afraid to travel sounds not quite right, and to be an assistant missionary bishop would make a furlough in England very difficult, so I wired back, 'No enthusiasm. Willing to act if necessary,' and I have heard no more since." At the end of the month he lunched at Maymyo with Bishop West who was on holiday there, and writes, "I think the idea of me as assistant bishop is more or less a thing of the past. There is the question of age limit at sixty-five, but the bishop says this is a case of 'special circumstances'. I do not agree."

Meanwhile the political situation was changing from bad to worse. In February a rumour was doing the rounds that the insurgents had taken Mingaladon airport and that a hundred miles of railway from Toungoo was also in their hands. There was a government strike of public servants, with all post and telegraph offices closed, and no telephone operators working. "Maymyo is reported to have been captured but no one knows whether this is true or not. Myitnge also, only twelve miles away, has changed hands more than once."

On 11th March came this: "I am writing early this week because a plane is expected today to take away women and children who may like to get out of town… I think I shall probably move from my hut and live with Firth (the chaplain) when his wife has left; the walls of his house will give more protection. There has been shooting in Mandalay." In due course he moved in, and a fortnight later reported, "Still here, and still safe and well. Firth and I occupy our house. We have no neighbours on three sides, but on the fourth side is a good block of five houses, so our little oasis of people number two or three hundred persons who can be relied on to help each other. There is a good supply of water in this compound, and we are able to help others who are short. About ¾ miles away is the leper house which is where we should make for if the worst should happen, and we have each sent a suitcase with a change of clothes there in case of emergency. The government officials have run away, mobs of people are going about looting whatever property they can find unattended. I had occasion to go to the hospital one day and found that the doctors and nurses had also run away, but the patients are still in hospital wondering what they should do. I am not at all happy about our S.P.G. compound, which has been part of the hospital these last three years. The Brotherhood House was the private patients' block, The Royal School the nurses' quarters, and the other building the servants' quarters. If they are left empty, no doubt they will be looted too, but the government commandeered them and has not handed them back, so I suppose they are still responsible. The Maymyo road is now opening; all English people have left for Rangoon. There has been a lot of fighting there but there seems to have been only one member of our church killed, a woman picking flowers in her garden and caught by a stray bullet. The Myitnge people are safe, and came to church on Sunday. We had a big offertory with their thank offerings."

On 3rd April Will wrote, "There have been more refugees in the S.P.G. compound lately, quite a number of them, the gaolers from the Mandalay gaol. The communists have released all the prisoners and given fire-arms to quite a number of them so the gaol staff have had to go underground, and some of them are Christians, and they have brought some of their friends with them".

Will's letter of 10th April reported "We are still under martial law and no communications are possible with the world outside, but things are quieter. The house is now more like itself again, and the bookcases back in their places. They served their purpose well as barricades, and a camp bed downstairs behind brick walls with the book cases guarding the doors proved quite effective. Things came to a climax on Wednesday afternoon and then suddenly ceased, when Fort Dufferin (the old king's palace) surrendered. For the last two days it was difficult to go outside, and we had no idea as to what was happening in the town. The electric light was off for more than a week, and the wireless was therefore out of action. Things are happier now and the corpses cleared away from the streets, and when the government returns, the military will retire out of sight, I hope."

On 16th April he wrote, "The military are still in charge and do not appear to wish to give up their authority to the civil people, who have now mostly returned, and want to get to work again, and so nothing is really started yet." On the 24th came this: "We all thought our troubles were over, as the People's Volunteer Organisation were welcoming the government officials and helping them to get back control. Last Sunday, Mandalay was divided into three parts, one part taken over by government, one part held by the army, and a third part still under the P.V.O.s (or levies). Then on Sunday night, something went wrong. The P.V.O.s made a complete volte face and attacked the army and the government and drove them into the fort, and there has been fighting ever since. Our doors and windows have had to be barricaded again and things are unpleasant. Twice we have had to open up everything and submit to being searched, and each time things disappear. The telephone receiver was taken once; and the other time my boots attracted their attention, and three pairs disappeared. My feet are size 9 and my boots are much too large for any Burman to wear, but they took them all the same. On Friday it was reported that more soldiers were coming from Maymyo and there was heavy fighting, and yesterday we were in hopes that things would have been quieter today, and we might have had church, but they are far from quiet and the P.V.O.s are said to be boasting they are mopping up the newly arrived reinforcements. The leper house, which is a mile outside Mandalay on the Maymyo road, had to be evacuated for a time while people chased each other round the buildings, but the patients are back again today and no lives were lost."

As 1949 continued its chaotic way, Uncle Will heard from Bishop West that Archdeacon Aung Hla and Francis Ah Mya were to be appointed as assistant bishops. On receiving this news, Uncle Will wrote home, "It is good for me to be alive to see a Burmese and a Karen bishop, but I wish the first indigenous bishop might have been someone of the calibre of old *Saya* George. The modern young Burmans do not have the character or the dignity of the people of those times, though I suppose their knowledge of English is a good deal greater."

Rev. Aung Hla now gave Will the task of looking after All Saints', Maymyo, as well as St Mary's, Mandalay, which in practice was going to be rather a problem. His letter says, "I do not think there is a single English person left in Maymyo, and I don't know where to stay, unless perhaps I ask for a room in St. Michael's school compound. As to getting to and fro, trains are unsafe and motoring impossible through attacks by *dacoits* and the exorbitant price of fuel." At the end of May, Will wrote, "Petrol in Mandalay is pretty well non-existent just now; a week ago it was Rs 12 a gallon, and on Thursday it was Rs 100 for 4 gallons. I don't know what today's figure may be, but the communists are sitting cosily in the oil fields, and the export of petrol is stopped. One advantage there is, as it makes cycling a great deal less dangerous, as beyond military cars, there are no motors on the road."

Despite all these problems, Will did his best to cope, managing services in both churches whenever possible, but he commented, "The situation of two churches in Maymyo is getting acute, and the congregation at St. Matthew's is large, while with the withdrawal of the English residents, All Saints is left high and dry. It seems such a pity, as All Saints is the most beautiful church in the diocese, whereas St. Matthew's was built for utilitarian purposes and is quite unpretentious."

In July the newly consecrated Bishop John Aung Hla was welcomed back to Mandalay at the big Transfiguration Festival and everyone was delighted, while in October a wonderful letter arrived from the Commissioner giving instructions to return the S.P.G. compound buildings to the Winchester Mission.

On 30th October comes this amusing passage: "Bishop Aung Hla is in Mandalay today for the dedication of the first local air strip, two miles away. I had arranged for a truck to be at St. Mary's church at 9 a.m. and we went, about forty of us, straight from our 8 a.m. service to the air strip. Bishop Aung Hla and *Saya* Chit Tway and others were doing the same at Christ Church, but unfortunately the bishop's car developed a flat tyre and he was late for his appointment. The aeroplane people came after me to take his place, but I had nothing prepared and asked that the Muslims should have their service first, while I went to look for the bishop. The Muslim worship was rather picturesque and at the end the spectators clapped! Then a Chinaman gave a long musical intoned monologue and he was also clapped! Then Aung Hla read a psalm and said a prayer in his red episcopal vestments and drew more clapping! Then others followed, and at last four planes arrived and made a big

Bishop Aung Hla.

dust on landing. Everything went off quite safely, but the heat was terrific and it was midday before we got back."

A week later, on a more serious note, he commented, "Now in Mandalay we have the planes flying just over the roof as they come down to land, and a worse noise still as they start to go up. Still, a lot of people feel safer with an air-strip so close, and think it would be easier to get away if a time of emergency comes again."

On 20th November, Will was back at last in Brotherhood House, which he was to share with Bishop Aung Hla. He wrote, "On my first night, the house had no doors at all upstairs or down, but by last night one room downstairs was able to be locked up, and in course of time we shall become fully fledged. The carpenter has ten men working with him. Everything is muddly, with dust inches deep and unsavoury smells, but one sitting room and one bedroom are now reasonably clean, and gradually the rest of the house will get better, though I am afraid the bishop and his wife will still find plenty of dirt on Tuesday when they are probably coming into residence. I shall have my own cook boy to feed me."

A week later he wrote, "The Bishop and his wife are now here and I think will be agreeable companions. The insurgents have been more active lately and I am afraid are developing a new technique. We hear shooting frequently at nights, but two nights ago there were specially loud bangs, two of them, which I am told were land mines. That is a new thing. Also, we had an air pilot in hospital this week, with a bullet in him which passed through his heel and his sit-upon and is still in his body. Fortunately, it turned out less serious than seemed likely and after three days he was able to be flown back to Rangoon hospital for his operation. But shooting at planes is a new idea and not to be encouraged. Our house now has all the downstairs doors on the side facing the road, and the upstairs doors on that side will have next priority. My study-office has doors too on the compound side. The bishop and I are messing separately, and I hope to continue my own establishment. The bishop has a wife and son, and sister, a Karen woman and child, and I think I am better alone."

By 1ˢᵗ January 1950, Uncle Will had been in Maymyo for nearly three weeks, deputising for *Saya* Chit E. He was enjoying it, but it was very cold and he had five blankets on his bed at night, and an electric heater both morning and evening. On Christmas Day he reports that there was a congregation of 225 at St. Matthew's church, with ninety-eight communicants, and a congregation of 153 at All Saints, with eighty-two communicants, so he was pleased.

In the middle of the month, he was back in Mandalay, where he had previously had trouble with his cook-boy. Now he writes, "Yes, I have a new cook. He has a face rather like Bill Sykes, but as far as I can see is quite a useful cook. At present we are getting on all right. My house warming party seems to have been a great success, especially the lovely tea. It was all done by the ladies of St. Mary's congregation, and I think home made patties and curry puffs are nicer than those which come from a shop."

On 19ᵗʰ February he wrote from Mandalay, "I do not think I have yet told you but I have to go to Rangoon in two weeks' time. Bishop West asked me to preach at the ordination service on March 5th, and since then he has also asked me to conduct a quiet day for the candidates, so I have said I would go if he would pay my travelling expenses. The only way to go is by air, and that costs a lot of money… I went to Myitnge one day this week and wish I had stayed at home. The engines on the trains nowadays burn wood and I was calmly reading my book as we went along when someone gave me a heavy thump on the back, and when I demurred, he told me that I had a hole burned in the back of my cassock by a spark from the engine! Fortunately, it was an old cassock, but even so one grudges anything in the way of clothes in these hard times. I am told that the engines on the Maymyo line are given coal to use on the uphill journey, but have to burn wood when coming down the hill."

In Rangoon, on 6th March he said, "I am writing this at Bishopscourt where I am now staying. I came from Mandalay to Rangoon by plane on Friday and did not enjoy it much. We bumped about quite a lot and most of us were distinctly thoughtful most of the way. We sat in two long rows facing inwards, and so could see each other, and we were various shades of green and yellow."

He reported home from Mandalay on 12th March, saying, "I think my little jaunt to Rangoon was probably good for me, though I hope it will not be repeated just yet. The journey back was certainly more pleasant than my journey there, but that was chiefly due to a small boy, or rather a big boy who came running to greet me when my luggage was being weighed, and told me he was a pupil of mine when I was at Shwebo. He has just finished his university exams and was on his way home for the holidays, and he chose a good place for me on the plane, so that I could see out of a window. Then, when we were properly started he produced a *Tit Bits* from his pocket for me to read – it must be quite fifty years since I read a *Tit Bits* but it was quite amusing without being vulgar – and about halfway home produced a paper bag with two slices of sponge cake."

In March, Will treated himself to a new saddle for his bike, his saddle springs having broken completely into two pieces after much pedalling to and fro. By April he was having more bilious attacks, and was commuting between Mandalay and Maymyo quite frequently, with life becoming something of a grind, as he found his energy sagging. Miss Cam had been very helpful with ideas about how to re-start the Union Hospital in Mandalay (the old Alexandra Children's Hospital) and he ended his letter by saying that, "Mandalay is very hot and I am trying to rig up a *punkah* to work with my foot as we used to do in times past."

The 9th July was a red letter day, when the new Burmese prayer books were delivered. "The large convoy of ships arrived safely on Wednesday after endless muddles, and a small box of fifty-eight books has come and I expect there is another box of ninety-two more somewhere not yet unloaded. The books look very nice and some of the worst misprints have been neatly corrected. Aung Hla is a very tidy writer and also a bit of an artist, and I think it was he who did the actual work."

On 30th July he wrote, "I have been having a field day with a broom tied on to a twelve foot bamboo against the spiders and the bats. This time next week, Bishop West and his wife will be here, and Bishop Aung Hla's wife is doing such a spring clean that I shall be all behind if I do nothing. So I have begun too, and it is dirty work. Bishop Aung Hla, *Saya* Chit Tway and I all went to Sagaing on Wednesday to re-dedicate the church. I felt a little like the people in the Bible and did not know whether to rejoice or to cry. The repairs are just the essential minimum to keep out the weather, and half a dozen very hard seats to sit on. There is no altar yet, so I have suggested we follow Myitnge's lead and have a brick altar as a precaution against further trouble and its being again removed."

CHAPTER NINETEEN

Farewell (1950-1951)

The beginning of August 1950 was to see Uncle Will suffering from a bad throat. On 13th of that month, he wrote, "The Bishop left this compound for Maymyo at midday last Sunday and was to return to Rangoon on Thursday, so I ordered breakfast for three. However he did not turn up, so I got out my cycle and went to the aerodrome. I badly wanted to see him because I had barely had five minutes with him while he was here, and mercifully the aeroplane was two and a half hours late, so I had quite a nice time with him. It was a very windy day and my ride to the drome was dead against the wind, and when I got there I was rather like a grampus. I have been having a cough and as it didn't get better I went to a doctor, and the bishop saw me at my worst, but I settled down and am a great deal better now."

But things didn't improve, and on 20th August Uncle Will was to write "My throat is still choky and I must try to get to Mohnyin to Dr. Middleton West; he is the only English doctor in the country I think. But from here to Mohnyin is a fearsome journey, three days each way, unless I go by air and then it will be two days."

Almost at once, through a chance meeting with Miss Stillman of Mohnyin, he was found a comfortable berth on a boat going to Katha, and set out immediately. From there he travelled by train, being welcomed by Dr. Middleton West only a couple of days later, when pleurisy was diagnosed. The normal treatment would apparently have been to inject a needle into the damaged right pleura to withdraw the fluid, but would have meant a stay in bed of four to five days, and this was impossible locally. There was no option but to return to Mandalay, where further x-ray photos were taken. Will wrote home, "I will keep you posted as to developments, but it looks as if I come home to England next spring, whether on furlough or for good must be settled later. I am not ill at all, only get out of breath easily and have a pain in my right side if I cough."

Canon William Rolfe Garrad.
(Uncle Will)

On 10th September he wrote from Mandalay, "I am glad to say that my chest is very much better, but the doctor makes me stay indoors except for going to church services when I drive in a *gharri*, and makes me lie on my camp-bed downstairs as much as possible. I am trying to take his advice seriously."

A fortnight later came this: "I have been on my back again most of the week, but am certainly better than I was. As long as I am lazy, I am perfectly well, but if I try to do something I get giddy and have to sit down. I managed to take Burmese service here this morning. I brought the credence table to the chancel step and used it as the altar, and I sat on a chair most of the service. The stupid thing is that I am supposed to be doing great things at St. Matthew's Church at Maymyo today, but *Saya* Chit Tway has gone there in my place." Bishop Aung Hla was away in Switzerland at this juncture, attending Moral Re-Armament meetings, and Will was trying to take some of his services when he should have been resting.

In October he continued with services at Christ Church, being able to remain seated most of the time, but his health did not improve. On 5th November he wrote, "I have had a set-back again and have been ordered to bed, and am having calcium injections intravenously every fourth day. Bishop West and the doctors are discussing my going to Rangoon hospital for two or three days to get some decent x-ray photos and then to go for a few days to a nursing home. I gather the x-ray machines in Rangoon and Mandalay are identical, but the Mandalay man does not understand his machine and his results are consistently hopeless. The Mandalay standard of doctoring is lamentably low, and this is the reason why I want to get our mission hospital open again."

By November Uncle Will was in Rangoon Hospital, having been flown there from Mandalay. The electric lift was not functioning when he arrived, and he had to be carried upstairs. "Dr. (Mrs.) Huffton met me at Mingaladon and took complete charge; she is on the staff here and very quickly had a hot bath ready, and next morning had me x-rayed. I had expected to be in hospital only for a few hours, but I overheard the words 'interesting case' several times, and a rather special mattress was produced for my bed, and I think I am to be here for several days. I have already been here three days, and I think what the doctors wanted to happen has happened by itself. They wanted one lobe of my right lung to collapse itself and I think it did so on my arrival from Mandalay. It means I shall be short of breath until I get used to breathing differently, now all I have to do is to eat and drink and sleep and rest and then I can be discharged."

Very many visitors came and went over the next month, while Will continued to write home every week, terribly bored with himself, but insisting throughout that he was getting better. On 30th November Miss Cam arrived and made her way in, despite a notice saying "NO VISITORS" – a preventative measure to lessen his over-tiredness. She had just returned from leave in England, and was staying alone at Bishopscourt (preparatory to returning to her nursing duties), Bishop West being away. She wanted company, and discovering her old friend was in hospital, came straight over to see him. Will writes: "I was very pleased to see her, and as she did most of the talking, it was not exhausting. Travelling in the Delta is not too safe yet, it is all right in places, but bad in others, and she has promised me that she will not attempt to go anywhere until the bishop returns. I am afraid she will find Toungoo impossible at present; the town is pretty well destroyed but both sides are manoeuvring for further fighting, and if she goes it must be for the shortest possible visit, just to get a general impression."

On 15th December he had a surprise visit from Dr. Middleton West from Mohnyin. "He has come to Rangoon for a few days and came to see the doctor and me. He was shown all the temperature charts etc. and the x-ray photographs and I think is quite satisfied with the treatment I am getting. His coming in like that has given me much confidence, and I really do feel much happier since he came. Bishop Aung Hla is now back from his travels and came in last evening when I was having my supper at 6.30 p.m. I had no time to learn where he has been and what he has been doing, but it is a joy to see him again, and to feel that Mandalay will now get more attention."

We know from Aunt Fan's diary that the Bures plum pudding had been despatched to Uncle Will in Mandalay well in time for Christmas, as usual, but whether it ever reached him in Rangoon Hospital is doubtful. The pudding always played such a central part in the annual festivities of the Garrad family at this time of year that he must surely have missed its non-arrival, even though, on this occasion, he was hardly in a fit state to eat it.

Will wrote on 27th December 1950 from Rangoon, "I have been lazy the last two days and have not written any letters, so I must get going again. Christmas was a very quiet day; no festivities of any sort in hospital. Padre Matthew brought me my Communion. The nurses had told me they were making paper flowers, chains etc. but apparently they are getting ready for Independence Day (4th January) which has superseded Christmas."

On 9th January, came this: "I have no news but am slowly improving I hope. The bishop is now back from Tavoy and has been in the last two evenings. Last night we started to go through the visitation of the sick service from the 1928 prayer book; it takes a different aspect when one is the person being visited, rather than the visiting priest.

"I do not think I ever mentioned Independence Day, 4th January, and the sooner it could be all forgotten the better. The nurses had been decorating most of the previous night and we were all woken up by guns, sirens, rockets etc. at 4.15 a.m., which continued for five minutes, making a hideous din. From nine till midday the hospital seemed to keep open house, and the Prime Minister and government officers were fed first and then a series of people in relays. The traffic on the verandah outside my room was six abreast for two or three hours, and though no one came into my room, I was quite exhausted before they stopped. To think that Independence Day has been substituted for Christmas seems very pathetic and tragic."

It was on 13th January 1951 that my uncle wrote his last letter home. In it he said, "I had another set back a few days ago, but not too serious, though disappointing. I have a nurse to myself at night now, so am less lonely, but the nights are very tedious. My love to you all. Will."

Canon William Rolfe Garrad died on 24th January 1951 in Rangoon Hospital. "A man of great humility, dogged faithfulness and quiet devotion" was how Bishop West described him, adding, "Canon Garrad was loved and respected throughout the diocese, as well as by members of all communities in Mandalay. After the liberation of Burma he returned to Mandalay where his wisdom and humility did much to build up the Burmese Christian leaders under whom he was serving.

Many a time when I entered his cool room in the hospital I would find him propped up in bed diligently reading his Mattins. Right up to the end, Padre Tidey said Evensong and Mattins with him, and he usually found enough breath to utter a response now and then.

His work lives on in the friendship and sacrifice which many are showing. Miss Cam found that difficulties which had been obstructing the development of the hospital melted away." (These had been acute, as the old children's hospital buildings in Mandalay had been used as a torture centre by the Japanese, and for a long time afterwards no Burman would enter them.) "The difficulties which were hindering Miss Sexton's coming also disappeared. *Saya* Ba Than volunteered to go up to Mandalay to re-start The Royal High School, and Edward Yarde is to proceed to Christ Church, Mandalay directly after his ordination."

Bishop Fyffe added later, "Will Garrad's body lies just outside the substantial brick church he built to replace the decayed timber church given to Dr. Marks by the Burmese King Mindon. At his funeral, the church was crammed, and round his grave gathered a crowd that must have numbered 1000. It included his kind Methodist friends, government officials, Roman Catholics, old school pupils, and Christians from Shwebo, Maymyo and other places. His Mandalay congregation provided a brick-lined grave, and on it is placed a stone slab he had once seen in a house in Maymyo, and then had said playfully that he would like it for his grave. The people there took him at his word and sent it down. He was the last of the 'little band of brothers' that started in Mandalay in 1904 at the instigation of Bishop Knight."

For me, by far and away the most poignant tribute is that made by Bishop Aung Hla, Will's one-time pupil, who wrote this about him: "I came back with Canon W.R. Garrad from Rangoon after the Clergy Synod in 1947. It was his first return to Mandalay after the war. He was very thrilled to get back to his mission. I can remember, before he left Rangoon, how he was showing his railway ticket to all his friends with great delight. He loved Mandalay.

Canon William Garrad's Tomb, Christ Church, Mandalay in 2007.

Once we told him that Mandalay was very hot and dusty. He said that it was sweet. 'Sweeter than honey, wonderful.' He really meant it. When he arrived in Mandalay there was no house for him. The house, the schools, the hospital and all the remaining buildings were requisitioned by the government. He did not mind. He lived with friends cheerfully and went round shepherding his old flock very happily.

He had a small-size bicycle. It looked like a racing kind. He liked it very much. He was seen on it everywhere in Mandalay. He did not care whether it was hot or cold, dusty or muddy. A friend of his once left a Jeep with him to try, because he could not bear to see the old man pedalling hard on the dusty roads in the blazing sun. Canon Garrad tried it. He almost bought it. Unfortunately, he had a few awful times in starting it. Two or three times he had to call for helping hands to push it in the middle of the town. Finally he gave up and stuck to his dear old cycle. He loved cycling.

Last August, I was taking the bishop to the airstrip outside Mandalay. About half a mile away from the strip we saw the Canon pushing his cycle. He could not ride it. The wind was too strong against him. He was going to meet the bishop and see him off. He was very tired when he came into the waiting room. He could hardly talk. He said that he was not very well. The bishop told him to see the doctor. He said, 'I don't want to see the doctor. He may stop me riding my cycle.'

He loved to work hard. During the first water festival after his arrival, he went to the cemetery, every day while the festival was on, and made a new register of the graves, as the old one was lost during the war.

He cared for his people very much. When Mandalay was overrun by the insurgents, there was severe fighting all over the town. It was insurgents against insurgents, and all insurgents against the government. Canon Garrad was seen on his bicycle going from place to place to see his people. He helped everyone who needed his help. He was known and respected by everyone on all sides.

The insurgents caused a great deal of damage to the town. The hospital was disorganised. The nurses' quarters which were The Royal School buildings were deserted. The Mission House which had been turned into private wards was empty. When the hospital was re-organised, the Mission House was not used. It was kept in reserve. After eight months the Special Commissioner was seen about it. Before long Canon Garrad received the de-requisition order. He was very pleased. He engaged the carpenters at once to make the doors and windows which had been stolen during the war.

He went in and occupied it long before the doors were replaced to make sure of the possession. He combined the Christmas party and the house-warming together and gave a very big reception on the 23rd December, 1949. There was plenty of food, games, entertainment and speeches. What a happy evening!

Everybody saw how happy he was. It was quite natural. He had got back his house to settle down after so many years in exile. He had moved his residence three times since he came back and before he could move finally into his old home.

The Union Christian Hospital Scheme which he started was getting on very well. They had drawn up a constitution. They had started collecting money. They were ready to start as soon as the buildings were available. One of his major wishes was being fulfilled.

The other worry he had was the schools. St. Mary's English School and The

Royal School. Both the buildings were occupied by the government. No one knew when they would be available. But he had some ideas on it.

After he came back from the doctor in Mohnyin I used to rub him with liniment every night. He said it helped him very much. He could sleep better. Once he said 'I should get better soon as I am getting the episcopal unction regularly.'

He knew what was wrong with him and started thinking about his leave. He had his name booked to sail with his friends in April. He had three ideas. To go on furlough to which he was entitled, or go for good, or stay on two more years and retire. He liked the suggestion given to him by the Burmese friends, to come back as it is a glory to the family to have an elderly person in the house. He could not decide and I was not able to help him. But he helped me in many of my decisions.

I had a letter from the Bishop suggesting that Bishop Francis and myself should go to Caux. (This was to a big Moral-Rearmament meeting.) I did not want to go but I did not want to miss this good opportunity. I consulted the Canon. He took time. After twenty-four hours, he said that it might be right that I should go. I went. But he was in hospital when I came back.

He was greatly relieved of his anxiety when I arrived home well in time for Christmas. He, too, had a good Christmas. He wrote to me and said, 'Christmas Day was very quiet. Padre Matthew brought me my Holy Communion. I had a nice vase of flowers and the nurses arranged my Christmas cards round it, and I thought what a difference had come into the world since Jesus Christ came. Before he came there were no such places as hospitals. No one used to help people when they were sick. In the evening Mr. and Mrs. Lewis came in. They had no sooner gone than Bishop West came in. So I ended very happily.'

After Christmas, when we went to the hospital we found he had begun to sink. He said, 'I am all lost. I don't know whether I am living or dead. Everything is muddled. Is it Christmas or Epiphany or Lent?' That was the last time I saw Canon Garrad.

His funeral was wonderful. We all felt that it was right to bury him in Mandalay. There was no train. It would take a long time to bring the coffin by boat. The Burmah Oil Company came to the rescue. Wonderful! They brought him in a special plane and the B.O.C. in Mandalay helped with a truck.

We kept him five days in the church. Friends of all races and religions and from far and near came and paid their last respects. It was one of the biggest funerals in the country and a most dignified 'PONGYI-BYAN'.

The Bishop of Rangoon and I stood at the head of the grave with *Saya* Chit Tway. We all took part in the service.

At the end of the service we all sang 'Lord, now lettest thou thy servant depart in peace.' May he rest in peace. His work continues."

***

Over seven years later, miles and miles away in England, Will's elder brother, my father Charlie, also came to the end of his life at the age of eighty-two, with obituaries in both *The Times* and *The Church Times* paying tribute to his long service and translation work in Burma.

His funeral was at Crewkerne Parish Church, Somerset, on 23rd December 1958. By contrast, it was a simple, relatively small service, with all the family present. Father's old friend, the Rev. George Appleton, was there to represent Rangoon Diocese, accompanied by George Kyaw Mya and John Shan Lone, two ordinands studying at the College of the Resurrection, Mirfield. The lesson at the funeral was the Christmas Gospel, taken from St. John, Chapter 1, verses 1-14, which was read from the Burmese Bible by George Kyaw Mya.

The Burma News of Spring 1959 reports that, "Mr Appleton (later to become Archbishop of Jerusalem) expressed the thankfulness of the Diocese of Rangoon for the devoted service of Charles Garrad, and said that he would always be remembered in Burma for the great part he had played in the Bible Society version of the Burmese Bible. He himself had been fortunate in arriving in Burma just at the time this translation was published. Later he had worked with Charles Garrad in the revision of the Burmese prayer book and had been deeply impressed by his scholarship and accuracy and by the humility with which he listened to other people's judgments, and the patience with which he worked until he had found exactly the right word or phrase. After his return to England, Mr Garrad still worked persistently to improve the translation and several volumes of comments and suggestions had been prepared for the next revision of the text; these had been handed over to the keeping of the Bible Society. The people of Barrow Gurney, where Mr. Garrad worked for nearly twenty years after his return to England, came to love their vicar and to recognise the simple saintly quality of his life."

***

My mother outlived my father by twenty two years, dying at a nursing home in Great Malvern on 21ˢᵗ May 1981 at the great age of ninety-four. A few days later, we had a wonderful family funeral in celebration of a life well lived, before adding her ashes to those of my father, burying them together just outside the porch door at Barrow Gurney Church, Somerset.

Mother always enjoyed life to the full. She adored acting and singing, and even in later life was often involved in conducting choirs and putting on plays. She was also a very fine speaker, giving talks up and down the country on the overseas work of the Mothers' Union, and I well remember her joy when she was elected as a member of the Church Assembly (the predecessor of today's Synod or Church Parliament) for the Bath and Wells Diocese. Perhaps her most famous achievement was being given number W/1 (Woman One) when the Auxiliary Territorial Service was formed in 1938. Somerset had been allotted the first numbers, and she joined up for immediate local service, a whole year before the Second World War started. She was given an arm band, I remember, of which she was very proud, and the rank of Senior Leader (the equivalent of Sergeant Major) and spent much of the next two years in and around Bristol, encouraging girls to join up. Her only brother had been killed in the First World War, and she felt strongly that women were badly needed for the future defence of the realm. Later she joined the Red Cross, and helped to run an army convalescent home at Barrow Court.

***

Aunt Fan lived with us at Barrow Gurney until she was needed by her doctor brother, Frank, in Harrogate in 1949, after his wife died, when she went north to care for him. How hugely we missed her is impossible to describe.

In the mid 1950s I still managed to see her from time, as I was by then married and living near Norwich, and Aunt Fan had returned to the family home at Bures, which was only an hour and a half's drive away. One evening in late January 1959, I received a telephone call from Aunt Katie (her younger sister) to say that she had just been admitted to Halstead Hospital, Essex, and 'was not at all well'. I had three young children at that stage, including an eight month old baby, but a friend valiantly stepped in to care for them, so I was able to set out by car immediately after breakfast next morning.

It was the last day of January and I was longing to see Aunt Fan again. But I was too late; she had died in the early hours. As I knelt by her bed, holding her hand, which still felt faintly warm to me, my mind was raging. How merciless, I thought, that our beloved Aunt Fan should have had to die entirely alone, away from home and in a strange bed, when, in life, she had never stopped giving comfort to everyone she met. And then I realised that of course she had not been on her own at all. God would have been with her, and with her great faith, she would have known that He was there. Indeed, His presence was with us at that moment, enfolding us, holding us close, as we held hands together in that funny little room. Although I still wished I had got there earlier, I now knew that all was well, and that she was at peace.

Later, we held an uplifting funeral service in her beautiful home church of Bures St. Mary, Suffolk (when her selfless work in Burma was recalled), and amongst the large congregation were her remaining brother and sisters, as well as Mother and the three of us, Anne, Douglas and Elizabeth, whom she had cared for so lovingly, both in Burma and in Barrow Gurney.

***

Sadly, my husband Claude died on 28th April 1996 at the relatively early age of seventy-four years, after a long illness. The years in Burma as a young man had taken their toll physically, but despite the many aches and pains he suffered from time to time, his life, I believe, was happy and fulfilled. All in all, we had had forty-five good years together, sharing this with our three stalwart sons, of whom he was immensely proud, and with whom we travelled widely from our much loved home in Norfolk. "I want them to be citizens of the world," he used to say, a wish that they have certainly fulfilled, the eldest serving in various remote corners of the globe in the British Diplomatic Service, the second living and working in Australia and the third mainly in France, and all in very responsible positions, with families of their own.

Soldiering was in Claude's blood. He had been in the Cadet Force at school, and in the Territorial Army before immediately volunteering for full time service when war broke out. After his time in Burma, he worked with his much loved father in Norwich, in his accountancy business, and rejoined the Territorials, which were central to his life. When in due course he retired he did so as the Commmanding Officer of 54 (East Anglian) Division Royal Corps of Transport, T.A., and later, while teaching army cadets to shoot at Bisley, was to become Norfolk County's Honorary Secretary and Treasurer of the Forces' Help Society and Lord Roberts' Workshops; posts he held for fifteen years.

On the morning of 1st May, after a brief committal at St. Faith's Crematorium,

Norwich, we held a Thanksgiving Service for his life at Fundenhall Church, with all our normally scattered family present. An army sergeant stood at attention throughout, displaying the Corps' Colours, and Claude's medals were on view, among them his Burma Star with Oak leaf clasp, and his Territorial Decoration with two bars.

It was a sad but proud day for the whole family, and amongst the many letters we received after his death are some affectionately addressed to 'Colonel Claude', these simple tributes being amongst those I treasure most.

***

I have always been bewitched by the enchanting country of Burma, and now that my childhood tale is coming to an end, it is time to thank the diarists and letter writers who have made this story possible. Their actual words, written at the time, seem to me to be worth the telling, painting – as they do – a very different picture from that of the world today.

The one constant factor, both then and now, is of course the Bible, the bedrock of belief for the Christian, and I remember how greatly Father longed for an update of his translation during his lifetime, though this was not to be. Now, however, a fully revised edition of 'the Garrad version', sponsored by our family, has at last been published by the Bible Society, much to everyone's delight. It will certainly be well used and has been worth waiting for, even if it's taken over eighty years for this to come to pass!

Recently, on returning from our Burma pilgrimage we were introduced to a valiant Burmese priest working in London, with a parish of his own. His name is David Haokip, and he has suffered much for his faith. Not only, he told us, was he brought up on Father's translation of the Bible and of the prayer book, but was also ordained at Christ Church, Mandalay, the splendid red brick edifice built by Uncle Will, to replace King Mindon's old wooden church, which has since become the cathedral of the Mandalay Diocese. David talks rather disarmingly of 'Big Father Garrad' (my father Charlie) and 'Small Father Garrad' (my uncle Will) as greatly respected, much loved figures in the history of the church in Burma, whose faith he is now continuing to share in the country from which they came. Our story has come full circle.

Epilogue

"When I was a child, I understood as a child, I thought as a child, but when I became a man, I put away childish things." (1 Corinthians, 13, v.11.)

But it wasn't until very much later in life when I was standing with my sons round Uncle Will's grave, in its simple isolation outside the main door of Christ Church Cathedral in Mandalay, that I began to realise the full force of these words. When we asked the young priest who was with to us to translate the Burmese inscription on the stone, we remained for some moments in thoughtful silence as he read "Blessed are those who stand firm in faith; they will be rewarded with the living crown."

Such integrity can never be over-valued. It is the one basic tenet from which everything else stems, this extraordinary ability to 'stand firm' against all the odds, to hold onto the truth as one sees it, whether it be in politics or religion or any other sphere.

The leader of Burma's National League for Democracy, Aung San Suu Kyi, has shown this quality in abundance through her long years of house arrest, and it is greatly encouraging news that she can at last take her rightful place in parliament, having won a landslide victory at the head of her party in the spring bye-elections of 2012.

No one knows what lies ahead, of course, but Burma is proving itself to be something of a sleeping giant, just waiting to be fully awakened in order to play its part once more in world events after a long period of isolation. There will inevitably be many difficulties to overcome and progress may be slow and bumpy, but, with the backing and encouragement of international leaders of good will, the warm-hearted Burmese people having at last begun to enjoy the right to choose the way they want to live, will not give up their struggle easily.

An extract from Miss Suu Kyi's moving book *Freedom from Fear* sums everything up splendidly, with words that I echo with my whole heart. "When I honour my father, I honour all those who stand for political integrity in Burma."

Sources

The quotations used in these pages come, in the main, from letters and diaries in the private possession of the author. These include:

Diary of Miss F.M. Garrad – 1919-1949
Letters from Rev. C.E. Garrad to his sisters – 1927-1931
Letters from Rev. W.R. Garrad to his sisters – 1947-1951 and *collected notes.*

Other material is taken from:

SOAS Bulletin of Burma Research, volume 1 and volume 2. (IISN 1479-8484).
Old S.P.G. Periodicals, including *Burma News, Burma Calling*, the *Rangoon Diocesan Magazine* and *Mandalay Chaplaincy Records*.
A Visit to the King of Burmah at Mandalay, Oct. 1868. J.E. Marks. (London, Bell and Daldy, 4 and 5, York St., Covent Garden).
Saya George (The Revd. George Kya Bin) – (No author is named in the photocopy that was given to me at All Saints', Maymyo, in November 2007.)

Three books which the author has found particularly valuable in the provision of background information are:

The River of Lost Footsteps, Thant Myint-U, Faber and Faber 2007.
Freedom from Fear, Aung San Suu Kyi, Penguin 1991.
Christian Missions in Burma, W.C.B. Purser, S.P.G. 1913.

Appendix

List of British Missionaries mentioned in these pages

Anderson Nicol Keith, missionary in Burma 1911-34. Archdeacon Rangoon 1930-34.

Appleton, George, missionary in Burma 1927-47. Archdeacon Rangoon 1943-47. Later Archbishop of Perth 1963-69 and Archbishop of Jerusalem 1969-74.

Atwool, David Courtenay, missionary in Burma 1910-40.

Beloe, John Seppings, missionary in Burma 1907-13.

Caldicott, Joseph George, missionary in Burma 1915-40.

Chard, C.H., missionary in Burma from late 1860s to'70s.

Clack, George Reginald Sadler, missionary in Burma 1907-51.

Colbeck, James Alfred, missionary in Burma 1873-88.

Cowper-Johnson, Wilfrid Harry, missionary in Burma 1909-31. Archdeacon Rangoon 1923-31.

Delahay, William, missionary in Burma 1919-39.

Dilworth, Arthur, missionary in Burma 1927-1939.

Dunkley, Ernest Hale, missionary in Burma 1912-1916.

Edmonds, Francis Robert, missionary in Burma 1906-24.

Fairclough, John, missionary in Burma 1866-1897.

Fyffe, Rollestone Sherritt, missionary 1904-10. Bishop of Rangoon 1910-28.

Garrad, Charles Edward, missionary in Burma 1906-32.

Garrad, William Rolfe, missionary in Burma 1910-1951. Hon. Canon of Rangoon 1945-51.

Higginbotham, William Harold Spencer, Missionary in Burma 1934-42. Archdeacon Rangoon 1942.

Jackson, William Henry, missionary in Burma 1917-31.

Jerwood, Henry Arthur, missionary in Burma 1904-05.

Knight, Arthur Mesac, Bishop of Rangoon 1903-1909.

Lee, Arthur Oldfeild Norris, missionary in Burma 1916-40. Archdeacon Rangoon 1938-40.

Marks, John Ebenezer, missionary in Burma 1860-1895.

Menzies, Wilfrid Roxburgh, missionary in Burma 1906-33.

Park, William Robert, missionary in Burma 1912-37. Archdeacon Rangoon 1934-37.

Purser, William Charles Bertrand, missionary in Burma 1904-29.

Seeley, George Henry, missionary in Burma 1894-1921.

Stevens, James Reginald, Principal St Matthew's Boys' School, Moulmein 1927-36.

Strachan, John Miller, Bishop of Rangoon 1882-1902.

Thursfield, Gerald Arthur Richard, missionary in Burma 1913-36.

Tidey George Lewis, missionary in Burma 1941-57. Hon. Canon of Rangoon 1950-57. Archdeacon Rangoon 1954-55.

Titcomb, Jonathan Holt, Bishop of Rangoon 1877-1879.

Tubbs, Norman Henry, Bishop of Rangoon 1928-34.

West, George Algernon, missionary in Burma 1921-34. Bishop of Rangoon 1935-54.

Whitehead, George, missionary in Burma 1899-1906.

End notes

[1] *The Glass Palace Chronicle of the Burmese Kings*, G.H. Luce, trans. (Rangoon University Press 1960).

[2] *Journal of the Burma Research Society* 27:3 (1937). From the Old Tang History "The Ancient Pyu".

[3] Quoted in G.E. Harvey, *History of Burma*, Longmans, Green & Co, 1925. p. 235.

[4] *The Daily Telegraph* 15 January 2011, 23.

[5] *The Making of Burma*, Dorothy Woodman (London: Cresset Press, 1962). 64.

[6] *A Visit to the King of Burmah at Mandalay*. Oct 1868. J.E. Marks. London, Bell & Daldy, 4 & 5, York St, Covent Garden.

[7] Full names and dates of British missionaries are given in the Appendix.

[8] *Forty Years in Burma*. John Ebenezer Marks. Hutchinson & Co (1917)

[9] *SOAS Bulletin of Burma Research*, Vol 1, No 2, Autumn 2003, ISSN 1479-8484.

[10] Ghosh Amitav *The Glass Palace* published by Harper Collins. ISBN 0-00-651409-X

[11] *SOAS Bulletin of Burma Research*, Vol 2, No 1, Spring 2004, ISSN 1479-8484.

[12] Miss Linstead ran the Mission School at Shwebo and Mr Stockings had a separate establishment, teaching blind adults how to weave cloth.

[13] They included St. Augustine's Burmese Boys' School and St. Agnes' Burmese Girls' School, St. Matthew's English Boys' School, and St. Matthew's English Girls' School, St. Raphael's School for Blind Girls, and St. Aidan's Chinese School

[14] Designed by Mr. A.G. Bray and built by the United Engineers of Rangoon.

[15] Chit Tway had been ordained deacon in 1918 and was to be made priest in 1931. He spent the greater part of his life working with the Garrad brothers at Mandalay, as well as taking his share of duty in the school and mission hospital. Father said he was a man of little formal education but of great practical ability and shrewd common sense, who was always there when needed, being much missed when eventually he moved to Shwebo.

[16] I think these must have been Rev. William Purser and Archdeacon Cowper-Johnson.

[17] These were 'All People That On Earth Do Dwell'; 'Come, Holy Ghost, Our Souls Inspire'; 'Now Thank We All Our God'; 'The Church's One Foundation'; 'Yet Saints Their Watch Are Keeping'; 'Salvation's Giver, Christ, the Only Son'; 'Be Thou Our Guide and Helper' and 'It Is the House of Prayer'.

[18] Popham Peter, 'The Lady and the Peacock. The Life of Aung San Suu Kyi of Burma.' p.172. (Rider, an imprint of Ebury Publishing, 2012).

[19] The Moulmein staff on the outbreak of war were the Rev. Vivian Whittam (the Anglo-Indian chaplain of St. Matthew's English-speaking congregation); the Rev. Taw Mwa (the Karen priest-in-charge of St. Augustine's Mission); Miss Linstead (the English principal of St. Raphael's School for Blind Girls); Mr. Tresham (the Anglo-Indian headmaster of St Matthew's English Boys' School); Miss Tilly (the Anglo-Indian principal of St. Matthew's Girls School); Mr. Buttress, (the Anglo-Indian headmaster of St. Augustine's Burmese Boys' School) and Ma Lucy (the Burmese principal of St.Agnes' Burmese Girls' School.

[20] The story of the trek to India is taken from notes in my possession belonging to my uncle, Canon W.R. Garrad, and written by his great friend Rev. George Tidey. Much of Mr. Tidey's narrative was published by S.P.G. just after the Second World War, and is reproduced here by kind permission of the United Society for the Propagation of the Gospel.

Index

INDEX